Decumbitures and Diurnals

Joseph Silveira deMello

No part of this book may be reproduced or transmitted in any form or by any means, electronic or mechanical, including photocopying or recording, or by any information storage and retrieval system, without written permission from the author and publisher. Requests and inquiries may be mailed to: American Federation of Astrologers, Inc., 6535 S. Rural Road, Tempe, AZ 85283.

ISBN: 0-86690-541-3

First Printing: 2003

Published by:
American Federation of Astrologers, Inc.
PO Box 22040
6535 S. Rural Road
Tempe, AZ 85285-2040

Printed in the United States of America

Dedication

To the memory of my mother,
who refused to tell me my hour of birth lest I become interested in astrology.
To all astrologers of the past who taught me
and to future students of astrology who will write, publish, teach
and keep the great science and art of astrology alive.

Acknowledgements

I wish to thank the many astrologers mentioned throughout this book
for the many charts they submitted for my study and for their constant support
throughout the writing of this book. Needless to say, this book
could not have been written if I had not read many other previously published
astrology books and countless astrology articles in astrological journals and magazines.
Most of what is written in this book is hardly the sole product of the creative self.
Kt Boehrer
Macelle Brown
Don Borkowski and his late wife Georgie Borkowski
the late Nan Burket
Karen Christino
the late Henrietta "Mike" Cramton
The late Edith Custer
The late T. Patrick Davis
Edward L. Dearborn
The late Shirley Decker
Guy de Penguern
Defiance Gregg
Eleonora Kimmel
Diane Lawson
J. Lee Lehman
Margaret Meister
Rev. Joy Morris
Rev. H. Lee Poteet
The late Lois Rodden
Mollie Sommer
Helena Stansfield
Norma Storey
Jan Van Schuyler

Contents

Introduction

Astrologers have used several strange methods to study the effects of transits on their own charts. Once upon a time, many astrologers began the day by constructing a map of the transits at dawn of any day they wished to check and compare that chart with their own natal charts. This is rather artificial since every day that is done is going to have the Sun on the ascendant. And astrologers further dumbed it up by putting the ascendant degree on every house cusp of the transit chart. It was still possible to get some direction from such a comparison, but there had to be a better way.

The author hit upon diurnals almost by accident. He brought up his own chart and then created a new chart using his own natal data, changing only the date being examined. He then brought up a bi-wheel where he put in the center the transit chart and its angles and his natal chart around the outside ring. Astrologers will quickly see if they do such a chart for their birthdays, the angles of the chart will be close to their own natal angles. If they do a chart for next day, the angles will have increased by one degree. For the day after that, they will increase another degree. Throughout the year the angles will travel all around the whole 360 degree circle.

What makes it important is that if only one transiting or natal planet is touching one of the moving angles, the day will be in the nature of the planet touched but not very productive of special events and experiences. However if two or more planets, either transiting or natal, hit the angles with only a one degree orb, the day will produce a significant event. Any astrologer studying such charts becomes immediately aware of the strengths of his natal planets and also the strengths of those same planets as they transit our charts. We will also see those times when transits hit conjunct to natal planets that there is far more impact when those conjunctions hit on angles than when they do not. This is a very viable technique, and the author treats you to a few examples from the lives of people whose charts he has followed.

Decumbitures are a technique not much in use by astrologers other than those of the Evangeline Adams school of astrology. Part of the horary technique, specifically decumbitures are done for persons at the time the actually take to their beds with sickness. Decumbitures are part of horary astrology in that they will reveal the course of the patient's discomfort. Since these charts are also capable of predicting death, should the illness be fatal, they have fallen into disuse as modern astrologers have little wish to make such predictions. Some will very strongly object that any astrologer is actually able to do so successfully. To some extent there are ethical considerations against making that dire prediction. Possibly the only the patient's relatives and friends may be prepared to deal with the outcome of the illness. But it is also a valid objection. For should you convince a client they are at death's door they can do one of two things, buy more life insurance right away, or they are free to go on a big crime spree that will leave their heirs financially well fixed, knowing that if they are caught, they will not have to spend very long in jail. Unfortunately the nature of humans is such that the second of the two choices is frequently found to be most appealing. This part of the author's work presents a number of old cases and shows how they worked out, and it is presented only because it is an instance where the workings of astrology get proven to go with the events after the charts were done and studied. What kicked off this study occurred when Karen Christino was writing the biography of Evangeline Adams and discovered that Miss Adams had in 1926 predicted the death of Rudolph Valentino almost to the hour it happened. Miss Christino applied to the author to help discover how Miss Adams had done this so successfully.

Decumbitures

As a technique, decumbitures are so old fashioned that only a few of the older astrologers know about them, what they are, when to consult with this sort of chart, and how to read it. Until quite recently, it has been little done since the death of Evangeline Adams, and she used these quite frequently. However, they were widely done in Elizabethan times by Lilly, Culpeper and Gadbury, and since I have begun to work with them, they seem to be having a sudden astrological resurgence. Decumbitures are a special part of horary astrology.

Evangeline Adams used this technique when she read of the sudden collapse of Rudolph Valentino, the celebrated Sheik of the Silent Screen. He was not her client, so she had no natal data for him. But she found the exact time of his collapse very nicely reported by the New York *Times*, fully datelined at 11:50 a.m. EDT, August 15, 1926, New York City. Modern newspapers, so afraid of stale news, no longer time and date news items. Idiots that the media are, they have forgotten that the word "news" has no relationship to a new item; `news' is a word made up from the four points of the compass. At any rate, she knew that it was only a matter of time before some enterprising reporter would remember her and come round to her studio to see if she would make newsworthy prognostications in the matter. And being naturally curious as any astrologer, but also being aware of the power of the press, she prepared herself to have something to say. Because of this, she is celebrated as having predicted his death almost to the hour it actually happened. And, it was this chart, sent me by New York astrologer Karen Christino, who was researching how psychic Adams was, that got me interested in decumbitures.

And thereby hangs a tale. I went to my computer and entered the data in my usual style and printed out the chart. I worked with the chart, and I puzzled over it mightily. It was some time before it dawned upon me that the chart I had done was different than the one sent me by Karen Christino. If I were checking out the work of Evangeline Adams, I ought to use the style she had used, and she used the Placidus house system. While the use of another house system does not change the chart angles, change of house system will express in the succedent and cadent houses, changing cusps and sometimes cusp signs, which will change the rulers of those houses. New house rulers will give different interpretations.

Before we set to work looking at this chart, we have to remember that Evangeline Adams would not have had Pluto or Chiron, and she probably would not have calculated the East Point or the Vertex, so, though they are in this chart, we will work only with what she did have. Adams had only the astrological knowledge and style of her times. Moreover, she had no foreknowledge of the outcome of this event. We are in a different place. We know what she predicted and what actually happened. Another astrologer with whom I chatted about this chart and the technique stopped me short to tell me he would have nothing to do with any technique which would predict death in an astrological chart.

As I hinted above, the great thing about this technique is that you do not need to have the birth data of the person involved. It is, of course, very helpful if you do, but the decumbiture is both an event chart and a kind of horary. *The chart is cast for the time, as closely as possible, when a person decides he is ill enough to take to his bed.* And the horary part is that you are essentially asking what is going to happen in this event.

Decumbitures started out as the natural offspring of horary, used by astrologers who had no compunction about predicting death if they saw it. And the first amazing thing we see about this chart is that we shouldn't even be reading it. The first rule of horary is that we not read charts with the Ascendant in the first three or last three degrees of any ascending sign. In the first three degrees it is too soon to ask the question, while in the last three degrees, as in this chart, in the final degree of Libra, it is already too late to ask. I have always quarreled with the notion that it is too soon to ask a question, but no trouble agreeing that the last three degrees of a sign on the Ascendant does mean that the matter is unalterably set. What is meant to happen will happen. But, alas, what is that? When I studied horary, I had a teacher who believed that every chart always had something to tell us. She herself had been trained by teachers of the Adams tradition. But it is plain from the outset here that we are starting with bad news.

In decumbitures, the first house is the patient, and the seventh house is the besetting ailment and the doctor. We cannot get mixed up on this. Ascendant is the person asking for help, and the seventh house is what is being asked about. In natal charts, we give considerations of health to the sign on the sixth house combined with the tendencies of the natal rising sign. Heavens, if what is being asked is "what is going to happen to me?" would not the second house the house to check? No, maybe not. That too is in the last three degrees and has no planets in it. Venus rules the patient and will be out of its sign in four days, will hit the Midheaven of this chart in seven or eight days, remembering that Venus travels at more than one degree daily. Mars rules the seventh house and is unfortunately in the seventh house thereby giving the ailment and the doctors more power than is given to the patient. Angular planets are always the strongest positions. Venus is not angular; but Mars is. This is another piece of mixed news.

That chart immediately shows us some oppositions. The Moon we see with the East Point (and since she probably did not use it we will slightly disregard it) are both opposite Mars, and these make a square to Mercury retrograde at the top of the chart. Mercury is applying to the Midheaven although it is almost stationary and would go direct in three days. In this chart Mercury rules the ninth and eleventh. It is not as important as it would be if it were chart significator. As a Mercury person myself, I am always on the watch for Mercury so close to any angle for it always brings a change, in this case, to the status of the patient. Remember that any planet making a station slows its daily movement considerably. Then it takes the planet a while to achieve its usual average motion. But in a decumbiture, the tenth house is indicative of the treatment and medication given to the patient. We see the Sun is with Neptune, both opposite Jupiter. Most people would not regard this as difficult, but what I see is that Neptune of confusing situations is going to be more powerful than the Sun, and I do not see that as a good omen. Worst of all, the North Node is conjunct Pluto opposite South Node over which the Part of Fortune recently passed. You will recall the ancients regarded placements conjunct the South Node as potentially severe, and I will allow my sight of South Node with Fortune as more superstition than good astrology.

If astrology in 1926 did not have all that we have today, certainly the world of medicine and doctors was no better off. The first published diagnosis was that Valentino was suffering a severe recurrence of his gastric ulcer, due perhaps to what he had eaten for dinner the previous evening. He was known to have ulcer problems, and doctors always go with the patient's history. With a Saturn ruled third house, the patient would have some delays in conveying to his doctors the proper origins of his pain. Ulcer pain is usually above the waist. Gall bladder pain is lower and to the right. The gall bladder is on the right lobe of the liver, and considering that, any doctor would look for jaundice. Had Valentino been able to say his pain was lower, that might only have sent some

nurse's aide scurrying for a vessel into which the patient might urinate, and everyone would turn aside while he did so.

It was not until his appendix burst and peritonitis set in (the patient's color would get a greenish cast) that doctors rushed to operate on him. In those days, the mortality rate from peritonitis was much higher than today. When an infected appendix explodes, what was contained therein begins to contaminate the lower body cavity. The doctor has to go, take everything apart, clean up these contaminants. If any small part remains, the patient eventually will die of the contamination. Doctors also did not have the antibiotics of today to help kill off the noxious invasions. We know Valentino improved over the next six days, but on the seventh day, his condition worsened, and on the eighth day he died, and we know this is what Adams predicted.

It is time we checked the path of the Moon through the rest of the sign Scorpio, also remembering that the past path of the Moon had been over the East Point, signifying an event, over the Ascendant, troubling our patient, and over Neptune which certainly added mystery to this ailment. Ahead the Moon first makes a trine to Pluto, then a trine to the North Node. Trines are well regarded by most horary astrologers, but I see them less than lucky, more as permissive, allowing things good or bad to happen. The Moon is then conjunct Saturn, square Sun, square Jupiter (dangerously retrograde) and square Neptune. Finally the Moon trines Venus and, lastly, it trines Uranus. A final trine usually means a good outcome, but if a trine to Uranus has to surprise us, and a trine to any retrograde usually produces a twist that skewers the basic meaning of any planet that may prove unfavorable to the situation.

A few words on this first house. In addition to the Ascendant, the first house viably describes the subject of the chart. his personality, and his current circumstances. There we see the Moon which we know is always rather ambivalent. The Moon there tells us he is constantly re-inventing himself. To have Saturn of obstructions and delays there, is also not favorable.

Saturn is a the planet of assorted ailments. Just about the only thing favorable about these placements is that they are not in the rising sign. First house planets in the sign of the Ascendant are always much more potent than they are if in the following sign. The Moon rules the intercepted portion of his ninth house, and Saturn rules the intercepted portion of the third house as well as his Aquarian fourth house of the end of the matter. I do not thing interceptions bode well as what is intercepted is private to the person of the chart, and make him impervious to outside intrusion. Moreover, Saturn is not in the most favorable degree of Scorpio I can think of, conjunct the evil star Serpentis, and providing lessons along the line of snakebite. You never know what sort of backlash is going to result from 19 Scorpio. To find irony involved in this degree is not unusual. We have already seen communication was going to be important. English not being his native language, and, coupled with a sense

Upper Right
Vallention decmbiture
Natal Chart
Aug 15 1926
11:50 AM EDT +4:00
New York NY, USA
40N40 073W58
Geocentric
Tropical
Placidus
Mean Node

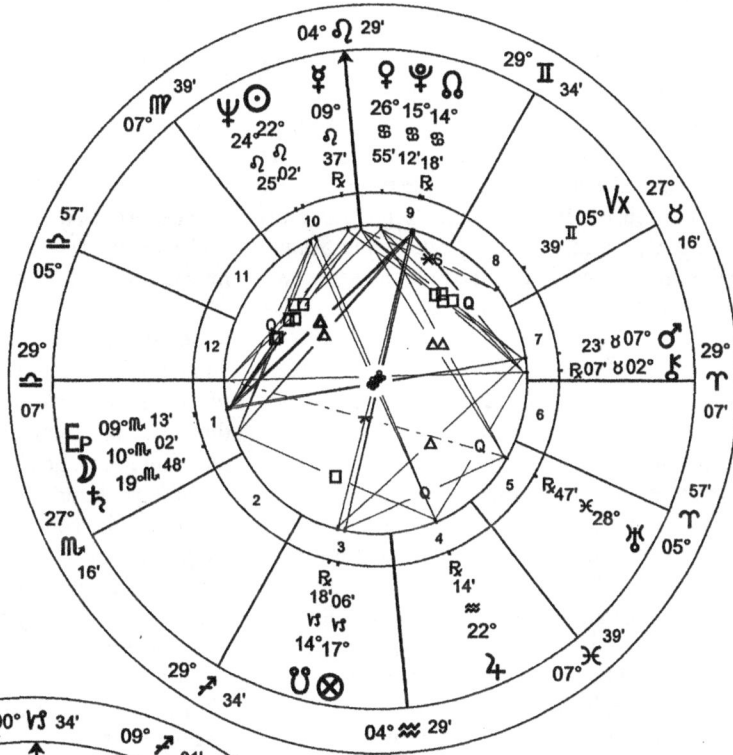

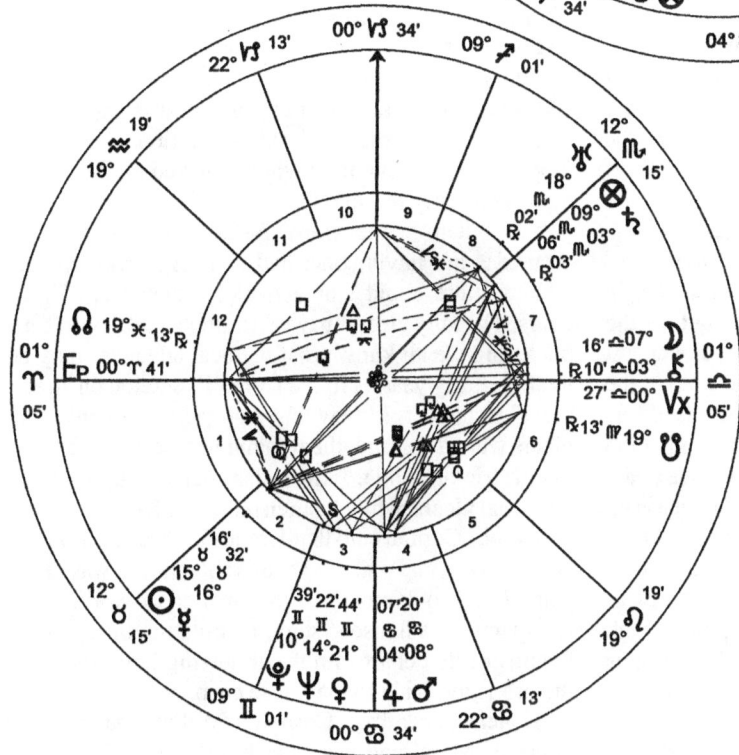

Mean Node
Placidus
Tropical
Geocentric
40N37 016E57
Castellaneta
3:00 AM CET -1:00
May 6 1895
Natal Chart
Rudolph Valentino
Bottom Left

of privacy, these do not aid necessary communication.

The second house is indicative of his immediate future, and this is Scorpio for whom Adams would not have Pluto and would use Mars which we already said is poorly placed in the seventh. The tenth house which rules medication and treatment has Mercury retrograde, Sun and Neptune, all in Leo, but since Mercury is closest to the angle and not in good condition, we have to go with Mercury as the most important of the three occupants there. The Sun of the patient is subject to Neptune, and, while this might describe the status of the patient (simplistically) as a very popular screen star, we can expect all sorts of confusion from Neptune to go with anything done to the patient under Mercury retrograde. As we said, Mercury would go direct in two days. In the same two days, Sun would exactly conjunct Neptune, and gave a false positive.

Checking the course of Moon aspects leads us to think of the course of the patient's problems. But the Moon will not long remain in Scorpio. The trine to North Node and Pluto, (and we should not check the latter) are what led to the operation. He was carefully watched through the conjunction to Saturn and the squares to Sun, Jupiter retrograde, and Neptune. They may have thought he was out of the woods by the time Moon trined Venus. But in a normal run, by the time Moon trined Uranus retrograde, the Moon had all told less than forty hours to complete its tour of Scorpio and this in no way matches to the patient dying in eight days. This final aspect to a retrograde planet is not much desired.

Now we encounter a major difference between strictly classical horary interpretation and the interpretation of decumbitures. In classical horary, we are done when the Moon leaves Scorpio. Now, in decumbitures, we follow the Moon into subsequent signs. That means that the things trined by the Moon will eventually become quincunxs, while the Moon in Sagittarius will trine the tenth house planets. But the Moon will only be two and a half days in Sagittarius, or any subsequent sign. The other big difference is that in classical horary we have regimented the technique to the point where we have excluded any attention to the movement of all the other planets. Remember that this is the chart of the moment when illness was admitted and help was asked for. The chart is a snapshot of the specific moment. But all of the heavens keep on moving. Without leaving the science of astrology, we go onward into the art of astrology. Science is all very well, certainly has its place, giving us the skeleton of the tools with which we work, but what is done beyond gets interpreted artistically. Astrologers must use their art just as the medical practitioner uses art it making diagnoses. I think I had already discarded the notion that Evangeline Adams had indeed been very psychic. We all have a certain amount of intuition, but everything about Adams was so practical, so logical that we could all be sure that anything she "saw" was right there for the rest of us to see in any chart.

As far as I was concerned, I had looked at this chart until it had made me blind. I had even checked out Arabic Parts, finding the Part of Peril at 8 Gemini 13 (uncomfortably close to the Vertex which is always a health problems indicator, and sextile Mercury retrograde), of Surgery at 11 Taurus 30 (opposite the Moon, and square that same Mercury), of Sick-ness at 16 Aries 40 (who can argue that placement in the sixth house, and square to Pluto and North Node), and the Part of Death at 16 Taurus 03 (waiting for transiting Mars). There are times when these things can tell us a great deal, but most of the time they just clutter the chart. And did Adams use Arabic Parts? I also checked the aspects between the rulers of the fourth and tenth (end of the matter and status), the fourth and eleventh (end of the matter and our hopes and wishes), trying to get three corroborating responses which we always need before we make predictions, but neither success nor satisfaction occurred. We were left with ambiguity.

I even went so far as to check timing for when his illness might come to an end. We had a fixed and angular Moon which would speak of "months" and had to be tossed out since I knew he had died in eight days. But what would Evangeline Adams have thought when the resolution was unknown to her. It became obvious to me that every technique of horary I had checked had failed me. The Moon headed for the chart's second house is not going to improve Valentino's immediate future. The Moon would continue onward until in eight days it would be coming to meet retrograde Jupiter in the fourth house. I did not see this as a good omen. And that is as close as I got to saying maybe that was what Adams must have seen. Because I knew what happened I could find myself led to make astrology fit what Evangeline Adams predicted. I knew this was a horrible temptation and not productive of good astrology.

Of course I checked all my books. I went to Cornell and found his section on ulcers a total disaster area, he being more concerned with skin ulcerations. I got into a loop of going to one item which referred me to see another item only to have that item refer me back to the previous item without any further enlightenment. It seemed to me, having once had an ulcer of my own, that I knew more about stomach ulcers than Cornell. Of course I had my ulcer thirty years after Cornell wrote his book, and we all know what medical advances may be made in thirty years. I found Cornell's section on "treatment" a shocker. I knew that eighty-five percent of all ulcers were duodenal, the remaining fifteen percent being gastric or peptic. I knew that men mostly suffered duodenal ulcers, while women mostly suffered the latter two kinds. Cornell said that Uranus in Pisces was an ulcer indicator, and that is what this chart has. It was time I paused and took stock. In my own chart work, using Campanus as a house system, I would not interpret the Uranus of this chart into the following house because the orb is too wide to the house cusp.

Under "appendix," Cornell said that was ruled by Scorpio (Mars) and secondarily by Virgo (Mercury). We have to admit that both these planets are strategically strong placements in this chart. A note was seen that some astrologers believe Neptune should rule the appendix for disturbances of this organ are "closely associated with psychic, spiritual and astral causes." At this point I closed that book in some disgust and agree with Barbara Waters that it is more than about time Cornell should be revised; it was already ten years out of date when it was published.

Next I went to *The Rulership Book* by Rex Bills, a more concise text but one without any medical credentials. Ulcers, especially gastric ulcers, we are told, are ruled by Cancer (Moon), and secondarily by Scorpio (Mars). Can we deny Moon opposite Mars? Bills felt that the appendix was ruled by Virgo and Scorpio, secondarily by Libra. But Bills is later and had Pluto, which Adams did not. As with Cornell, peritonitis is not mentioned.

I recommend any astrologer interested in decumbitures to read *Horary Astrology and the Judgment of Events* by Barbara Waters who discusses decumbitures in her seventh chapter. She also recommends for our study Andreas Argolus and his many examples in *Concerning Critical Days and the Decumbiture of the Sick.* I should have liked to read that book, but had no idea how I was going to get my hands on a copy of it. And then, to my great surprise, after the Orlando Convention in 1998, I visited Lee Lehman, mentioned Argolus, and she went to a bookcase and brought out a sheaf of xeroxed pages of this 15th century book, and rushed to make copies of those pages for me. The text is in Latin, that dead language in which I am more interested these days than I was when in the schoolroom, and it was printed in a font where the letter "s" was printed as "f". Watters tells us that Argolus relied heavily on natal charts when he could get them. If I say the decumbiture chart can stand alone, here we have two prominent ancient and modern astrologers who preferred to have both.

Returning to the notion of Uranus interpreted in its next house, I came to a stop. I knew that users of Placidus had no compunction about pushing planets into the next house from a system where its users normally say that they can already feel a planet in the next house when it is within ten degrees of the next house cusp. But the situation in the sort of astrology done by Evangeline Adams went a great deal further. In "olden days." users of Placidus divided every house in half, and any planet showing up in the second half of the house is automatically interpreted in the next house. I know quite a few older astrologers who do this halving of the houses, and they give excellent readings to their clientele. If we do that to the placements of this chart, we certainly boost a lot of planets to other houses.

And then a brilliant flash bulb lit in my imagination. If there was one astrologer who might be able to help me with this chart, it would probably be my astrologer friend Henrietta "Mike" Cramton in Tulsa, a person who reads everything but still does astrology quite closely to the way Evangeline Adams worked. Astrologers should spend more time remembering the work of past astrologers before ego tripping into making new discoveries. It hardly took her any time to see that the Sun was coming to the final degree of Leo and going into zero Virgo. Her rationale was that when the Sun comes to the end of its sign (in eight days, in fact), death is highly possible. The way "Mike" put it was that the last degree of any sign has about it great sorrow. Put that with Moon meeting retrograde Jupiter, disposed of by retrograde Uranus, and you have a good scenario for the actor's demise.

I conveyed this information to Karen Christino who originally sent me this chart for study. She wrote back that I had done exactly what John Gadbury would have done, that he too checked out the path of the Moon and other planets as they moved around the chart or changed directions. I was a bit perked up when Karen told me of this as I have never read Gadbury and not chanced on his way of doing things. I might add that Karen's original research was prompted by her question of whether Adams relied solely on her astrological knowledge or took into account some personal psychic sense. Many people today are quick to agree that Adams was strongly psychic. But if we allow this notion, we would then logically say the same of all the great Elizabethan astrologers, which I think is a highly unlikely conclusion. It is very denigrating and rude to say the successful conclusions and predictions of an astrologer are arrived at psychically.

Another book I consulted was the *Encyclopedia of Psychological Astrology* by Charles E.O. Carter which contains an article on appendicitis. He wrote: "This trouble occurs readily where there are Virgo and Scorpio afflictions, but the special degree areas are rather numerous and ill-defined. Eighteen degrees Taurus-Scorpio is probably the chief, and afflictions are also commonly found to the first three degrees of the mutables, and also 22 degrees of the same as well as 22 degrees of Leo-Aquarius. Uranus is a common afflictor. Mercury is commonly in the first decanate of the mutable signs. Out of 16 cases, I find it in this position in eight (cases). It is nearly always in a major bad aspect to one or more of the malefics." Thank heaven for Carter, who then directs we look at his example chart #3 at the end of the book and to look at the charts of King Edward VII and of his son Prince George, later King George V of England.

Back to this decumbiture chart where we see that the Sun and Jupiter are opposite each other at 22 degrees Leo-Aquarius. Saturn is at 19 Scorpio. In the course of all this I had found in *Sabian Symbols* data for Valentino's birth and erected the chart for 3:00 a.m. CET, May 6, 1895, Castellaneta, Italy, 40N21, 7E04. Unfortunately the source for this data is not recorded, so we can take it as data astrologers have found reason to accept. However, I must voice some objection to Aries rising. I hardly saw an Aries resemblance to the subject. Had he been Pisces rising, as remarkably superstitious as he was, I would have given less argument. As superstitious and serious as was Valentino, the man could get inarticulate and obsessed. But this natal for Valentino is Aries rising with Mars in Cancer, the Sun in Taurus, and the Moon in Libra.

At the time of this decumbiture, the Sun and Neptune were transiting his natal sixth house, transiting Mars was coming to his natal second house, the transiting Moon was going from his eighth house, over the top of his chart toward his natal twelfth house, and Mars was sextile natal Mars. Saturn was in orb of his natal Uranus at 18 Scorpio thus transiting his natal eighth house. Later in Carter's book he gives us under "peritonitis" "usually shown by afflictions to 18 Virgo-Pisces and to the Moon or Cancer."

Now, there is yet another interest here. According to family history, and of course no exact date, I was myself a nine month old infant and very ill. We had in June moved into a new house. I cried continuously and was not wet. The family doctor had made several house calls, and each time, he gave a new and more dramatic devastating diagnosis. He ran the list right up to the dread meningitis. I forget what others but all were irreversible and fatal. I was only getting worse, and suddenly he had to go out of town. A Jewish couple ran a grocery store around the corner, and the lady there had a brother who had just set up private practice four blocks away.

My father was convinced to get this new doctor to see what could be done for me. The doctor walked back with him, picked me up and noted that my diaper was dry. He asked my mother when was the last time I had wet. She was flabbergasted she could not remember, but I had not wet in days. He asked her to boil some bath towels in water, and it took a while to activate fire in the big black kitchen coal stove in August. When he had the towels, he wrapped me in them until I let go a stream of very bloody urine, and my mother mopped up the mess while the doctor applied more steaming towels around me. I must have been both relieved and shocked enough to stop crying and to fall into exhausted asleep. I was more inarticulate than Valentino. Obviously I had a blockage somewhere in the kidney-urinary system, and the towels had provided a shock that relaxed or shocked me into letting go.

I certainly was in no position to declare myself ill and in need of attention. But from my first look at Valentino's decumbiture and then my first look at his natal chart, I could not resist looking at my own natal chart with the Valentino decumbiture. You understand the problem. I had been born the previous November. It was as if I had just been born, and he was dying. Ever since she had refused to give me my time of birth when I was 11 years old, she was sufficiently Piscean to remember to deny me specific information I might use astrologically. I have smiled frequently to reflect that my mother more pointed me to astrology than deflected me.

Shingles

I first met Henrietta "Mike" Cramton, who found a solution to what Evangeline Adams had seen at the AFA convention in San Francisco 1974. We were great friends until her recent death, and no wonder. She was was a Scorpio with Gemini rising, as am I, but I my Moon is in Gemini, while hers was in Aquarius. Her Ascendant is with my Mercury. If she read something she found interesting, she passed it on to me, and I did the same. Sometimes it was she who telephoned me, as she did in early February 1996, with a problem of her own.

She had awakened one morning the previous week with an uncomfortable itch and was horrified by what she saw in her mirror. She discovered a rash belt across the front of her and going around to the back. She knew something was wrong immediately and made arrangements to see her doctor. He told her she had shingles, an ailment which has much in common with chicken pox and herpes. Indeed, some doctors say that you cannot get either shingles or herpes unless you have had chicken pox. Psychologically, shingles is the product of stress, perhaps of some inner resentment of duties and responsibilities which seem to be imposed on us by others. I remembered the first person I ever knew to suffer shingles had come down with this discomfort on a leisurely ocean voyage returning from a European vacation. But now "Mike" and I agreed a decumbiture chart should be set up for 7:30 a.m. CST, January 25, 1996, Tulsa, 36N08, 95W58. Astrologer's natal data: 6:00 p.m. EST, November 19, 1917, New York City.

The chart we get has early Aquarius rising (in the "too early" frame). I have to confess to being a bit out of patience with the "too early" and "too late" designations. And here I have a chart where Uranus and Ascendant fall on her natal Moon. This decumbiture has unavoidable significance to the patient. First of all, everything, almost, is on her side of the chart, most notably that the seventh house ruler is in her first house. Since the Sun is below the horizon, I determined to use the old rulers for the outer planets. And now we bump into Moon in Aries, ruled by Mars, Mars in Aquarius, and Uranus in its own sign. Or with logic, Mars is ruled by Saturn, and Saturn in Pisces is now ruled by Jupiter so that this latter pair are in mutual reception with Saturn.

In decumbitures we can rid ourselves of this "too early to read" Ascendant. I went to my bookshelves again. Bills says shingles is a condition ruled by Mars, and we see Mars at almost 13 Aquarius. Remembering the Valentino chart, we now see Sun as significator of the ailment and the doctor and is in the house of the patient. The degree of Aquarius which Ebertin correlates to the lower left leg, was not of much help. Nor is Cornell of any help for he lists too many variations.

I really ought to check when her natal chart ruler Mercury went retrograde for it is now in the twelfth house of the decumbiture. It had made a station at 5 Aquarius, quincunx her natal Pluto, and it would make a direct station on January 31 at 19 Capricorn. Are we really happy to see Fortune in this decumbiture chart at the top of her chart and in Scorpio? Fortune in the area of medication (even if Pluto is also there), but this might spell out that the medication is going to have Pluto significance in Sagittarius, disposed of by Jupiter. Indeed, with so many twelfth house planets, we find that there might be some delays in dealing with this problem. Of course we are checking the chart against her natal chart and the fact that her natal Moon was 1 Aquarius. Her natal Saturn was 14 Leo, and Mars is opposite that in this chart. Ah, but Mars here is 13 Aquarius. No better indication can we have of a chronic condition and frustration and stress. Of course with Aquarius rising, this is a chart for a long-time professional astrologer. Jupiter of this chart just happens to be opposite her natal Pluto, and Neptune now is sextile her natal Chiron.

Cornell identifies shingles as herpes zoster. He gives as indicators the Moon afflicted in Cancer, Leo or Virgo, not the case here. He tells us this is a Mars ail-

Shingles decumbiture
Natal Chart
Jan 25 1996
7:30 AM CST +6:00
Tulsa OK, USA
38N08 095W58
Geocentric
Tropical
Campanus
True Node

Compliments of:-
Joseph Silveira deMello
1755 Franklin Str #204
San Francisco CA 94109
Tel (415) 775-8939
email jsmelscorp@AOL.com

ment or of Mars afflicted in Leo. But here we have Mars in Aquarius and only afflicted by a semisquare (friction) to the Saturn of this chart, but opposite her natal Saturn (in which case, Mars is doing the afflicting). On the other hand it may be an Aries disease, the product of affliction in Aries, or of Aries on the Ascendant and afflicted, none of which is the case here. Well, the Moon is in Aries.

Hoping for better, I turned to *The Rulership Book* by Rex Bills. There all we find is that Mars is in parenthesis, meaning that the author considers this a secondary involvement. He may have done this because shingles is a derivative of another ailment. We better do some work of our own.

If we use the old rulers, Saturn is the chart significator and robs Uranus above the Ascendant of a sort of rightful place in this chart. Let us remember that this illness came on suddenly and unexpectedly. Shingles manifests as itchy blisters on the skin. Saturn may rule bones, but we also know Saturn rules skin afflictions. Here we see Saturn headed for the second house of her immediate future, probably going to be around for quite some time, as is the nature of shingles. I attacked this chart with trepidation, knowing shingles is a long-lasting condition and that I would have to tell of things as I found them, aware that those things are seldom comforting. The second house is significant of her immediate future ruled by Jupiter (in the twelfth). In the second house we find the Moon in Aries, and since it is approaching the South Node which should show that she will suffer some discomfort before she finds relief. But, though she might lose patience with all this chart evaluation, it has to be pointed out that it is nice that she has ascendancy over the ailment and the sympathy of a Leo doctor. Since the seventh house is also the doctor, he went to work right away to alleviate her discomfort.

Resorting to horary techniques, the outcome of the matter is ruled by the MC-IC axis ruled by Mars and Venus which are semi-sextile in this chart. In this sort of thing we consider only Ptolemaic aspects. If we check out our hopes and wishes in the outcome, we get Jupiter and Venus and do not find them in any aspect. So we get not much help here.

Charting the path of the Moon through the rest of its stay in Aries, we get a mixed path, but this should mirror the progress of the ailment. Venus is at the midpoint of Moon and Mars. Perhaps we can consider semisextiles when they make midpoint patterns. We see the Moon will come opposite to Chiron, go on to a square to Mercury, an opposition to the North Node which also means a conjunct to the South Node. Then there is another semi-sextile to Saturn, and there is a final square to Neptune, an unfavorable ending aspect in horary. But we have not had other corroborative either favorable or unfavorable indicators.

Following up the course of actual events, first of all, the patient had problems with medications. Although it effectively controlled the constant annoyance of nerve ending pain, the medication so doped her up that she could not drive her car and mostly just wanted to sleep. She found she could not concentrate on anything, could neither read nor watch television. Why she had called me was to see if I could tell her how long all this was going to keep bothering her. Now I am not really well versed in medical astrology, and I certainly am not a doctor, but if there was one thing I knew about shingles, it was that this was not an easy condition to get rid of. I also remembered Barbara Waters said that how long an affliction would last was not a matter of the decumbiture chart but was best seen from an examination of the natal chart.

By the time we got around to February 13, her doctor gave her an epidural spinal block injection, telling her it might or might not work. Everybody I have ever known to have such spinal blocks has been told the same thing, but it has worked for all of them. That is, it works for a goodly period of time, and then the procedure has to be repeated. At any rate, the day following the spinal block was the first comfortable day the patient had since the onset of this condition. This is a whole week earlier than Mercury getting back to the point over which it went retrograde.

Jupiter as ruler of the second house of the immediate future is important. It is in the twelfth house of this chart, the famous Guardian Angel placement of Jupiter, but the trick of this Jupiter is that the person who has it has to wait until she is as far gone as she can be before it works at the very last moment. The chart shows Jupiter semisextile the Sun and trine to the Vertex, the latter always having to do with health matters. The Vertex, at the same time, is not very helpfully quincunx the Ascendant and Sun, and we known the quincunx is more than somewhat a health aspect, though I personally regard this aspect as being an indicator of nervousness, the very sort of aspect that drives us up a wall.

Both "Mike" and I have Sun in Scorpio and Gemini rising. We have laughed with each other about this, but we understand the stages of any Scorpio discomfort. The first stage of any Scorpio illness is that they want to be left alone and as much as possible continue their daily routines and not talk about it. When that stage is over, Scorpio enters the complaining stage and everything gets complained about. That is how other people can tell Scorpios are getting better.

But in this case, getting better means that the scars are somewhat healed and the discomfort somewhat abated. But there still remains a background itch which makes itself felt now and then. We all, at a certain age, begin to feel our physical responses (every darn twinge) and think in terms of our mortality. This is where having her natal chart comes in handy. I wanted to see Mercury move through her natal eighth and ninth house and past her 27 Aquarius natal Midheaven.

This would be as important as watching Mercury in the decumbiture. Mercury as her natal chart significator has very definite action going over the angles. Any astrologer might snort that any planet moving over an angle brings change. When your chart significator goes over your angles, it is always worth noting and watching. When Mercury goes over the Midheaven it usually connotes a status change, the triumph of ideas or communication, the start of a new job. Here I had to act as both astrologer and old friend. I could see the treatment would work, ask her to trust in her doctor's treatment in which I had faith, and predict improvement, and I could even predict improvement if I could not say when the condition would be completely cured.

Feeling Unwell

I had barely dealt with Mike's problem, still studying decumbiture and natal charts, when on February 27, 1996, I received a telephone call to tell me that Ruth, one of the first friends I made in San Francisco when I moved here in 1964, had been hospitalized and suddenly died. I was devastated as we had only a few days before been scheduling our next monthly luncheon date.

When I first knew her, Ruth was a vivacious blond public relations woman handling special events for a large department store where I was to become book buyer. We quickly discovered we were both Scorpios, that I was interested in astrology, and she had told me that soon after she was born her mother had her horoscope done. No, she did not know who had done it, but I thought it might have been done by Evangeline Adams and would be a fine historical document. But Ruth could only say that it was a huge sheaf of written out material, and that she had not seen it in years. It sort of embarrassed her. So that no visitor would casually open a desk drawer in her house and find the thing, and think her a huge ego for keeping it so close at hand, she had stored it in a trunk which was inconvenient to get at.

Ruth was what the French call a lady of a certain age, and that age was as uncertain as she could make it, always a secret. Since her school days, she had carefully done nothing that would reveal her age. No one could catch her referring to events by what age she was when they happened. Although I had met and had chart data for two of her schoolmates, she explained that because their parents traveled a great deal it was not unusual that girls of various ages found themselves in the same classrooms, which should leave me to understand she was much younger than they. Stating that such a chart might well be a historical manuscript (she hardly cringed), I said I would very much like to see it. Alas, any document which would reveal her birthday was simply not going to be available.

At work she coordinated celebrity book signings for my department, and away from work I got to know the real San Francisco of fine eating places and great friends. She had a great sense of humor, and scandal delighted her to the point that she would let out a huge peel of raucous laughter. If you walked into a crowded room, you could always tell she was there before you could actually see her. And thereby hangs a story. Her father had been a mining engineer, and her mother was a lovely Edwardian lady with much gusto for life and a laugh so raucous that, as a young lady, it rather embarrassed Ruth. One day, at a favorite restaurant where we knew the owners, the bartender placed a tape recorder on the bar while we dined in a distant alcove. After dinner, when we returned to the bar, he played the tape recorder back, and she was amazed when she heard herself laugh for it was exactly the sort of laugh her mother had. We had to urge her not to think of curtailing it because it was one of the things which gave us much joy.

Ruth began her career in public relations with the Las Ve-gas Chamber of Commerce before the days when Bugsy Seigel arrived there to start the strip development with the building of the Flamingo Hotel. She had aided in all the promotion for his opening. "Of course we never called him that, he was always Benjamin or Mr. Seigel." Las Vegas had been a dusty cowboy town in those days. Lucius Beebe, western historian, author and bon vivant, has credited her with putting Las Vegas on the map. She brought to every Las Vegas opening all the Hollywood celebrities she knew. When she decided to move to San Francisco, screen star Norma Tallmadge, who had a house in San Francisco, loaned it to Ruth if Ruth would baby sit it. And, no sooner was I promoted to book buyer, than she decided to resign her position and hang up her own shingle in public relations. There were some snide speculations that she had resigned so no one would know when age forced her to retire and everyone would know that she had reached age sixty-five. Mind you, all this was in the 1960s, and we are now more than thirty years later. We can all count on our fingers and make wicked guesses.

When I first knew her, she lived in a lovely garden apartment with a view of Alcatraz. When her landlady died, the landlady's relatives wanted to move in, so Ruth had to move. She was very careful to inform me that she had found the trunk in the storage room had been broken open and that the horoscope was one of the things which had been taken. And that kept me from asking if I could see it. Of course, throughout our friendship I kept thinking of what other signs she might be other than a Scorpio Sun. It seemed to me that all her responses were decidedly Scorpio or Pisces. But without a year of birth, I could make no attempt to do a chart for her. In November, the previous year (1995), a group of us attended a special dinner party for her birthday. We often joked that Mickey Mouse was born on her birthday. One of her colleagues had managed to inveigle her a very impressive executive birthday greeting from the White House signed by both President Clinton and his wife. Since such greetings are forthcoming usually to centenarians, I teasingly asked what special group you had to be in to get on that list, for after all she could hardly yet be a hundred years old. Her resolve was firm. She wasn't telling.

A few minutes after receiving the bad news, I decided to do a decumbiture chart for the time she was hospitalized, 4:30 p.m. PST, February 27, 1996, San Francisco. To my great surprise this came up with Leo rising, the Sun in Pisces and the Moon in the last degrees of Gemini. I was not happy to see the Sun conjunct Mars in the seventh house, and above it, Saturn in the eighth house. If the Ascendant did not declare the matter as set, a void of course Moon in this case certainly needs no other comment. The Moon had been void of course since 10:20 a.m. PST, its last aspect a square to Saturn (Moon ruling twelfth, Saturn ruling sixth), and had gone into Cancer at 8:10 p.m. that evening. She had nothing in the first house, nothing on her side. The seventh house is the ailment and the doctor, and the Sun was over there in bad company. Another disquieting feature is Venus,

Decumbiture Chart
Natal Chart
Feb 27 1996
4:30 PM PST +8:00
San Francisco CA
37N47 122W25
Geocentric
Tropical
Campanus
True Node

Compliments of:-
Joseph Silveira deMello
1755 Franklin Str #204
San Francisco CA 94109
Tel (415) 775-8939
email jsmelscorp@AOL.com

ruler of the tenth, was in the ninth house and on the South Node. Astrologers in olden times, seeing a malefic on the South Node, had no hesitancy to predict death. Here with a benefic, we can only see blessed release, bad news in any case.

After I had done this chart, I telephoned our mutual friend and her colleague who had taken Ruth to the hospital. In mid-morning of twenty-seventh, she had called Ruth, and the conversation developed that Ruth was not feeling very energetic that day. Our friend was convinced that Ruth did not eat properly and suggested she bring by luncheon, which she did. After luncheon, she insisted that if Ruth found herself really unwell she should telephone. And finally at 4:30 p.m. PST, Ruth did telephone and said that she was very dizzy and something was not quite right.

Immediately her friend dialed 911 and dashed from her own office two blocks away to be there to let in the ambulance people. They packed Ruth off to the hospital where she was taken into intensive care and where she regained consciousness. Our friend stayed at her bedside, and Ruth was sardonically laughing about unawareness of the ambulance ride. Her friend went home and was home barely a half hour before Ruth's doctor called and said Ruth has lost consciousness and was slipping away quickly. At 9:40 p.m. the doctor called to announce that Ruth had died twenty minutes earlier. Cause was an aortic aneurysm, internal bleeding, cause of the dizziness (decreased blood pressure) which was her only discomfort that day.

At death, all things become known, and we finally had her birthday as November 18, 1907 in Los Angeles, California. All of three years younger than her eldest schoolmate. I rectified this to 1:14 p.m. PST and was surprised to come up with Pisces rising which so much fit what of her was not Scorpionic. The surprise was to find a Taurus Moon, but it was no surprise to find it in the second house. A good test of rectification is always to watch the movement of Saturn in a chart. I noted that she went into a business for herself with transiting Saturn through her first house and a Saturn return, and that she had just had another Saturn return just prior to her death. The day she died the Sun was approaching her natal Ascendant and transiting Mars was on it, while transiting Moon was going through her fourth house. The Moon was at 0 Cancer 34 when she died. We can say the Moon is never exactly on time, or we can remember that patients usually die before the doctor gets around to certifying the event. But in this case, the doctor was in attendance.

Of course I did other charts, the most recent solar and lunar returns, as well as a diurnal chart for that day, and finally an event chart for the recorded time of death. In the latter chart I found that the Ascendant had moved down to her natal North Node and quincunx her natal Saturn. For Saturn watchers, she was born with Saturn retrograde and was just past her fourth Saturn return, having had her first Saturn return in early infancy.

Let me summarize by stressing that decumbitures, much used by Bonatus and then Lilly and his contemporaries, thoroughly involve our use of the art of astrology. Although we are scientific and mathematical when we set up the chart, and although we start off by observing the techniques, rules and strictures of horary astrology, we can take those and stretch them carefully to the limits our imaginations can take us. If horary teaches of discipline and routine which will seep into any other astrological techniques we study, here with decumbitures we are permitted to stretch the whole distance all planets will travel in the days after any serious event.

Enrico Caruso

Let us now look at another pair of decumbiture charts I have from Karen Christino which were originally done by Evangeline Adams. These were done for one of the most celebrated of opera tenors Enrico Caruso (1873-1921), and he was an Adams client. He was never at the Metropolitan Opera that he did not regularly consult her, and all his closest friends knew of his faith in her. She had worked to rectify his natal chart to 3:07:48 a.m. LMT, February 27, 1873, Naples, although many other astrologers have used various times ranging from 10 a.m. to 12:15 p.m., and Marc Edmund Jones gives Caruso's data as 12:14 p.m.

We therefore see that Adams had worked with Caruso's unusual natal chart more than from casual interest. Caruso had Capricorn rising, was a first house Saturn in Capricorn, so we should prepare ourselves to see Saturn as a strong influence in his chart. He was born going into a New Moon with Moon and Sun at seven and eight degrees of Pisces, respectively, probably interpreted by Adams as being in his third house. Since this is her natal chart for him, it is given in the Placidus house system. Any placement falling into the second half of the house, no matter how distant from the next house cusp, was automatically read in the following house. She would therefore interpret his Saturn in the second house, his Moon, Sun and Mercury in his third house, his Neptune and Venus in the fourth house. She would not have had Chiron, and had she Pluto you can be sure she would have pushed it into the fifth house, his Uranus in the eighth house, and his Mars in the eleventh house.

So we find the consummate artiste's Venus and Neptune conjunction at the end of his third house, to be read in his fourth house. Venus should testify to an easy death, and Neptune to its occurring while he was in a coma. Notice that these two are opposite the Midheaven and square to Saturn within orb but not exactly on the midpoint of the opposition. This square of artistic planets to super conservative Saturn obviously led him to Italian Opera and traditional music. We also stop to notice that the fourth is ruled by Mars, and his creative fifth is ruled by Venus. His sixth is ruled by Gemini and his third was ruled by Jupiter retrograde.

We are now brought up short by Moon ruling the seventh (interpreted in the third) and the creative eighth with Leo on the cusp is ruled by the Sun in the third but has it in Uranus and Jupiter. Though these planets are fire and water, all of it leads to communication and type of communication. Those who have heard recordings of Caruso have to rank him with the elite tenors whose voices have the bell ringing tones few singers actually

11

have (Melchior and Bjorling who are in German called heldentenors. Caruso was also only married once, and he never divorced. As a creative person, of course, he created only with his voice, and the works he sang were the creative works of others. This chart has a plethora of aspects and just as many midpoints. Note the sequence of semi-squares from Saturn to Moon-Sun, to Venus. All of this makes it a complicated chart. But Adams was familiar with it. He was one of her many celebrity clients.

The first decumbiture chart she did for him involved his being stricken on Christmas Day 1920 at age forty-seven with an attack of pleurisy. This is an ailment in modern medical disrepute. When I recently told a doctor that I had suffered pleurisy, he told me without hesitation there was no such thing. Any ordinary dictionary defines it as an inflammation of the tissues surrounding the lungs. Even in the 1950s when I had it, the only cure for it was bed rest. Any sharp intake of air due to excitement or laughter was utterly painful. And woe unto the smoker who should go into a sudden fit of coughing. It was intensely debilitating and must have been unbearable for Caruso who had to sing three or four acts of grand opera every evening. The danger was that pleurisy could develop into pneumonia which would be life-threatening. Even in my time there were no antibiotics to prescribe and take against this ailment. Evangeline Adams was to write of this episode herself in American Magazine which appeared a year later in December 1921, four months after his death.

She relates that she was called to the telephone three times between five and seven o'clock in the morning. The woman who called her was in such a state of anxiety that Adams could not put her off. At five in the morning, she wanted to know if Caruso would live or die. Adams had tackled the matter immediately and told the woman that Caruso would not die of this illness. She had gone back to bed only to get another call at six o'clock. The same question was repeated, and Adams could only repeat what she had said earlier. At seven o'clock, the same woman was again on the telephone with the same question. (Some people never learn that one should never repeatedly ask the same question.) Now the asking woman was distraught. She said, "But Miss Adams, he is dying. The doctors have given up on him, and the priests are administering the final sacrament. He's dying." Nevertheless, Adams told her caller that Caruso would come through.

And he did in fact recover and eventually returned to Italy at the end of the New York opera season. In mid-June 1921, transiting Uranus went stationary retrograde one degree before hitting Caruso's natal Moon and Sun, to which it was natally trined. With transiting Uranus still two degrees retrograde of natal Moon, it was at the end of July, 1921 that the same woman who had called at the time of the first illness once again consulted Adams. This time Adams did the chart for Naples, Caruso's birthplace, where he was then residing, and this time Adams told the caller that it was very likely that Caruso could die suddenly at any time. He died two days later on August 2, 1921.

In the first illness, she had the time of his onset of illness, 12:30 p.m. EST, December 26, 1920, and he was in New York. The chart done for that time and place, and with Placidus houses, has Aries rising with Mars in Aquarius in the eleventh house. Mars also ruled the eighth house of the decumbiture, and Mars as his ruler was with Venus as ruler of the seventh, illness and doctor, and both ere in the eleventh house. Adams must have seen that the transiting Sun has just come over Caruso's natal Ascendant and Fortune. Now Fortune is in the second house in Pisces, not a good omen. The chart of this decumbiture is neither too early nor to late to read, has its Ascendant in his natal third house, afflicted his ability to communicate. The Moon of the decumbiture, in Cancer with Pluto (which we may see as serious but which Adams did not have), was trine his natal luminaries and would have made its last aspect as a sextile to Saturn, Caruso's natal significator, so I am sure Adams found that favorable. She probably saw Mars with Venus and saw their location as favorable to the patient.

Now, for a reality check, let us check the question as asked by the woman who roused Adams so early in the morning. Those of us who do horary astrology are always at pains to decipher the questions we are asked. If we get a "yes" answer to the question, "yes" means he is going to die. Adams told her caller that Caruso would not die, so she must have been getting "no" for an answer. So we have to find "no" in this chart. The conjunction of Venus and Mars is a "yes" answer, but it has qualifiers to bother us. While Venus is harmonious in Aquarius, Mars is not. Ruler of the fourth is trine ruler of hopes and wishes eleventh, another "yes" response. Fourth ruler to tenth, Moon to Saturn are in no aspect, productive of no answer at all. Perhaps she was working with reference to his natal chart, seeing the decumbiture positions in relation to the natal chart, seeing the Sun into his first house and Fortune there. That can hardly have been enough for a definitive answer. Adams would have hoped for negative answers to those questions. Perhaps she based her negative response on the basis of what was simply not present, and what had to be discounted as not aspecting his natal chart. Could she have abandoned the question as asked and, in her work, simply put matters in what was pro client or against client.

Remembering to disregard the things Adams would not have had or used, it is still difficult to see why Adams was so sure Caruso would recover. Of course she would have seen the Moon so early in Cancer would aspect everything in this chart, lastly making a sextile to Saturn well before leaving its own sign. Both Jupiter and Saturn went retrograde on the fourth of January, but which time the Moon would have been well through Leo. She would have seen Uranus trine the North Node and sextile the South Node, again favorable mitigating aspects. Thinking again of the ailment, pleurisy is an inflammation of the tissue surrounding the lungs (more Mars ruled than Mercury ruled). I think Adams was looking ahead to transiting Uranus coming to the patient's natal luminaries was not going to happen soon. The following June, Uranus having come to his natal luminaries, made a retrograde station at 9 Pisces.

12

Enrico Caruso
Natal Chart
Feb 27 1873
3:07:48 AM LMT −0:56:48
Naples, Italy
40N37 014E12
Geocentric
Tropical
Placidus
True Node

Compliments of:–
Joseph Silveira deMello
1755 Franklin Str #204
San Francisco CA 94109
Tel (415) 775–8939
email jsmelscorp@AOL.com

Enr Caruso 1st decumbiture
Natal Chart
Dec 25 1920
12:30 PM EST +5:00
New York NY, USA
40N40 073W58
Geocentric
Tropical
Placidus
True Node

Compliments of:-
Joseph Silveira deMello
1755 Franklin Str #204
San Francisco CA 94109
Tel (415) 775-8939
email jsmelscorp@AOL.com

Enr Caruso 2nd decumbiture
Natal Chart
Jul 31 1921
7:30 PM CET −1:00
Naplels, Italy
40N37 014E12
Geocentric
Tropical
Placidus
True Node

Indeed Caruso did recover, and he journeyed home to Sorrento for further rest and recuperation. He was hardly back from death's door when he began to experience abdominal pain and fever. This we have from Howard Greenfeld's *The Great Caruso* published in 1922. Doctors who arrived to treat him in July of 1921 found an abscess between the liver and the diaphragm which they felt was going into peritonitis. If science can laugh at astrology, and we are dealing with medicine in the Twenties, it is difficult for us as astrologers to see this diagnosis, but we usually do not argue with such things. Anyway, to get the best of medical care, they scheduled the great tenor for surgery with the best of doctors and in the best hospital in Rome on August 3.

Caruso became delirious the night of July 30, and his wife arranged for a private train to take them to Naples, the first leg of a trip to Rome. They went to the Hotel Vesuvio on July 31, arriving at about 7:30 that evening. Now the doctors scheduled an operation next day in Naples, seeing how the patient's condition was so quickly deteriorating. As was later quoted in his biography, his wife said that Caruso had arrived at the hotel, immediately taken to bed and went to sleep and never got up again. His condition took such a bad turn for the worst at 4:30 a.m. on August 2, 1921, and he died at 9:00 a.m.

In the second decumbiture, it is not pleasant to see Leo ruling the seventh house with the Sun behind it in the sixth house and Neptune in close orb to the seventh cusp. I would wonder that his doctors had the correct diagnosis. How difficult was it to see his affliction on an x-ray film? The decumbiture Moon is about to make its final aspect to Venus before going void of course. It does not help at all to have the luminaries below the horizon. Neptune in the seventh easily leads us to see the confusion and lack of confidence, the usual Neptune lack of reality and abundance of mystery, impairing the effectiveness and diligence of his doctors. In this chart, the illness is serious, the doctors mystified. We may pause to see the nodal axis at 21 degrees and also find Saturn so placed even if in minor aspect. This is not a matter of merely considering Ptolemaic aspects but underlining the point that a difficult planet is in the same degree as the nodal axis. If Saturn is semi-sextile to the north node, we automatically think of this aspect being much less than benign, and realizing that this planet is also quincunx to the North Node. The Sun coming to the Descendant is not going to bode well for the patient. The Descendant is the doctor and the what afflicts the owner of this chart. Saturn the significator is fenced off in the seventh house. Would Adams had disregarded the interception and put it in the eighth? That is very likely. What then would she have thought of Uranus intercepted in the first house? But the really crucial warning of this chart lies in the Sagittarius Midheaven. This is by far the most potent indicator of the seriousness of this chart. Those who do returns charts know that a Sagittarius Midheaven is special. Jupiter ruling treatment is with Saturn in seventh or read in the eighth.

We have to see this second decumbiture from the standpoint of astrologer Evangeline Adams. She did not quarrel as we might with the patient's diagnosis, but she would never have overlooked Neptune. Do we really have a void of course Moon since it makes no Ptolemaic aspects. She ex-

pected him to die on this occasion. It certainly boggles our imagination that he was taken to a hotel rather than to a hospital as soon as his train arrived in Naples. But of course they assumed he would be going on to Rome next day. Due to Caruso's fame, his doctors may well have deferred to his celebrity, and not wanting to rush him into hospital when he might be going on to Rome. But the really startling thing with this second decumbiture is its bad fit with the patient's natal chart.

Joseph Jefferson III

This is the third Evangeline Adams subject we are going to check. Joseph Jefferson III was one of the great actor-managers of his day. A fourth generation of his family on the stage, the first Jefferson had come to colonial America prior to the Revolution and died in 1807. This man, his grandson, was born February 20, 1829, in Philadelphia, an early Pisces by Sun sign with Aquarius rising and the Moon in Virgo. Evangeline Adams did have a natal chart for him, but because all particulars of his being taken ill were published in the New York *Times*, she did a decumbiture chart for him for noon CST, April 13, 1905, Palm Beach, Florida. We know that now Palm Beach is in the EST zone, but in her time it observed CST. Again we must look at the chart she used and do so with Placidus houses, though it little changes the chart when done in the Campanus house system I prefer.

Not only did Karen Christino contribute the chart data as used by Adams, but she also sent me a sheaf of xerox copies of the story of his illness as it very fulsomely appeared in the New York *Times* of April 14, 1905, reporting he had been taken ill at noon the previous day. He had been staying at his home, The Reefs, in Palm Beach, where he was having a fishing vacation. He was seventy-four years of age. The previous day, he had gone to his son's home in nearby Hobe Sound to meet with ex-President Grover Cleveland. There, in line with the luncheon menus of those days, he had eaten to the point of subsequent severe indigestion, his first complaint. The following day, he somehow developed pneumonia. His own doctor found it necessary to call in a specialist from St. Augustine, who came by train almost 300 miles to examine the patient. Between them they concurred in the opinion that this was no more than a routine case from which the patient would rally with proper bed rest. And indeed the patient did rally, but only too briefly, before going into a final sinking spell and dying at 6:15 p.m., April 23, 1905.

Such was the actor-manager's prominence that his obituary was given front page space on the Monday New York *Times* and continued on page two. His career, which began before the Civil War, was given extensive coverage. In the style of the great leading men of his time, Jefferson often wrote entire plays and personal adaptations of other vehicles to give himself the best parts. Most notably he had adapted Washington Irving's *Rip Van Winkle* and defined the role so that he owned it, and no other actor would ever attempt to do that role, put on

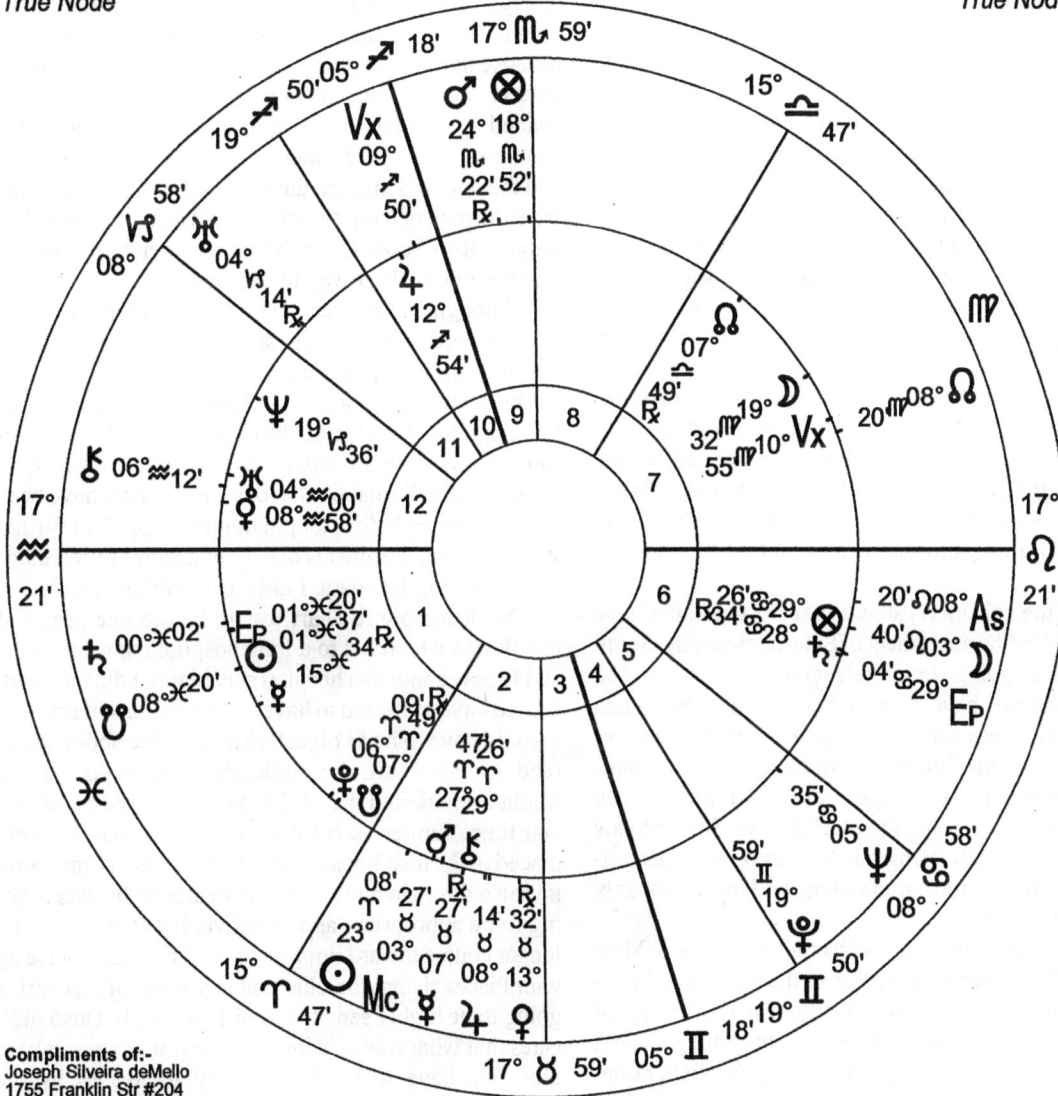

Inner Wheel
244. Joseph Jefferson III
Natal Chart
Feb 20 1829
6:13 AM LMT +5:00:40
Philadelphia PA
39N57 075W10
Geocentric
Tropical
Campanus
True Node

Outer Wheel
243. Actor's decumbiture
Natal Chart
Apr 13 1905
12:00 PM CST +6:00
Palm Beach FL
26N45 080W02
Geocentric
Tropical
Campanus
True Node

Compliments of:-
Joseph Silveira deMello
1755 Franklin Str #204
San Francisco CA 94109
Tel (415) 775-8939
email jsmgemscorp@juno.com

that play. He was not only famous but quite wealthy. He had married twice and had eight children. At the time of his death, three of them were actors and one of those a very important actor-manager. Despite his fame, he was seldom seen in public off stage, preferring to devote himself to fishing and was well acclaimed as an excellent amateur painter.

From her decumbiture, Evangeline Adams had predicted his death "within the month."

But he had died in ten days, literally when the decumbiture Sun reached the Midheaven of this chart. Adams had no trouble equating Leo rising as descriptive of so prominent an actor. The Sun is chart significator. Too bad it was in a cadent house going to his Midheaven. We do not normally look upon the Sun as a debilitating influence. In fact all the things we look at in this chart bedevil us. The illness was sudden and unexpected, ruled by Uranus, and, in accordance with her style of looking at a chart, she did not hesitate to interpret Uranus in the sixth or Saturn in the eighth house, neither of them speedy movers. One wonders why she did not give a ten-day prediction. The Moon was in early Leo in the twelfth house but would make only squares to Mercury, Jupiter, Venus, a trine to the Sun, and again a square to Mars, all but Sun and Jupiter retrograde. The Moon's final aspect is a square to Mars retrograde and retrogrades have a habit of giving a special twist of their own to any event. Though difficult to see, he was only 66 years old. The Moon rules and varies the tides of life, gone over the chart Ascendant and will square Venus in the ten days predicted, but only by direction. Doubtless she saw the Moon headed for the fourth house of the decumbiture, but he did not in fact die until the Moon was at 3 Capricorn, within orb of the decumbiture Uranus retrograde and out of bounds by declination.

A check of the ephemeris shows that she could not have been influenced by the movement of Saturn toward the South Node. Saturn was going station retrograde at 2 Pisces. The interesting thing we have to remember is that meanings change when the Moon aspects retrograde planets. Mercury retrograded to meet the Sun on the Midheaven of this chart. The four retrograde planets dispose of the affairs of seven houses of the chart, including the fourth house. She also saw the Sun would trine with retrograde Uranus or the Sun coming to an opposition to retrograde Mars, and these probably expanded her time frame.

I have talked about this chart with other astrologers. Most rightly consider the Sun as the ruler of the patient and treat the Sun from that point of view rather than as significator of the chart. I was prepared to get the arguments I did get about the ailment of the patient being indicated by the sixth rather than seventh house, hence ruled by Uranus rather than Saturn. All gave the seventh house rulership of the patient's doctors, which is fairly basic, but then could not equate the patient's illness with Capricorn on the sixth house, even though Capricorn's only indication was that we were looking at a chart of someone of advanced years. All could see Gemini and Mercury as ruler of pneumonia. It would appear the actor (Sun) and his ailment (Mercury) were going to meet their fate (Midheaven). Some time was spent dealing with Palm Beach being thought by Adams to be in the Central

time zone. For those wishing to do further work, the actor was born at 6:13 a.m., February 20, 1829 in Philadelphia. I did this natal chart for LMT. EST was not universally accepted until 1883. According to the data we have for Florida, EST was adopted in May 1889, so it is not known why Adams used CST, the original designation for Florida.

Jim Haynes

Jim Haynes is both an old friend and a well-known sidereal astrologer. Although he began his astrological studies as a tropicalist, he is now firmly a siderealist and not at all enamored of either horary or decumbitures or any type of astrology which might predict death. I have argued with him that my interest in decumbitures is not because they might predict death. Anyone's demise is a natural consequence of having been born, not to be evaded by denial. Decumbitures easily predict what course an ailment will take, whether treatment is correct and the doctor's mind in the right place, and it can show what the patient has going for as well as against him. It is important to know these things in order that plans be made about the best way to proceed.

Although Jim Haynes and I correspond regularly, it was not until after a long hospital stay that he informed me about his indisposition. And, to my surprise, he gave me full data. On January 21, 1996 at 8:45 a.m. PST in Los Angeles, California, Jim decided he was ill. Because I have his natal chart, which I am not at liberty to reveal, I did a diurnal for that day. He can only have been surprised when his doctor put him in hospital for further studies. Then, despite his dislike of decumbitures, since I had the complete data, I did a decumbiture chart.

The decumbiture chart was to be the interpreter of this illness which led to a long hospital convalescence, and I knew about this hospital stay before I did the chart. I could have preferred to have been sent that data earlier, I would have to be as objective as possible about what I read in the chart. Immediately Sagittarius on the Midheaven alerted me of this as an important and crucial time. Jupiter as ruler of the Midheaven is nicely placed in the next house, and although it is in Capricorn, it is also direct in motion, so the treatment he gets is going to be appropriate and effective, but it might take a longer course toward improvement. The chart comes up with Pisces rising, the clue that any work of this sort is going to be highly sensitive to the patient, but also indicates that what was causing his illness was a mystery to him. We have to be immediately impressed by the crowd of planets and both luminaries among them in the twelfth house, another underliner to say that convalescence is going to be drawn out. Neptune the chart significator is in the twelfth house and exactly conjunct a retrograde Mercury which rules the ailment and the doctor (and the Moon impacts on the illness) but all these planets are on the side of the chart which is the patient. Jim is the sort of person who attends to his well being and does everything the doctor recommends. All other twelfth house planets are in intercepted Aquarius

245. Haynes decumbiture

Natal Chart

Jan 21 1996
8:45 AM PST +8:00
Los Angeles CA
34N03 118W14
Geocentric
Tropical
Campanus
True Node

Compliments of:-
Joseph Silveira deMello
1755 Franklin Str #204
San Francisco CA 94109
Tel (415) 775-8939
email jsmelscorp@AOL.com

and fenced off and of private significance to the patient.

Although an abundance of planets in any one house complicates matters of that area, the interception allows us to deduct some considerations. It is a problem here that the Moon makes no Ptolemaic aspects to anything in the chart but a quincunx to the Vertex, and may be considered void of course. Such a Moon indicates that nothing will come of the matter. This is, of course, a stupid cliché to pass on to a client. Does that mean that nothing will happen, that the patient will not improve, that the patient cannot do anything about the matter? The Moon in a fixed sign and in a cadent house does not reveal the length of time this indisposition will last. The Sun is with Uranus, but the Sun will take 34 days to get out of the twelfth house, while the Moon will have come all around the chart in the same time frame.

The first house should indicate what the patient has going for him. Venus is in the first house, where it rules the third and eighth. Venus is exalted in Pisces, but would have to be remarkably poorly aspected to not be in the patient's favor. Saturn in the first house testifies to his indisposition and the fact that it might last longer than he would like. The fact that Saturn is together with an unhelpful Fortune in Pisces does not speed up matters. Moreover, Saturn and Fortune are opposite the Vertex, a health indicator, and so on the anti-Vertex, an axis which is as much a secondary Ascendant as is the east and west point axis or the Ascendant-descendant. It does not help that Saturn and Fortune are in the same degrees as the nodal axis. Saturn rules the eleventh of the hopes and wishes in this regard, and the twelfth house of the enforced convalescence. Saturn in the first house is not detrimental to the patient, but it does curtail personal expression. I felt that with Saturn in the first house the patient would be long incapacitated; a prolonged convalescence was in order. Barbara Waters says that longevity of ailment is best seen through a study of the patient's natal chart, but this particular patient does not want us to have recourse to his natal chart. We would like to see as many of those twelfth house planets leave out of the twelfth house. When we cannot use the Moon to predict that path of the matter, we have to turn to the Sun. I felt that if he had survived the Moon going into Aquarius, he would survive it leaving the twelfth house. Actually, Jim was pretty down most of the Winter and Spring and did not really begin to feel more himself until well into the Summer months. Most of the time, he felt pretty washed out.

The aspects in this chart also have their tale to tell. The Nodal axis makes a T-square to retrograde Mercury. Then the North Node makes a trine to the Midheaven, but the Midheaven is square to the Vertex. Then the Vertex is trine to Mercury, which is in sextile to Saturn and Fortune. Ascendant and Venus might be square to Pluto, but a separating aspect, and Pluto is in the ninth house which it rules.

A Very Different Leo

Because of the persecution of astrologers at the turn of this century, many astrologers lived and worked under pseudonyms. There were at least three astrologers who used the name Sepharial, and then there was W F Allen who is best known to the world as Alan Leo. A friend of mine sent me a xeroxed page from *The Traditional Astrologer,* issue #12,

August 1996, wherein Brian Carrington of Gloucester, England, presented a horary done by Leo's colleague H. L. Green, done when Green got a letter from Bessie Leo asking "Will Mr. Leo's illness be serious?" This original horary chart was given in *The Life and Work of Alan Leo* (p. 82). Greene did the horary for 3:10 p.m. BST, August 29, 1917, and for where he was, Bournmouth, England. The strange thing is that neither Leo nor his closest colleagues put much faith in horary astrology. Mr. Carrington believes that Mr. Green resorted to horary as a way of reassuring Mrs. Leo, and he came up with the same diagnosis as had Leo's doctor, which Green did not know, that the situation was not serious and would work itself out in a day or two. The fact is that Alan Leo died less than 24 hours after this horary was done, 10:00 a.m. BST, August 30, 1917, after two more violent seizures and at age fifty-seven. Since that article mentioned the actual time of when Alan Leo took to his bed, I decided to try to see what a decumbiture for that time would show.

There is some confusion over the birth time of Alan Leo. It is reported as late as 6:10 a.m., which would have given him Virgo rising, and we know that many people, astrologers included, would rather be Leo rising than Virgo rising. Actually he was already a Leo by Sun sign. He rectified his chart to a time with which he himself was satisfied even though it put Saturn on his Ascendant. He was born at Westminster, downtown London, 51N30, 4W40. Leo himself said he always understood he was born at 6:00 or 6:10 a.m., and later on his wife reported that he had rectified his own chart back to 5:49 a.m. He first became interested in astrology when he was about twenty-five years old. At that time he met Walter Richard Old (who was later to be better known as Sepharial). Old was then connected with the Theosophists and a friend of Mme. Blavatsky. With another friend, F.W. Lacey, Leo started the influential and popular periodical, *The Astrologer's Magazine,* which grew as a result not only of hard work but by the offer of personal horoscopes to all new subscribers. There was soon a name change to *Modern Astrology.*

Leo himself was twice tried for foretelling the future. The trial in 1914 got thrown out of court, but at his second trial, in 1917, he was found guilty and fined 30 Pounds. It was then that he decided to move from London to the north Cornish town of Bude. He was working hard to rewrite his books in such a way that all prophesy and prediction was taken out of astrology. Leo was working at least five hours a day at this task when he became ill.

For all his involvement in astrology, especially as publisher and author, it is difficult to believe that he could neither read nor write. He met and married a rich divorcee who was also a palmist. She took his dictation and helped make him the best known astrologer of his time. The marriage enabled him to devote his full time to astrology. Once in a while, his wife's name appeared as author of articles in his magazines to make it seem he was not the only contributor.

246. Alan Leo Decumbiture
Natal Chart
Aug 27 1917
5:00 PM BST -1:00
Bode Cornwall
51N04 004W40
Geocentric
Tropical
Campanus
True Node

Compliments of:-
Joseph Silveira deMello
1755 Franklin Str #204
San Francisco CA 94109
Tel (415) 775-8939
email jsmelscorp@AOL.com

247. Alan Leo
Natal Chart
Aug 7 1860
5:49 AM GMT +0:00
Westminster, London
51N30 000W07
Geocentric
Tropical
Campanus
True Node

Compliments of:-
Joseph Silveira deMello
1755 Franklin Str #204
San Francisco CA 94109
Tel (415) 775-8939
email jsmelscorp@AOL.com

Leo's books are the most Leo part about him, which is not to say that they might not also be quite thoroughly Virgo in style. His big books are solid and substantial. His little books are pocket sized manuals which include books on mundane astrology and another little jewel *Notable Nativity's* in which he gives the data and chart particulars of many charts he had studied. Unfortunately there is a lack of consistency in his data. In some he misses completely place of birth, time of birth, and sometimes year of birth, and nowhere does he give us any sources for his data. Since he gave us house cusps and planetary positions, we can only try to replicate them taking what data he did give as true. But trying to replicate them met with some frustration. We know of course that it is not beyond any Leo to fail to give pertinent complete data in his exercise of infallible supremacy. In the case of the data of his own wife, he left out her time, date and place of birth entirely. I find it incredible that no one has ever studied or published anything about the chart of Bessie Leo who must have been a remarkable woman.

Again it is useful to remember that Alan Leo did not know of Pluto or Chiron, and to be aware that he never used any other points in his charts such as Vertex, East Point or Fortune. He could not read for himself the works of any other astrologer (and Leos don't have to read anyone else). As Mr Carrington himself comments on the Green horary, they did not in those days know of the Part of Death as it was known to Dorotheus of Sidon, which in that horary would have been at 28 Capricorn and would moved right along as the Moon moved to get to it. Essentially, the horary has a void of course Moon. Had he known it, he would not have said that Leo's illness was trifling.

Leo took to his bed at about five in the evening on August 27, 1917. Very late Sagittarius was rising with the Moon just above the Ascendant. What we have here is that both Ascendant and Moon are pretty much void of course. The usual dictum in this case would be that it is too late to ask, that the matter is already and unalterably set, or that "nothing will come of the matter." I vastly dislike both these descriptions no matter how often they turn out to be true. In my mind it is never too late to ask. In any case, Moon Void of Course should be disregarded in Sagittarius (Bonatus aphorism #64).

A chart always has something to reveal to us. What hits the eye has already been mentioned, Moon on Ascendant. The other thing is that most of the planets are on the other side of the chart. Good heavens, the Sun is in the eighth. Pluto, which was not known then, is of no help for him in the seventh. Mars, which rules the Midheaven, is in the seventh, firmly with the doctor who is in charge of the treatment. The chart ruler Jupiter is in the sixth house. also giving the ailment supremacy.

I did this chart in my usual style, with Campanus houses, but I also checked it out with Placidus houses where MC and ASC angles remain exactly the same and only intermediate houses change. Neither style is going to put Saturn in the eighth house. What we are told happened is that on the morning of August 30, 1917, Leo suffered two cerebral aneurysms which caused severe convulsions. He must immediately have gone into coma. In any case, he died about ten o'clock that morning. Note that this decumbiture is based on a time said to be "about" 5:00 p.m. BST. This does not mean British Standard Time; it means Summer time, and we must remember that Britain was then in WW I and clocks were advanced an hour for what we would today call War Time.

We are given a cause of death which we would normally associate with Aries. The part of the body afflicted was his head or brain. Yet Aries rules the third house of the decumbiture, and Mars is in the seventh house. The rather curious thing is that the decumbiture Mars is exactly opposite his natal Mars. In a case of aneurysm, a burst blood vessel, severe internal bleeding occurs, and anything involving blood is Jupiter which in the decumbiture is in the sixth house. The occupants of his seventh are Mars, Neptune and Saturn, and again we have another anomaly. The decumbiture Saturn at 8 Leo is exactly on his natal Jupiter at 8 Leo.

Sudden Onset of Vertigo

On October 15, 1996, my sister and her regular foursome finished their round of golf and adjourned to the club snack area for coffee and soft drinks. Getting on to 1:00 p.m. MST Denver, she was seriously discomforted by an attack of vertigo that she asked her friends to call in a 911 emergency ambulance alert. She was immediately taken to hospital and went rapidly from emergency room to intensive care where she was treated and medicated for the vertigo and released about four hours later to the care of her primary physician.

Her own doctor discussed a viral attack to her ear that might have been responsible for the vertigo, and they discussed whether this involved some sort of small stroke. An appointment was made for her to have an MRI the following day. Following that exam, the doctor informed her that he had good news and bad news. There was no indication that a stroke had occurred, but they had found a tumor inside her head which he felt was benign. He referred her to a neurologist and neurosurgeon with whom he had already discussed her case.

By the time they got to the neurologist, it was October 30. She was thoroughly examined for physical capabilities and coordination, and together they examined the films of the MRI scan. The tumor was located on the left side of her head, forward of the ear and rather higher up. The size of it was slightly more than an inch. In any case, the situation was going to require surgery, and, in his opinion, the sooner the better. The operation would pose only a minimal risk as the tumor was outside the membrane covering the brain itself but under her skull.

He also happily told her that the tumor was benign. Surgery was scheduled for December 19. Since all she had to do was rest and take things easy, she and her husband went to visit a sister in Florida in November, returning only in time for the annual family Thanksgiving reunion in Texas.

There is no recorded or family history of her time of birth, but she was born December 22, 1926, at Newport, Rhode Island. She would have a 0 Capricorn Sun and

Moon in Leo. She had married a Navy man who graduated from business school with a Phi Beta Kappa and spent his entire career in the oil and natural gas business. They had four daughters and a son, and four of these five children are Aries rising, while the middle child, a daughter, is Cancer rising. Throughout her life she pursued all sorts of various interests, art school, ceramics, Biblical studies, golf and shopping, shopping and more shopping.

The decumbiture chart was done for 1:00 p.m. MST and must stand alone. It gives 3 Capricorn rising (and her birth Sun was zero Capricorn). It really was too early as diagnosis was only arrived at after much testing. The decumbiture Moon is in the first degree of Sagittarius which would aspect everything else in the chart except that its last major aspects are a sextile Sun in Libra, a trine to Mars in Leo in the eighth house and a sextile to the Libra Midheaven all favorable aspects. The odd thing is that the Moon of the chart is in the eleventh house, engaged in recreational activities with friends, but then exactly conjunct Pluto almost at her twelfth house cusp which may account for the sudden attack of vertigo.

We wonder about the nature of the ailment with Cancer on the seventh house, with Gemini ruling the sixth house and Mercury in Libra in the ninth house. The ninth house leads us to considerations of why things are as they are, to intellectual philosophizing, to brain operation. Saturn the ruler of the patient is in the third house in Aries, the sign of the head. Resorting to Elspeth Ebertin's *Anatomical Correspondence to Zodiacal Degrees* as translated by astrologer Mary Vohryzek, we find: "cerebellum (abscess)." Part of my charting of this situation involved a diurnal for this day. In the diurnal, natal Fortune was on the diurnal Midheaven, and natal Uranus was on the diurnal MC. There was nothing on the diurnal Ascendant, but it was at the midpoint of her natal MC and natal Mercury which, in Ebertin's *The Combination of Stellar Influences* gave the biological correspondence of Mercury-Midheaven as "the motor nerve centers of the brain." Oddly enough, soon after, movie actress Elizabeth Taylor was found to be similarly afflicted and to require the same surgery.

I hope that as astrologers we have all learned when we find the sign Cancer on the sixth or seventh house that this does not correlated to a diagnosis of cancer. In my sister's case, there is no known family history of cancer although she has had skin cancers on her neck due to golfing in the sun without protection. In the three years past she has had several minor procedures to take care of such exposures. Our family history, maternally, runs to dietary allergies and kidney problems. However, she strongly resembles our father's side of the family, and his middle age was plagued by a series of subcutaneous cysts on his head, all benign, and all outside the skull. However, she did inherit a lot of the maternal family allergies. Checking Carter was not much help until I checked "abscesses" and he comments about them in the area of the ear, noting these as afflictions at 3 Aries-Libra. In this decumbiture, Saturn is backing off from 3 degrees of Aries.

Anything in the first house is going to impact the patient. There we see Jupiter and Neptune in Capricorn and Uranus in early Aquarius. Jupiter rules the twelfth and is nicely placed in the house ahead of what which it rules. Jupiter and Neptune both rule the intercepted portion of the second house, and Uranus and Saturn rule the second house with Uranus in the house behind that which it rules, and Saturn in the house ahead of where it rules. Oddly enough, Uranus is at the midpoint of the trine from Moon-Pluto to Saturn. But notice how many square aspects exist from the first to the ninth house. Squares provide us with energy which we have to control ourselves.

I tried to put a positive spin on the Cancer seventh house as indicator of a caring doctor and then noted the Moon with Pluto on the edge of the twelfth house of the decumbiture. Moon and Pluto are trine to the Saturn of this chart with Uranus at the midpoint of the trine. The chart also has a mutual reception between Mercury and Venus. By the time she would be operated upon, the Sun was going to be getting out of her twelfth house, coming to the Ascendant of this chart.

Every detail of the operation was discussed with her. She knew of the location and shape of the incision the doctors would have to make, that she would have to either partially or totally shave her hair. And this was so thoroughly discussed that she opted to shave her hair entirely so that the wigs she would be wearing right after the operation would fit properly. And since she loves nothing better than shopping for anything, she immediately went out and bought several models. Another thing she did was to sit down and write a round-robin letter which was issued to all family members regarding her condition and prognosis.

Her doctors prepared her thoroughly. Perhaps you can see in the chart that she would have some temporary disfunction of speech after the operation. She did suffer small episodes of *petite mal* or aphasia, and things she tried to say got twisted up in the saying. And all she could do was to wait for a better time to say the same things and get them right. Her attitude was fabulous both prior to and after surgery. The procedure went well and she was out of hospital in time for Christmas. Several of her children journeyed to be with her while she was hospitalized and for the holiday. The horrible thing to her was that when she again got out on the golf course, she had totally lost her golf swing. She could not connect with the ball. That was immediately remedied by scheduling golf lessons with the club pro. Her swing, she admits, was never of the best, but she was determined to regain her coordination. With the Sun moving to the Ascendant at the time of the operation, all the convalescence would take place with the Sun in the first house. Note, too, that the Moon went around the chart twice from decumbiture.

As decumbitures go, this is not a bad chart. The Ascendant is just to the point of allowable reading. The Moon, early in Sagittarius is going to start with a trine to Saturn and end with a sextile to the Sun. The Sun of the chart is the highest planet in the chart and will surely influence her treatment, status and prognosis. Although I was inclined to superstition about the surgery being

248. Vertigo decumbiture
Natal Chart
Oct 15 1996
1:00 PM MDT +6:00
Denver CO, USA
39N45 104W59
Geocentric
Tropical
Campanus
True Node

Compliments of:-
Joseph Silveira deMello
1755 Franklin Str #204
San Francisco CA 94109
Tel (415) 775-8939
email jsmelscorp@AOL.com

scheduled just before her next birthday, I restrained myself. She was even able to joke about the operation by having a camera shot without wig and bandages to say that this was a shot of what Elizabeth Taylor looked like after her operation.

Collapse Decumbiture

I am amazed at the amount of support I got when I told friends and astrologers the subjects about which I was writing. From so many, I was flooded by charts and data, and even requests for autographed copies when the book comes out. One of the first to respond was Karen Christino who also sent this decumbiture of the collapse of her father. It is not specifically a chart for this section since he had little to say the moment he collapsed. Karen underlined that this chart has Mercury and Mars out of bounds, her reason for sending it to me.

Her father was at his club or living room away from home. The bar was just opened at 7:45 p.m., January 7, 1993, Seaford, New York. The nice thing about this chart is that the time of it is officially recorded. He had just sat down at the bar, and his first drink had just been put in front of him. He suddenly collapsed, hitting and breaking his nose against the bar. The fire department was just around the corner and immediately responded and took him off to the hospital.

Donald Christino began his career as a motorcycle policemen. After years of doing this, he became a mechanic in the maintenance and repair garage. Then, for a brief time, he got into credit card tracing, and finally he became and is a courtroom bailiff, a job he very much enjoys and from which he has no thoughts of retirement.

We notice that the Ascendant is not yet in the final degrees of Leo. This is ruled by the Sun on the edge of his sixth house, all mixed up with Vertex, Uranus and Neptune and has opposed the Moon and is opposing Mars retrograde. Saturn rules the sixth and seventh and is in the sixth with Fortune. Saturn and Fortune are semi-sextile stellium on the edge of the sixth house Sun-Saturn mutual reception. Sun is semi-square Venus, a nice occupant of the seventh house which rules the tenth of treatment. We are making the usual effort to see what the patient has going for him and how strong the ailment against him might be. This is not going to be easy. Only the Moon, Mars, Chiron and Jupiter are on his side of the chart, and Jupiter is T-square to the oppositions to Mars and the stellium. Uranus and Neptune show us that the onset was both unexpected and mysterious. Everything else is on the side of the doctor and the illness. And these are all very woven with each other. The patient's doctors are going to be ruled by Aquarius who always knows what is best for other people. Saturn rules Aquarius in a nocturnal chart. Keep an eye on this Fortune in Pisces, even with Venus is in the seventh, as we tell of his experience in this problem. We also have Saturn in the house it rules and behind the house it rules, this latter not a good omen, and we remember that Saturn is a steadying influence, conservative, and given to practical considerations. I think it favors the doctors in charge, and the doctors will be working on him with a world of experience. It is not bad to have a steadfast Saturn working in a twelfth house position. But Saturn also rules the sixth of the illness which may prolong it.

Now, since we have declared this a nocturnal chart, if we have opted to work with one old ruler, we should consistently work with all old rulers. This means that we can discard Neptune as ruler of the eighth and substitute Jupiter which is on the patient's side of the chart, in the second house of his immediate future, and that we can discard Pluto as ruler of the fourth for Mars which is not too well placed in Cancer but is also on the patient's side in the eleventh house. Note that Pluto in opposition to the Midheaven is T-square to Chiron and the Ascendant.

Now we have Mars making a counterpoint to Sun, Uranus, Neptune which brought all this on (though Mars also had some responsibility in the problem). We are not happy to see that Mars is retrograde, so we can foresee that whatever Mars help will be coming, it will be somewhat tainted. A description of retrograde Mars that I have always liked tells that Mars retrograde is like trying to drive with the brakes on. Being retrograde, further thought is going to weigh in with the unappealing probability that any Mars solution is going to have to be reconsidered at some later time, and that in the balance with the Sun and a couple of outer planets, in their fight for supremacy over the Sun, sets up a war room situation on the enemy side of the chart. The ego is fighting the sudden and mysterious disability which is going to prove itself superior to the patient's ego and that temporary measures (due to retrograde Mars) may not be as effective at this time or under these conditions. Remember that Mercury and Mars are out of bounds, and that has to have significance here. Of course I charted the course of the Moon in the sign Cancer, seeing the path of square to Jupiter, quincunx to Saturn, opposition to the Sun, conjunction to Mars, sextile the Ascendant, quincunx Fortune, opposite Uranus, opposite Neptune, and, finally, a trine to Pluto. Notice the prominence of things in 17 and 18 degrees, and although the nodal axis is not on a degree of any other placement, in times ahead the North Node will move to 18 and 17 Sagittarius. This well may time future developments.

And, if we have arrived at the notion that the seventh house is well ruled, and we see in the seventh a Venus exalted in Pisces (and we have seen Saturn trine Jupiter). The semi-square between Venus and Sun-Uranus-Neptune may produce friction and some impatience between patient and his doctors. Are we ranging too far afield, mixing apples and oranges in our swing between traditional and modern astrology?

Karen Christino also contributed her father's possible natal chart data as 10:00 a.m. EST, March 21, 1924, Brooklyn, New York, 40N38, 73W56. She had never worked with his chart. It was unsupported family assumption regarding his time of birth. She knew I was working with diurnals, and I did immediately set up his natal for the given time and did a diurnal for the day of his collapse. The diurnal (Chart #205) came up with the diurnal nodal axis on the diurnal vertical axis and natal Jupiter on the diurnal Midheaven, sufficient touches to show applicability and to prove the assumed birth time correct. She also knew that I was interested in Saturn

250. Collapse decumbiture

Natal Chart
Jan 7 1993
7:45 PM EST +5:00
Seaford NY, USA
40N40 073W39
Geocentric
Tropical
Campanus
True Node

Compliments of:-
Joseph Silveira deMello
1755 Franklin Str #204
San Francisco CA 94109
Tel (415) 775-8939
email jsmelscorp@AOL.com

251. Donald Christino

Natal Chart
Mar 21 1924
10:00 AM EST +5:00
Brooklyn NY, USA
40N38 073W56
Geocentric
Tropical
Campanus
True Node

Compliments of:-
Joseph Silveira deMello
1755 Franklin Str #204
San Francisco CA 94109
Tel (415) 775-8939
email jsmelscorp@AOL.com

and Jupiter at zero declination, and was as surprised as I to see the Sun and Moon of his natal chart both at zero declination, born just after a Full Moon and with his Natal Mars out of bounds. This is a man who had gone through life doing what he wanted to do and, at over seventy, is not taking a retirement back seat. At birth he was a Gemini rising with Aries Sun and Moon in Libra. He has always enjoyed his place in the community and led an active life.

Every astrologer cannot resist comparing any chart he sees with his own. It is a way of seeing what affinity the astrologer has with the subject he is studying. In addition, I could not help but see on the occasion of his collapse (in the decumbiture chart) the Uranus-Neptune con- junction. In 1993, the stations of those two planets caused me two very bad computer failures. Would there be a repetition of Uranus-Neptune for Donald Christino?

The day after his collapse, a pacemaker was installed, and the patient left the hospital to be given time to recuperate. Although he eventually went back to work, the pacemaker was not quite satisfactory. He found himself able to function, but he felt he was not regaining his old pep and vitality, and he complained that he was not doing better. And, sure enough, persistent complaining eventually impressed his doctors, and he was to return to hospital the following September for by-pass surgery which helped to restore the patient to greater well-being.

Edith Custer

Edith Custer was a well known astrologer who won a Regulus Award for publishing *Mercury Hour* for more than twenty-five years. In it, astrologer-subscribers correspond with one another. She was not feeling well on November 30, 1996 at her home in Lynchburg, Virginia (37N23, 79W08) and called for an ambulance to take her to hospital at 10:55 a.m. EST. This may not be quite exact data for a decumbiture, for presumably, she must have admitted earlier that she was ill enough to go to hospital, but I must say that any decision to call an ambulance is too far away from a definitive admission of serious problems. What must have brought on the final decision was the evidence of rectal bleeding along with discomforting pain. At any rate, we get a chart with a very early degree of Aquarius rising, and Aquarian she is not, but it does say the patient is an astrologer. Uranus on the Ascendant underlines that as it obviously speaks of a sudden and unexpected turn for the worse.

No question of it being too early to read this chart, but it certainly was indicative that tests and studies had to be done until a diagnosis was achieved. There is, however, a striking consideration to make between this decumbiture chart and her own natal chart (January 5, 1923, 12:58 p.m. EST, Whitestone, New York, 40N48, 73W48. She is a Taurus rising with Capricorn on the Midheaven, and Neptune that day was within orb of her natal Midheaven. This gives us a cautionary moment. When any planet leaves a cadent house for an angular house it seems to deal out one last swipe at the person of the chart. Neptune rules the second house of her immediate future, and Jupiter twelfth is the well known Guardian Angel placement in critical situations. Even though she is an astrologer, I very much doubt she planned to go to hospital with Uranus on the Ascendant.

Another consideration is that this chart has a Leo Moon, which is almost making a lunar return, so the curious astrologer would do that lunar return. By birth she has Moon conjunct Neptune, and now Moon will come to a quincunx to Neptune. In this decumbiture, the Ascendant falls in her natal tenth house of her status, right on natal Mercury, so decumbiture Uranus also on natal Mercury. Under such circumstances, even a Taurus rising could get very intuitive and not delay making decisions.

That decumbiture Moon in Leo, in the seventh house, can afflict the doctor in a decumbiture. The Moon can bring indecision to the doctor, perhaps even emotional problems. The last thing anyone wants is a doctor who is not at his best. The Moon was last over Saturn, traditional ruler of the decumbiture, and retrograde in this chart is enough for us to stick with Uranus for chart significator here. That Moon last past Saturn which signifies conditions prior to the chart obviously involves a situation coming on for at least ten days. The Moon makes a trine to Mercury and a sextile to Chiron before leaving Leo. This chart appealed to me with Venus on my Sun and Jupiter on my Jupiter, sharpening my interest in how these work in the charts of other people.

Even prior to doing a lunar return, I did a diurnal for the day she went to the hospital. And I am glad I did so. I found Mercury close to the diurnal Midheaven. Now the diurnal Midheaven moves at one degree per day, and transiting or diurnal Mercury (the same thing) generally moves quite a bit more quickly and needs a quick look at the ephemeris. Much later on in December, Mercury would be turning retrograde, but at the moment, Mercury was up to speed. Mercury on an angle is significant. After all, in the decumbiture chart, that Uranus on the decumbiture Ascendant is also on her natal Mercury.

It is not normal to look at a decumbiture with the natal planets around an outer ring, but we all know to look at specific touches of the planets of any technique to natal placements. Indeed, I checked these when I did the diurnal. I saw diurnal Neptune coming to natal Midheaven, and right next to that, diurnal Uranus was on natal Mercury. Diurnal Pluto was conjunct natal Venus (and that always seems to involve problems in that part of the body). In the diurnal, diurnal Mercury at the top of the chart, was making a T-square to diurnal East Point and Saturn in opposition to diurnal Vertex the latter always significant in a health problem.

Edith was immediately put in ICU for testing which continued all weekend until on next Monday it was revealed that she was suffering from diverticulitis. Quick, the dictionary, to find out what sort of condition this is. Dorland's *Medical Dictionary* is explicit. This is a condition marked by the formation of small pouches along the border of the colon which get infested and sometimes sets up irritation and gives rise to inflammation and abscess. Since the whole digestive process is a Virgo thing, we are not now surprised to see Mars just past an opposition to her natal Mars and now in the sev-

252. Edith's decumbiture

Natal Chart
Nov 30 1996
10:55 AM EST +5:00
Lynchburg VA
37N23 079W08
Geocentric
Tropical
Campanus
True Node

Compliments of:-
Joseph Silveira deMello
1755 Franklin Str #204
San Francisco CA 94109
Tel (415) 775-8939
email jsmelscorp@AOL.com

253. Cancer decumbiture
Natal Chart
Dec 13 1996
4:00 PM CST +6:00
Rockford IL, USA
42N16 089W06
Geocentric
Tropical
Campanus
True Node

Compliments of:-
Joseph Silveira deMello
1755 Franklin Str #204
San Francisco CA 94109
Tel (415) 775-8939
email jsmelscorp@AOL.com

enth house of the decumbiture chart, and then we notice the eighth house is ruled by Virgo, sort of leading us in the right direction.

Of course we run the risk when we do to many things to a chart (diurnal, lunar return) when we have a perfectly substantial decumbiture. Remember, the decumbiture is a sort of horary, and horary is supposed to teach us to remained focused only on the essentials. A check of decumbiture Mercury locates it almost on the cusp of a twelfth house Sagittarius, and there we find that Capricorn, the natal Sun sign of the patient is intercepted in the twelfth, the interception holds Jupiter and Neptune, both rulers of the decumbiture second house of the immediate future. The patient's condition background involves blood and a mystery, and I expected Jupiter in the twelfth to manifest as that Guardian Angel position which is going to come to the rescue of the patient in extremis. I would judge that the patient had more going for her side of the chart. The rulers of the ailment and doctor were on her side.

There was a successful operation but a long uncomfortable recuperative period at home. All of this happened during the deteriorating health of her late husband and also coincided with the mailing of the winter issue of *Mercury Hour* which nevertheless went out on schedule.

Norma Storey

Norma is the astrologer who came to my rescue in discovering the identity of John B. Anderson of Rockford, Illinois when I was working with the declinations section of this book. Our acquaintance in astrology goes back to the fabulous 1974 AFA San Francisco Convention where I first came into contact with many people who are astrological friends today. In the meantime and over the years, time has not treated her well. She has had an very debilitating stroke, and just after Edith's operation, she reported that on the 13th of December 1996 that she had been examined at her doctor's office where he found cancerous tumors in her right breast. To make matters worse, one week later, similar tumors were found in the left breast, and her doctor scheduled her for an operation at 1:00 p.m. CST, January 8, 1997. The first diagnosis was made at 4:00 p.m. CST on December 13, 1996, and it is for this time and date that the decumbiture was done.

It is immediately plain that we are not going to like this chart. First of all, it is Gemini rising and her own natal rising sign is Sagittarius (September 2, 1935, 1:50 p.m. PST, Bellingham, Washington, 48N46, 122W29). Here, the Sun is in Sagittarius in the seventh house, and she is in the hands of her doctor and at the mercy of her ailment. The chart significator Mercury is also in the seventh, underlining doctor's care. Jupiter ruling he seventh is in the eighth which also has Neptune and then Uranus which rules the tenth of the treatment. One hopes the convalescence is not going to involve difficult therapies. A small blessing is that none of the planets of this chart are retrograde. There is little on the patient's side of the chart, while the side of the doctor and the ailment has everything but Saturn and Fortune. With the Moon in the Aquarius ninth house, we can agree that the patient did not go into this situation with equanimity. Over the years, she has learned to live with left side paralysis, and this

was sort of an unexpected and dismaying coup de grace. How many trials can a person be expected to suffer?

The Moon in early Aquarius will aspect a lot of the chart during its stay in that sign. The list is nicely curtailed if we leave out all minor non-Ptolemaic aspects. But it does not help that the final aspect is a square to Venus intercepted in Scorpio in the sixth house and ruling the sixth Libra cusp. But we have really a final trine to Chiron, looked upon by some astrologers as a healer. But I look upon Chiron as indicator of something obvious which we castigate ourselves for not seeing, which if it causes us to laugh at ourselves, might just have some healing influence. Chiron here is also in the sixth house. Perhaps the situation is not as serious or radical as it might be, something that must be done, perhaps not too disfiguring. Certainly at the time of this original diagnosis, something was being overlooked. And it was. The same tumors were also in the other breast. Chiron was about to leave Libra and go into the intercepted Scorpio of this chart, where it would surely be at the time of the operation, and perhaps of benefit to the patient.

The operation itself was performed as we were going into a New Moon, a good time for corrective surgery. Mercury which was direct at the time of the chart, was, at the time of the operation, retrograde, another good indication for successful corrections. She was able a week after the operation to call and tell me that the surgery had gone well, that she was out of the hospital and mercifully not scheduled for either chemotherapy or radiation. The operation itself had not been as radical as originally supposed, and that the cancerous tumors had not spread to her lymph nodes which was what denied a need for radical surgery.

Notice that Mercury in this decumbiture is out of bounds and out of orb of parallel to the Sun. Declinations sometimes move with the speed of their planets, and by the time of the operation, it was parallel Venus and well within bounds. In working with decumbitures, it is always helpful to keep an open ephemeris easily at hand. By the time of the operation, the Moon had gone almost completely around the chart toward a New Moon in Capricorn, and she no doubt got the good news from her doctor before the Moon got into Aquarius again, and was probably able to breathe a sign of relief the next time the Moon went over the Midheaven.

In looking at this decumbiture, I had full natal data on her, and I was able to do all kinds of derivative charts, secondary progressions, solar and lunar returns, not to mention diurnal charts for the dates of diagnoses and operation. I had a great deal of astrological information, though we can too frequently not have enough. Throughout, information was both positive and negative, and it is the work of any astrologer to discover which indicators outweigh the others.

Heart Attack

On March 13, 1996, an astrologer I have known for years had a heart attack at 2:30 p.m. CST, Dawson, Illinois, 39N48, 89W29. The chart came up with Leo ris-

255. Heart Attack decumbiture

Natal Chart
Mar 13 1996
2:30 PM CST +6:00
Dawson IL, USA
39N48 089W29
Geocentric
Tropical
Campanus
True Node

Compliments of:-
Joseph Silveira deMello
1755 Franklin Str #204
San Francisco CA 94109
Tel (415) 775-8939
email jsmelscorp@AOL.com

ing, which is also her natal rising sign (November 4, 1930, 10:25 p.m. EST, Buffalo, New York, 42N53, 70W53; she died of a stroke on May 3, 2001 in Dawson, Illinois). But there the similarity ends, for while she has a Scorpio Sun and an Aries Moon, this decumbiture had a Pisces Sun and the Moon in Capricorn exactly on this chart's sixth house cusp and still in orb of her natal Saturn. From first sight I did not like this chart. The Sun as significator is surrounded by Mars and Saturn, and besiegement is never an indication of fine things. These were in the eighth house and Mercury was on the cusp of this eighth house. The sixth house is not better signified by having Saturn as ruler and containing Jupiter, Neptune and Uranus.

Uranus which rules the decumbiture seventh, the sudden need of the doctor is opposite her natal Ascendant and natal Mars, and Uranus is in the house behind that which it rules. The decumbiture Moon has last been over the Vertex and Pluto of the chart. Moon's final aspects would be a sextile to Saturn and a conjunction to Neptune, and this is said to be not bad. Once again, there was little on the patient's side of the chart, mainly Venus on a Venus ruled Midheaven which is a fine indicator for medication and treatment. I was reassured that she would respond well, but I was not reassured that the event was really mild and a mere passing affliction. Knowing her rural location, what worried me was her distance from hospital and medical attention.

My friend, the patient, is a tiny lady, quite attractive, with, if not vigor, at least the determination of a racing greyhound. She is, after all, a Leo rising with natal Mars in Leo in the first house which gives decided Aries overtones so strong they cannot be denied. Moreover, her natal Moon is in Aries. She is not exactly in the best of health, on a strict diet, but, nevertheless, always on the go. There was absolutely no mistaking her natal Scorpio Sun sign. A Scorpio may become ill, as can any of us, but Scorpio illnesses take three stages. At first they want to be let alone and not fussed over. Secondly they always follow doctor's orders. When they get around to grumbling about their situation, you can be certain a cure is on its way. Her inherited chronic condition is sure to someday surely carry her away, but this chart has two mutual receptions, Jupiter and Saturn and Saturn and Neptune, rulers of the fifth, sixth, seventh and eighth of the decumbiture, I felt convinced of that there were not sufficient confirmations of danger in this chart.

And here again I had birth data and a sheaf of charts with which I worked. I met her through the pages of *Mercury Hour*, and I had visited her at this and a previous home, both of them charming and in dramatic settings. Over the course of years, I had the charts of her family connections, ex-husband, three daughters. As an astrologer, she had been very much involved in the breeding of horses and dogs and used astrology extensively in planning the breeding and engineering the sex of foals and whelps. Once upon a time she used to issue an almanac for horse breeders. And where she had been interested in Shelties, more lately she has been highly involved with Sussex Spaniels which she has shown and for which she has garnered many championship ribbons.

Another interesting thing about decumbiture charts is that they are more evocative when any placement degree number

repeats in the chart, here Neptune is opposite the East Point and trine Fortune which is sextile the East Point of the chart. Moon and Venus are exactly trine. A heart attack when the Ascendant is going on 13 Leo, according to Elspeth Ebertine, is indicative of problems in the right chamber of the heart. She, by the way, has no previous history of heart ailments and those are not the source of her really serious malaise, celiac sprue. The Moon which ends its stay in Capricorn with a conjunction to Neptune, generally regarded as favorable by all astrologers, meets an almost superstitious line of thought with me. I am as ambivalent about the Moon as I am suspicious about Neptune.

Serious Fall

I originally had a serious fall just after 9:00 p.m. PST, January 10, 1998, San Francisco, California. I had returned home in good order and just opened the door to my apartment and stepped into it. There was no one else present. I turned on the entry light fixture and was about to turn to close my door when I was pushed in the middle of my back just a bit lower than my shoulder blades. With rather unusual force, I landed against the left door jamb to my living room, felt myself hit the wall, and lost consciousness until I hit the floor with great force on my right shoulder and head. I managed to turn on my back and catch my breath. I noted the scatter rug in the doorway was all ruched up, and a chair which partly rested on that rug was moved out into the doorway. As I reconstructed it, I must have scuffed up the rug, moved the chair, hit it with my lower back to account for the pain in my lumbar spine, and spun off that to hit the floor on my right side. There was silence all around me. I managed to get up, note the keys were out of the door, I was later to find them flung across the room. I hurt so badly that I found Tylenol with codeine and took two, undressed on the spot and crawly across to my bed. Needless to say, I was in great pain next day, but I got up, took two more pills, took the elevator down to get my newspaper and proceeded to live my day as best I could at my usual routine. I did make an effort to lie down on my sofa during the day, but that was more uncomfortable than sitting in a chair.

I only considered going to the hospital when on the twenty-third I was running out of pain pills and was not improving. There I was fully examined and it was found I had a couple or herniated disks in the lower spine. Another kind of pain pill was prescribed, and I came on home. During all this period I was much involved in astrology. I was updating the chart of a friend's birthday and heard his mother was hospitalized and promptly predicted her death. I had been unable to get hold of another old friend, so I walked five blocks to call on her when during all that time no one responded to her telephone. There I was told by a neighbor she had died just prior to Christmas. I also did readings for several clients and had two other old acquaintance die. My bartender where I went daily for two evening drinks said I must indeed have a high pain threshold to be walking around

257. Emergency decumbiture
Natal Chart
Jan 30 1998
9:00 AM PST +8:00
San Francisco CA
37N45 122W26
Geocentric
Tropical
Campanus
True Node

Compliments of:-
Joseph Silveira deMello
1755 Franklin Str #204
San Francisco CA 94109
Tel (415) 775-8939
email jsmelscorp@AOL.com

with a broken back. By the twenty-seventh, the new pills were making me depressed, and I went back to Tylenol, but my back was increasingly more painful.

The morning of January 30, I was in such great pain that I called a friend for help. While I waited for him, I managed to dress in gym clothes, and left my door ajar, but I could not get up on my feet. As soon as my friend arrived, he called 911 to get me to the hospital. This was not easy. In tight quarters, I had to be lifted into a rolling chair, wheeled to the elevator, and got on the ambulance gurney down in the lobby. Off I went to the hospital and there was put into a curtained cubicle and hooked up to intravenous feeding and a morphine IV. I lay on my back, people came and went, but mostly I was left alone and went to sleep. At some time in the wee hours of morning, I woke gasping for breath, felt I was not getting enough air, and was claustrophobic and paranoid. I wanted to see daylight and people. They immediately realized I had overdosed on morphine and gave me the oddest smelling oxygen. I can remember seldom being as depressed as I was. The triage nurse, still the same one who had admitted me, and I did not think to wonder why, said I did not require hospitalization, but I would have to go to a nursing home until my medication could be stabilized and my back improved.

This I did not want to do. I wanted to be hospitalized. No one told me they were in the second day of a nursing strike and I did not remember until later that I had read about that in the newspapers. But it seemed nothing was being done to get me out of that curtained off cubicle. I told the nurse I would go home. I got dressed and called a taxi and did in fact come home. I was glad to sit up at my computer, and I did a diurnal of the day and found Saturn on my IC to tell me that home was not where I should be. Moreover, Saturn was quincunx my natal Saturn. I moved from my computer to my sofa, slept a couple of hours, talked to two friends on the telephone and looked at my chart. Everyone tried to convince me to bite the bullet and go to the nursing home. It was now I found out about the nursing strike. So I found a shopping bag, but in some books, desk diary, ephemeris, and a pad of paper, and called a taxi. I hurried back at the hospital and there was the same triage nurse. She immediately got me by her desk and talked me into the nursing home, called me a taxi, and back I came to a nursing home three blocks from where I live.

The nursing home was hell. No account was taken of my diet. Often the food was not identifiable. Toast was a problem they never solved along with how to serve a hot cup of coffee. I was daily out of bed by five, but food did not come until eight. I sat at the desk and read and did some writing, limped down the hall to the television and turned on the news. Everyone else was sleeping. A senior visiting nurse came to see me, check that my pills were working, listened to my complaints and assurances I would be fine at home, had food, could cook meals and could make hot coffee. She went off to consult with the head nurse and finally agreed after three days that I could go home. This process was incredible, too. I decided to have a shower and shave before I left the nursing home. I showered sitting down, a thing I had never done, and then found no way to get to a dry towel without slipping on the wet tiles. I am glad no one saw me accomplish this maneuver. I got into my clothes, filled my shopping bag,

was ready to go when suddenly a bag of supplies materialized. Or two bags. One was small and contained medication. The other contained all I would have needed to perform daily ablutions, razor, shaving soap, deodorant, shaving cologne, a veritable rash of supplies, all of which I had at home. I even got tooth paste and mouthwash. And I was off to the lobby with a new cane, to await my taxi home. My taxi and a fire engine responding to a silent alarm on the nursing home top floor arrived at the same time. Luckily I got a helpful cab driver who arrived in a van taxi. I was glad to get home.

I hobbled around and managed pretty well, and truly the pain was somewhat abated. It was obvious to me that the only way the pain could be surmounted was to think of other things, to get really involved. Nothing can be so disciplinary as working with the computer. It has its own way of operating. I had been thinking in terms of a new computer as the one I had was old and lacked a modem, and I noticed new computers came with built in modems. I saw that in March Mercury would go retrograde, so I got out in the second week of February and walked to the computer store three blocks away. I propped myself up on a counter, since my most painless position turns out to have been sitting, and let myself be sold a new Compaq. The salesman delivered it in two days and helped me set it up. The task was to transfer to my new computer the documents I had in my old computer. This was quite a process, taking on disk the stuff from my old computer, deleting personal stuff, entering it under DOS in the new computer and generally having more trouble than rustling livestock. I ordered a new astrology program, and when it came, I immediately tested it by doing a decumbiture for when I called my friend to get him to take me to the hospital, for which we actually needed an ambulance. This chart was done six weeks after I returned home from the nursing home.

The decumbiture chart came up with Pisces rising, the East Point at 21 Pisces, exactly my natal Uranus, was in the first house. Neptune as my significator in this case was in the eleventh house, minutes from going into the twelfth house. Now, while this is on my side of the chart, the placement is not endearing. I do remember in the trials and depression with pain killers that I had been depressed almost to suicide. One does not want Neptune in one's first house or angular, and it has never proven felicitous in the twelfth house of the subconscious. Mercury as ruler of the descendant is in the eleventh house. The Midheaven of medication and treatment is ruled by Jupiter also in the twelfth house. Neptune reminded me of my problem with morphine and further treatment was merely a watch to make sure I was getting effective pain killers. The Sun which rules the sixth house is also on my side of the chart but in the twelfth for the nursing home stay, the enforced inactivity. At least Neptune would be mundanely dignified in the twelfth, but I still found this little consolation. Doubtless there are some blessings to having Uranus in the house it rules, even if the Sun in Aquarius is square my natal Sun. Also on my side of the chart is Saturn though it is intercepted and private to me in my first house, still quincunx natal Saturn. I see that there are some things working for me, and that the only thing retrograde in the chart is Venus in Capricorn. In this chart Venus retrograde in the eleventh rules my second house of the immediate future, and the unoccupied intercepted part of my seventh house. The last aspect the Moon makes is a sextile to Mercury, and this is regarded as favorable to me. But there are no aspects between the ruler of the fourth and tenth of my status, nor of the ruler of the fourth and the eleventh of hopes and wishes. The Moon's previous aspect was to the South Node and Mars before that, and Mars has in recent years involved falling accidents. Reflecting on Chiron in the eighth and on my natal Saturn, what is the so obvious thing that I am missing. Is Pluto beyond the house it rules saving me for something else? Do I heed Noel Tyl's remark that when one system fails, all other get in line to take their turn, for such is the result of living a long life. I was due for a long convalescence, no doubt, and this does not bode well for someone as determined as I that nothing gets in the way of my daily tasks, my routines. The opposition of East Point and Vertex are somewhat tied in with trines and semi-squares instead of sextiles, notably the semisquare from Mars to Saturn which just might speak to us of chronic pain, a prolonged chronic condition. In the course of the twenty days from the fall itself to my going to hospital, the Moon has run the gauntlet from Gemini, opposing and conjuncting all those fourth quadrant placements and was still in the twelfth house until I got out of the nursing home.

Well the chart has Saturn square Neptune, mentioned only to say that I did see that. And I did see that the East Point opposite Vertex is T-square the Midheaven. I began to be aware of yet another problem. I was finding it difficult to read. One's sight does deteriorates with age, and long sessions with a computer monitor are not easeful. I forced myself to take regular breaks, but perhaps these measures were too late. Nothing in this decumbiture indicated eye problems. My right eye was the problem. Had I jarred something when I so solidly hit the floor.

I was getting a strange optical effect. If I looked at two pages of a book in front of me, the pages were exactly in front of me. They did not moved when I closed my right eye, but when I closed my left eye, the two pages would move one entire page-width to the left. My oculist, first, hardly believed me, and did not like it any better when he did a vertical test that proved I did have a problem. He could not make his apparatus bring together left and right vertical vision. But also he refused to discuss the matter. It was after all his specialty and I a mere layman patient. I felt I was being just barely tolerated as a nuisance. When he said that I had to get two pair of eye-glasses, one dedicated to distance vision, the other dedicated to reading, I balked. I wasn't going to spend the rest of my life swapping between two pairs of eyeglasses. He said it would be difficult for the optometrists to combine my prescription into the bifocals I have become used to wearing. He wrote out his prescription and left the room. Since he had not said he was through with me, I sat there awaiting his return, and when he did not, I went on to the optometry department where I was assured they could give me bifocals. And although these glasses eased my vertical distortion, it is still only partially corrected. If I look at a bright star, I soon get two of them. Scorpio like, I thought in terms of what it actually meant if he admitted to a condition that had not been checked when I first consulted my regular doctor at my first examination and tests. Doctors and HMO doctors particularly are very queasy about giving patients fodder for future litigation arising from any hint of patient neglect.

Perhaps decumbitures are not much done today because the very name for them sounds so old fashioned. Nevertheless the art of the decumbiture should never be so cavalierly dismissed. Its roots are legitimate and its services to the astrologically adept are marvelous. Do we leave all inquires of illness to the medicine men? Nonsense. We stretch our knowledge of horary and use it with artfulness. In decumbitures we are not bound by strictures except that the condition must be a true decumbiture. The ailing subject has to have made a conscious decision to take to bed and made an effort to summon help. All astrologers should expand through all the many techniques.

Diurnals

Diurnal means daily, which of course means transits. We habitually look to transits to trigger events in our lives. The soul of astrology is prediction, forecasting for ourselves and our clients. There are several ways of looking at transits and the most prevalent is to place them around our natal charts. We are well aware of the fallacy of Sun sign columns in our daily papers, and deplore them. When I started studying astrology in the 1960s, many astrologers discovered sunrise charts, but this is a very artificial method of working since the Sun is always put on the Ascendant, and then the same degree is given to all the house cusps around the chart to maintain the feel of the Ascendant to every activity of life.

It occurred to me ten years ago that astrologers watching the transits are too prone to give themselves much needless worry. A fellow astrologer clucked seriously about what would happen to me when Pluto transited my sixth house, failing to see that in my natal chart Mars does not aspect my natal Pluto, that Sun and Saturn are natally trine to Pluto, and that Mercury is in no aspect to Pluto. But it was he who died before the transit of Pluto failed to produce any serious events in my life. Not that things did not happen, but they occurred without touches of Pluto. Carter said nothing can happen that is not in the natal chart, but do astrologers really believe that? I think not. It sounds too intellectual, too pat, meaning impractical, so astrologers wait for the sky to fall. Astrologers who have studied horary astrology might force themselves to remember there must be more than one indicator, preferably three indicators, to bring serious difficulties.

The diurnal technique came to my attention. Once upon a time, astrologers did diurnals to create a personal daily horoscope. This is not a new technique for it was in greater use over fifty years ago. It may have fallen into disuse, because it required a little more than just placing transits around the natal chart. Philosophically, the diurnal technique works along the same line we use for secondary progressions of a day for a year. Here we assume that every year we are reborn on our birthdays. It even goes one step further to say that every day, at the time of our birth, we are reborn. The diurnal technique moves our natal angles about one degree each day until on our next birthday, our angles return to their natal positions. Those of us born during normal waking hours easily experience the daily moment of rebirth when our energies seem recharged. Those of us born at a time while we are normally sleeping simply have to believe that it is not merely sleep itself which is recharging us.

Of course, we know there are 365 days a year and only 360 degrees around the chart, but the slack is taken up because the speed of angular movement varies, some signs move faster or slower. From Cancer through Sagittarius the signs rise more slowly, and from Capricorn through Gemini, they quicken. Even taking leap year into account, we always come back to our natal angles on our birthdays, give or take a degree. In 1998, checking this out on my own chart, the return of the natal angles happened on November 2, rather than on the third which was my birthday.

As these moving angles proceed around the chart, they will hit all our natal placements four times each year. But what makes every year different is that they will also hit many of the transiting or diurnal planets. Some of the diurnal or transiting planets which move at the speed of a degree a day (the Sun), the same speed at which we are moving our angles, so the Sun, if it was natally in the fifth house, always stays in the fifth house of diurnals. Others move at more than one degree (Mercury and Venus) are rarely hit by our moving angles, usually doing so only when Mercury or Venus take time off to go retrograde. Mars goes more slowly, about one-third the speed of the Sun, but the diurnal (transiting) Moon know as the speediest of them all, outdoes itself by hitting all four angles each month. We will see how important this is.

In the course of these movements of diurnal angles to natal and diurnal planets, we achieve events in our lives only when the angles hit any two natal or diurnal (or a mix of them) on the same day. A single touch to an angle does not an event make. The single touch may provide a pleasant day, but significant life events only occur when there are combinations of two or more placements. If I had merely been looking at transits around my natal chart, I would have seen on March 11, 1999 that the Sun would be on my natal Uranus, that Uranus was coming to my Midheaven, that transiting Mars would be on my natal Sun and about to turn retrograde. Nothing special happened. Setting up a diurnal, not one of these transits touched a diurnal angle. In my natal chart, Sun and Uranus and Sun and Mars are in no aspect, and Uranus is in no aspect to my natal Midheaven. On the other hand, as an example, you will later see the chart for when the verdict was read to O.J. Simpson at the outcome of his criminal trial for murder, the trial where he was found not guilty, all four angles of his chart were occupied by natals and transits. That was an important day for him.

Now there are always rules, and this is the first of them. We check the angles, but traditionally we are told not to try reading the diurnal Descendant. If you think about this for a moment, you will see the rationale. The Descendant is the cusp of the seventh, the house of other people. We can hardly know for certain what someone else is doing to or for us on dates when the Descendant is activated. We might think ourselves all very cognizant astrologers, and we might dare make educated guesses, but guesses they will always remain until hindsight reveals otherwise. Our best significance comes from the Ascendant, the IC and the Midheaven. And, even then, we should behave as if we saw any approach to natal or diurnal Neptune, with delicacy and caution..

Diurnal charts are very easy to do. If you work by hand, and astrologers who do are becoming increasingly rare, you can run up an approximate diurnal chart very quickly. Somewhere you have the calculations you made to get your Midheaven and house cusps. These calculations involve your time of birth, the corrections you make to that basic time, and the sidereal time you take out of the ephemeris for your date of birth. This all adds up to what we called our calculated sidereal time. Deduct from this final calculation the sidereal time for your birthday that you copied out of the ephemeris. What you have left will be only the time calculations and we call this our diurnal constant. Make a note of this constant so you won't have to find it every time you want to do a diurnal chart. To this constant figure, all you have to do is to add the sidereal time out of the ephemeris of any day for which you want to construct a diurnal chart. The constant figure and the new sidereal time will give you a new calculated sidereal figure to take to your table of houses and write the house cusps on a new chart blank. Then, from the ephemeris copy the planets into your new chart, making a note of the rate of Moon movement that day. Place around this new chart every natal placement you used in your natal chart.

One very big warning: you must use the same kind of ephemeris you used when you made your natal chart. If you used a noon ephemeris, you must now use a noon ephemeris. You cannot do diurnals using a midnight ephemeris if your natal was done with a noon ephemeris, or vice versa. If you do, the chart will be twelve hours wrong. A major test of the correctness of you work will be determined by the diurnal Sun which will always appear in or close to the area or house where the Sun was in your natal chart.

The only permissible variations will when you work with the charts of people born at sunrise or sunset. If, in the northern hemisphere, you are doing a diurnal chart for a summer date, naturally the Sun will be over the horizon. People born in winter, with the Sun below the horizon, in the first or sixth houses, will find that, as the Sun rises earlier and sets later in the day, the diurnal Sun for a goodly portion of the year will creep up from first into the twelfth or from sixth into the seventh house. Any showing of the Sun in more wildly varying house placements always indicates some problem with your calculations. The other test of diurnal correctness involves the distance of the date of the diurnal chart angles to the birth chart angles. If you are an Aries rising and are doing a diurnal for an event two months later, you should have a diurnal Ascendant sixty degrees later than your birth Ascendant, some place in Gemini. Likewise, the same applies to your diurnal Midheaven. If you had Capricorn on your natal Midheaven, now, two months later, you should have Pisces on the diurnal Midheaven.

Such a chart as this quickly hand calculated chart is a very rough chart. For instance, you will not have an exact Moon position, and, since the Moon moves so quickly, this is very important. There is one thing you can do about that. Check the Moon movement of the day you were born. Compare it to the Moon movement of the day you are now working on, and make the proportionate adjustment. You will then find your rough chart fairly reliable. Do watch this Moon movement as it can always make the second or third angular touch which will really make this as an important day. The Moon moves at about twelve degrees daily. If your diurnal Midheaven is 22 Leo and the Moon is at 20 Leo, you can see that sometime during that day the Moon will be exactly on the diurnal Midheaven and, as smart astrologers, we know that is going to mean action from a woman to happen in four hours from the time of your natal birthtime which is always the time for which you do your diurnals. For example, my birth time is for a few minutes after six in the evening on the East Coast. I live on the West Coast. This means that it is 3:00 p.m. where I am living, and four hours later is going to be 7:00 p.m. The Moon, normally, is a so-so timing device. For some of us it works applying, for others it works separating, and sometimes it will surprise by being exactly on time.

Another important warning: Diurnals are always done for our birthtime no mater where we now live, and they are always done for the natal time zone and the natal birth location. Do not tamper with your basic data. The only thing which changes is the day for which you are doing the diurnal. I have always advocated that it is every astrologer's responsibility to test and experiment with any new technique. In this case. Other quite experienced astrologers have already done all the experimentation with this technique, so that it is not necessary for you to go through the ramble of experimentation to find out what works best for you. Lois Rodden who attended my first lecture on dirunals went home and tried doing diurnals every conceivable way, and years later she lectured on her quest to "find the perfect diurnal." She reported that, as far as she was concerned, she had not found it. You will see from the examples to be given later what you think of diurnals.

With the advent of computers, the computer will do the chart for you with all the angles, house cusps and planets exactly mathematically correct. Computer astrologers have their chart files and can bring up any natal chart they want to check. Open your chart and then ask to enter a new chart, label it "diurnal" or label it according to the event you are checking. Be sure you type in the correct date of the day you are checking. These are the only two changes you make. Leave all other data stand. Check to make sure the time for the chart is the original time of birth for the person involved. Make sure the place of birth is not changed, that the time zone is the same as you used in the natal chart, and make sure the latitude and longitude is correct for the place of birth. The only thing you change is the name of the chart and the date for which you are doing the diurnal chart. The computer will bring up a chart with all house cusps corrected and all planetary positions. Use in this diurnal chart everything you used in your natal chart.

As with solar or lunar returns, you want to study the chart of the technique, so you will view the diurnal chart as the main chart of the technique. Computers allow you to bring up a double ringed wheel. In the inner ring, choose to put your diurnal chart. In the outer ring, elect to use your natal chart. The computer allows you to view this data as you should be looking at it. But pause a minute, another thing the computer allows you to do with your chart set up is to press the "swap" button. You will see the natal chart go into the center, and the diurnals will appear around the outside as transits. So transits and diurnals are the same. We maximize importance of the diurnal technique by putting the diurnal at the center with the diurnal angles, then refer to natals around the outer side.

Yes, you can do diurnals for where you live. You can, in fact, do anything you want, but you will not then be doing viable diurnal charts. Let me make this quite plain. I was born at latitude 41 North, and I now live at 37 North. If I do a diurnal for the same day at both locations, the diurnal Midheavens will be the same, but the diurnal Ascendant will differ by two degrees. Because we only work with one degree of orb, a two degree difference is playing too loosely. Jim Haynes was born in Kansas and lives in Los Angeles, and the same thing happens in his chart. Mollie Sommer, a Los Angeles astrologer, was born in Washington State about on the same longitude as where she now lives. However, here we have a great difference in latitude, and it is such that it puts her Ascendant a distance of ten degrees off. Since each degree is equivalent to one calendar day, any prognostications made for her residential location, she has found, are ten days from exact. She agrees that the only way to do diurnals is for time, time zone, and place of birth. Ezekial says "I will judge a man from whence he came," a good axiom for diurnals.

The significance of multiple "hits" is the crux of the diurnal technique. They can happen in combinations of natals and diurnals, but there must be more than one hit for the day to have special significance. On the other hand, having mentioned the heavily hit outcome of the first trial of O.J. Simpson, I must add, when O.J. Simpson came to the end of his second trial, where a guilty verdict was reached, he had no touches to any of his angles. According to diurnal practice, the lack of touches means that this event was not particularly important to him. You may be of the opinion that the outcome of both trials should have been important to Simpson, but here is astrology to tell you that it was simply not so. I will later mention the deaths of each of my parents. The death of my mother shows up very clearly as important in my life. The death of my father does not, and I would be sentimentalizing to say that it was of great or special significance to me. More of that when I show those charts.

Think of your own natal charts as I now show you mine. I have 9 Gemini rising. Ten days after my birthday every year, the rising degree will take ten days to get to 19 Gemini and my natal Moon. I have 15 Aquarius on my Midheaven, which means 15 Leo on my natal IC, so every year nine days after my birthday, the IC will move onto my natal Neptune at 24 Leo. Since we use orbs of one degree, you can see that one of those days I will have Moon and Neptune both within orb of diurnal angles at the same time as well as any other transits which happens to be going through Gemini or Leo, Sagittarius or Aquarius adding to the two hit significance of the day. On the other hand, my Descendant is 9 Sagittarius, and it will take fifteen days for the moving Descendant to reach my natal Venus. At any time in the year transiting or diurnal planets can be at any of those degrees and give us the additional touches which will make that day important to us. Sepharial gives us a few axioms:

"1. Those days on which the malefic planets Neptune, Uranus, Saturn and Mars (and Pluto or Chiron, had he known them), are in transit over the meridian or Ascendant of the diurnal horoscope are evil in their import: and also those on which the Sun, Moon and Mercury, when in evil aspect to other bodies, pass these points of the diurnal horoscope.

"2. Those day on which the radical (natal) places of the malefics pass the angles of the diurnal horoscope, are evil, and also the Sun, Moon, and Mercury when radically afflicted. (Radical meaning natal.) (Notice by the wording that this is not a repeat of the previous axiom.)

"3. But the transits of Jupiter and Venus, when not afflicted, or the Sun, Moon and Mercury when well aspected, are uniformly good. (This axiom means that we have to decide whether Venus and Jupiter are afflicted by other aspects on the day we are checking.)

"4. The daily aspects formed to by Moon, must be taken in regard to the houses occupied. Thus, if the Moon forms a conjunction with Neptune in the 2nd house of the diurnal horoscope, it will indicate danger of being defrauded of money on that day. At the same time, the Moon may have a good aspect of Jupiter in the eleventh house, and the advice of a friend will be a corrective. (This definitely shows that Sepharial looked at everything in the chart, not just at those planets hit by the diurnal angles. More about that later.)

"5. The chief effects are due to the transits over the angles of the diurnal horoscope. Next, the conjunctions that are formed by the major planets with the Sun, next to the mutual aspects and conjunctions of the planets, and lastly to the aspects formed by the Moon to the planets in the ephemeris (other transits).

"6. The place of the New Moon in the diurnal horoscope is important, as it shows in what sphere of the life changes may take place during the month, good or bad according to the aspects to the luminaries."

To these six axioms from Sepharial, I should like to add one of my own devising. We cannot do diurnals for every day of our lives. There are many "down times" when we get only single touches or no touches at all to our angles. We have to decide when diurnals are going to be significant. One of these most significant times is when a new sign comes to the diurnal Ascendant. Another equally significant time is when a natal house cusp becomes diurnally angular, especially on the diurnal Ascendant. As you know, that will tell us on what activities we should focus our energies for the coming period. So there is that and the lunations to watch. We also want to look at any diurnals in conjunction with any natals. The final check should be of other aspects between diurnals and natals. Never lose from sight the very fast diurnal Moon which because of its speed, will touch the angles four times each month, always the most likely body to give us the second or third hit to classify any day as more important than any other day.

1991 Trip to Seven Hills

I first lectured on diurnals at Edith Custer's Seven Hills Conference in the spring of 1991. I knew as early as the previous Fall that I was invited to speak there, but new vacation requests were not accepted until January. I began an early campaign for a specific vacation time, and luckily no one else wanted the same dates. Then I set up diurnals for the days prior to the conference and the days after it, to see if it was best to take days prior or after for being a tourist.

I did a chart for April 23, 1991, which covered the twelve-hour period from 6:04 p.m. to 6:04 p.m. next day. My flight time was 9:00 a.m. the next day. I flew to Dulles Airport, rented a car and drove to an overnight motel in Culpeper, Virginia. The next morning I drove through a countryside of Springtime azaleas and dogwood in bloom to Lynchburg. After the convention, I would have three days to visit Monticello and get into Washington for another look at the National Gallery.

In doing these charts, I noticed that at this time of the year, with the days getting longer, sunrise coming earlier each day, and sunsets later, and with the slow down of my diurnal Ascendant sign, the diurnal Sun had crept up into my seventh house. I was glad to see diurnal Jupiter at the top of the diurnal chart. It would be in orb of the Midheaven for three days, the day of my flight, the day before the conference, and opening day when I was scheduled to make my presentation. I was not so happy to see diurnal Saturn taking over from Jupiter but at the diurnal IC. On the rising sign of this chart I saw I had dodged natal Mars, that natal Fortune would be in orb of the diurnal Ascendant to match with Saturn at the bottom of

the chart, and less than happy to see my not so great natal Fortune in Scorpio to be followed by natal Vertex, usually a sign of ill health coming up next in orb of diurnal Ascendant. Across the chart, the diurnal Descendant moving as slowly is never going to catch up with the diurnal Sun. Just as I had missed natal Mars, I had also missed the influence of natal Chiron.

I thought I could live with those indications, but I also checked around the chart for obvious aspects of diurnal to natal. I could see Mars coming to Pluto but could discard that as Mars and Pluto are in no natal aspect. Mars is trine natal Sun, also not in natal aspect. I rather more feared diurnal Mars coming square to its natal position, but that was way on ahead. I did not much care to see diurnal Pluto at 19 Scorpio. Nor was I much alarmed by Neptune with my natal Jupiter. The diurnal Moon was moving toward diurnal Ascendant which would at the same speed carry the diurnal Part of Fortune to the Descendant. For this I simply shrugged and crossed my fingers.

On the twenty-sixth, the conference opened in the morning, the diurnal of the twenty-fifth still in effect. Jupiter was still in one degree aspect of the diurnal Midheaven, and diurnal Saturn was in one degree orb of the fourth house cusp. I had to look upon this as especially significant to me as I was born with Jupiter and Saturn almost exactly sextile, and the only time Jupiter works well for me is when it is in any aspect to Saturn. The diurnal also had a fixed square, plus the diurnal East Point was with my natal Sun. The East Point always involves special events. I was scheduled to do the opening session with the basics of diurnals. It was the only event happening, so I had almost total conference attendance. The audience was in the palms of my hands. It went beautifully. I had a half hour rest period before resuming with the second half of my presentation. In it I would present diurnal examples and also look at the diurnals some of the audience had hurriedly asked computer people to do for them in the product and book room during the half hour rest period. I swept on through without any thought to myself until the luncheon break. And then I sagged. I had done two sessions back to back. Jupiter had given me the public eye, and Saturn had thoroughly wilted my energies. Never again would I let myself be thusly programmed.

It was a great conference, and I attended something every session. As with all conferences, the main thing was meeting and talking to people at every turn of the day and deep into the evening social hours. Up to then, I had never been to but one other small conference, and I found the experience delightful. On the twenty-eighth, the final lecture was given by Batya Stark who is not only knowledgeable but also very humorous. I was listening to her raptly, my right leg crossed over my left knee. When it was over we applauded and I undid my knees and found my right foot had gone to sleep. We had a Full Moon in Scorpio that evening and the fixed grand cross was still in operation. I waiting for my foot to regain normal circulation, but it just was not happening.

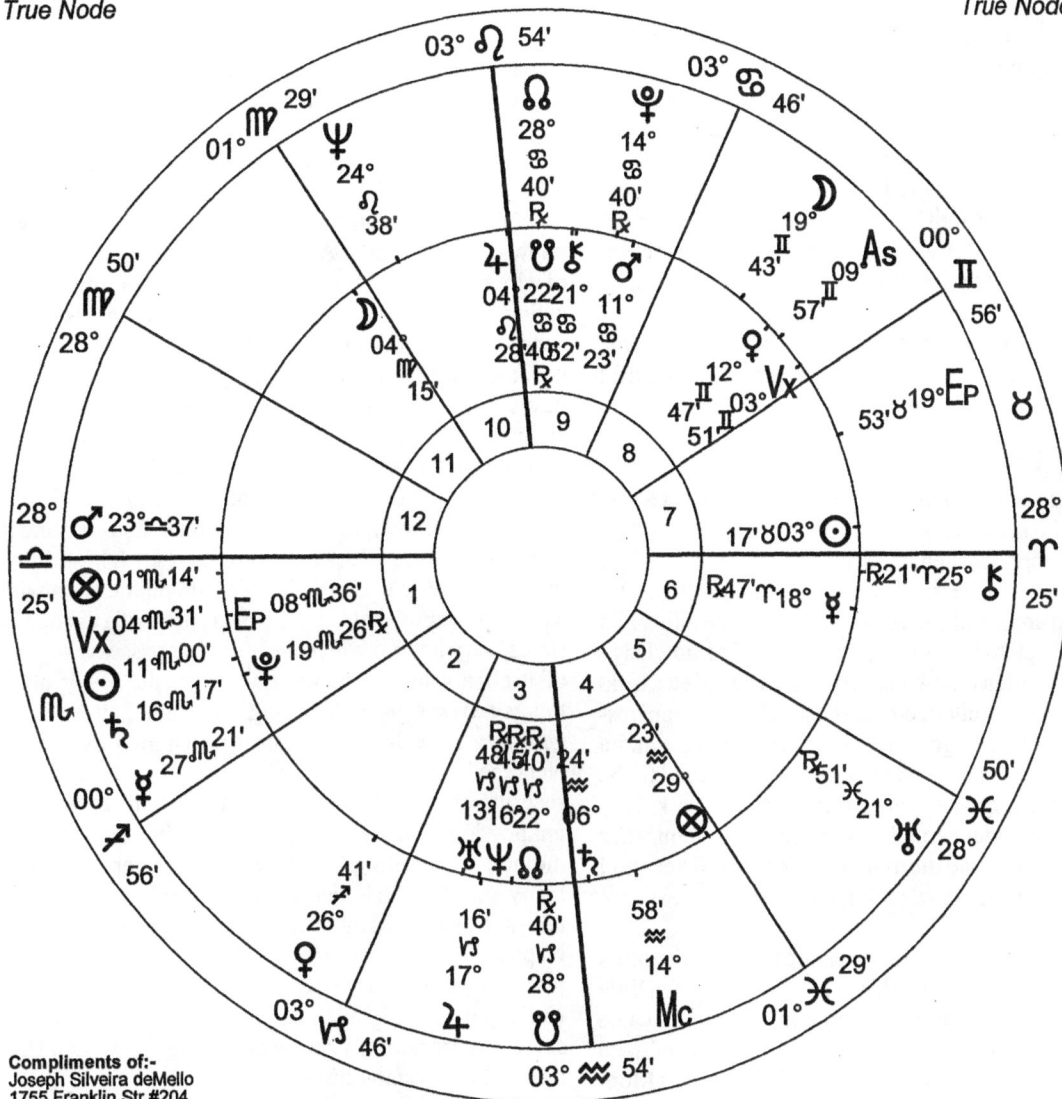

What is more, it was painful.

Nevertheless, I hobbled to the final evening's festivities. The pain in my foot was of the sort that resembled gout pain I get from having eaten something two days earlier which is not on my diet. Not only that, but I realized I had eaten the same shrimp dish for luncheon two days in a row, and duplicating shell fish is a definite dietary no-no with my gout condition. But, heck, it had been a fine luncheon and just as good on repetition. Now I was doomed to pay for my indulgence. This was a Chiron-Pluto-Mars situation. That night I slept fitfully, the pain accelerating in the wee hours of the night. Gout pain is like that, and next day it is gone until you commit your next excess. I woke in the morning and the pain had toned down considerably, but I still felt as if I had a dead section running the length of my right foot as if every step I took was similar to trying to walk a gym bar.

I had a quiet breakfast and drove to Charlottesville where I spent a long afternoon at Monticello. Even though much of the house was in scaffolding, house and garden and the vistas were superb. I drove on to Fredericksburg. Feeling fine next day I drove up to Alexandria, parked my car, and took the Metro to Washington where I spent most of the day at the National Gallery before going back to my car and Fredericksburg.

For examples to use at Seven Hills, I decided to check the days of the deaths of my parents as examples of meaningful events in my life.

Death of Mother

When I heard of the death of my mother, I was yet a few years prior to the serious study of astrology. I was spending the day writing reports when, at 11:00 on January 23, 1961, I got a telephone call from one of my sisters. Another sister back on the east coast had called to tell us that our mother had died. It was a shock to both of us since we had no knowledge she had been ill. But a month earlier she had suffered a mild stroke, was briefly hospitalized, had been released from hospital and was making a good recovery with therapy and a walker. But three days prior to her death, she returned to the hospital in kidney failure. Neither the stroke nor kidney problem seemed serious enough to warrant telling family at a distance right up until the morning she died. My sister and I agreed there was little sense taking on emergency expense now she was dead.

After I hung up, the sense of shock increased to the point where I could not continue working. I took a break to a little Spanish church behind our office building, but when I came back to the office, I was till unable to work. I checked with my boss and took the rest of the day off. That day was Monday, and we were not to learn any more until the weekend and after the funeral.

This was one of the first diurnal test charts I did almost thirty years later when I got into studying diurnal charts. Note that this chart is two months and twenty days after my birthday. My natal Midheaven has moved from natal 15 Aquarius to 10 Taurus (a bit slow), and my Ascendant has moved from 9 Gemini to 19 Leo (also a bit slow). Right away we see the diurnal Moon (mother or woman) about to go over the diurnal Midheaven, and directly opposite is diurnal Neptune on natal Sun are in orb of the IC of home and security. Looking at the diurnal Ascendant, we find nothing in orb, but we cannot fail to see that diurnal Uranus was on natal Neptune and that diurnal Pluto and diurnal North Node were together, all in the first house. On the Descendant we see that diurnal Mercury is exactly on natal Midheaven (although not in orb of that angle), and since Mercury is my chart significator, I always pay special attention to when that planet moves to any angle, and that day square to diurnal Neptune and my natal Sun were conjunct on the diurnal IC.

This is where having a computer and being able to switch to look at diurnals as transits can immediately show you transits such as the one we have here of Mercury about to go over natal Midheaven. Diurnal Venus is on natal Uranus, and then I these and Mars were making a grand trine to the natal Vertex, as if the angular touches had not been enough.

This is the sort of event I suggest every diurnal student to study. We know the event itself and anything to do with it which came to our knowledge later, and we know our own charts. Astrology provides the specifics of which planets were involved. It will not permit us placating bias. Any incorrect assumptions nudge us to the right conclusions, and we are there to agree, disagree, become fully aware of what really happened and tell us how we should realistically think of the event and its real significance to ourselves.

I checked the chart was correctly done, the angles increased, the sixth house position of the diurnal Sun. I also looked at my natal chart with the transits around it to see what those told me, and compare with how much more the diurnal told me. Transits around the chart with Mercury over my natal Midheaven spoke of a change in status, very natural when one's mother passes away but of itself not indicative of such an event. Many other things can be signified (getting a new job, getting fired, getting a raise in pay). Transiting Uranus over natal Neptune happens in my natal fourth house of home and security, bringing a surprise event with a the mystery of unknowing. I know the event was the death of my mother, so transiting Moon through intercepted Taurus in my natal twelfth house, if it is a clue of this event, was not that obvious. But it does underline my transiting Neptune over my Sun. The strange thing that Jupiter is just past natal Jupiter does not remind me of any especially good thing happening prior to this event. And the same with transiting Venus just coming to my natal Uranus in the eleventh house.

So, going back to the diurnal, the first thing is the Moon will go over my diurnal IC later that day and the diurnal or transiting Neptune is in orb of natal Sun and diurnal Midheaven and will remain in orb for two more days. But what of the future? What happened later? Because diurnal Mercury moves more than one degree daily and will be on the diurnal Descendant in three days. Diurnal IC will go on to touch natal Saturn in five, six and seven days at which time diurnal Uranus and natal Neptune will be then on diurnal Ascendant. In a

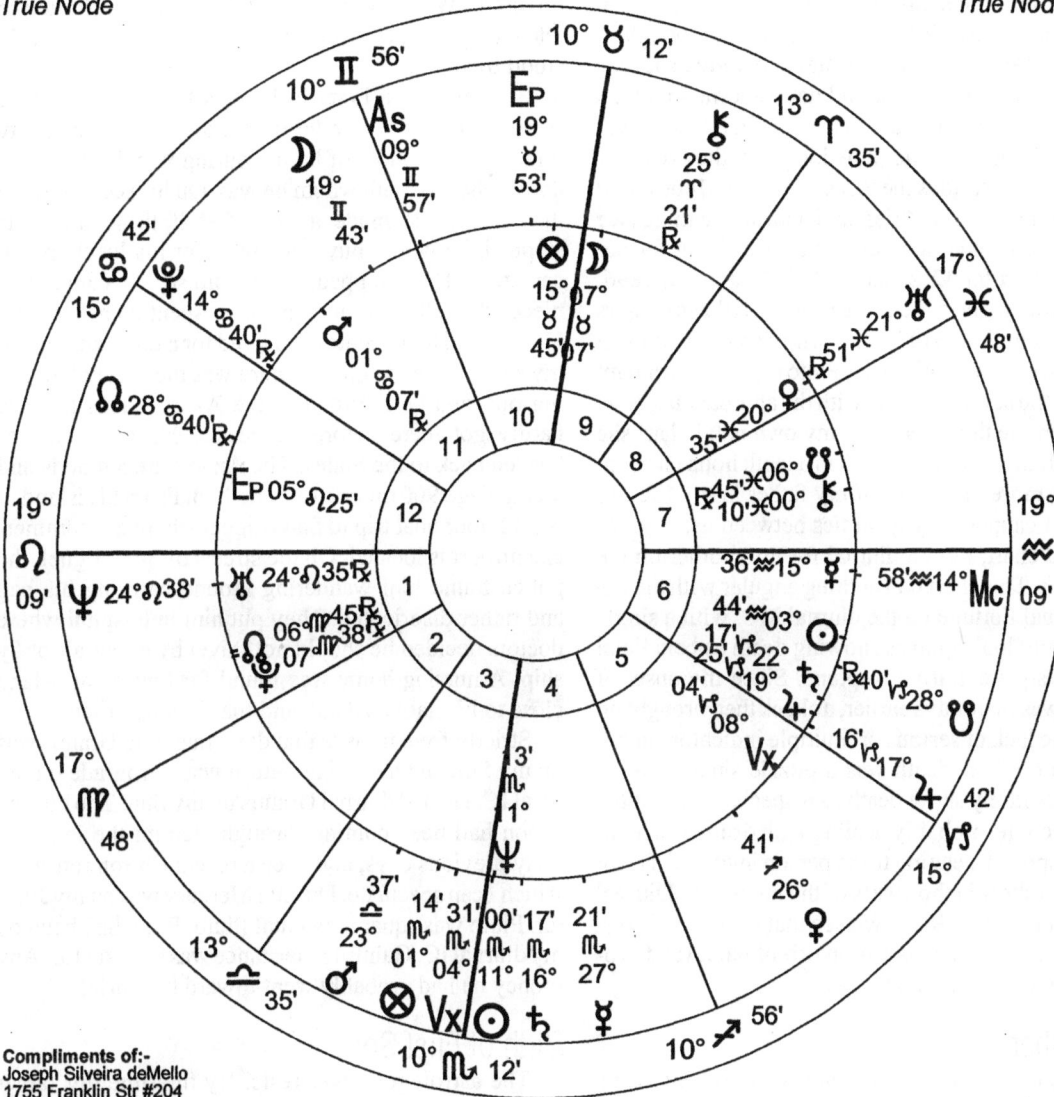

Compliments of:-
Joseph Silveira deMello
1755 Franklin Str #204
San Francisco CA 94109
Tel (415) 775-8939
email jsmgemscorp@juno.com

week, diurnal Moon will be also at the diurnal Ascendant. So there will be further times right then when there would be two or more planets on angles. There were subsequent telephone calls home, and bit by bit more was learned. No date was given for the initial stroke except that she was released from hospital after Christmas. Somehow, the family at home failed to remember that kidney problems are inherited from the maternal side of our family. With the onset of the kidney failure, she herself knew and said this was the end. We were to learn she had asked for the presence of those of us not at home. The family at home then realizing it was too late, simply did nothing and waited for the end.

I have never had my mother's natal data, and she always refused to give me mine. She found it strange that a son should want to know his birth data, and when she thought it was for astrological reasons that I wanted to know, she was superstitious about astrology and did not want me involved in astrology. Mind you, she was a Pisces, and if a Pisces ever refuses you anything, no matter how long ago, they remember and never relent. Besides the Pisces Sun, her Moon could have been either in Pisces or Aries, and with all the things we do as astrologers, I came up with Sagittarius rising for her (rectifying her chart for 12:26 a.m. LMT, March 14, 1896, Pico, Azores) which gives the Pisces Moon. All astrologers will go to these lengths to study any family chart. This natal chart fits her life very well, gives her Pluto on the Descendant and Neptune in the seventh house, with the approaching New Moon waning in the third house. In my own natal chart she comes out as a fourth house rather than a tenth house person, the latter being more indicative of my father in my life. As her eldest son, I cannot deny great ties between us.

As an added chart, I did a diurnal for my mother on the date of her death. This chart had nothing angular with the exception of diurnal Fortune on the diurnal MC, with a single touch we can only look upon as showing death as beneficial release. It was square diurnal Neptune. Since the onset of kidney failure was three days earlier, a check then brought no revelations. The lack of serious or multiple indicators in her chart at the time of her death was a puzzle since then resolved. Diurnals rarely show death as a special event in the chart of most people, probably dealing with death as a natural event of no special meaning to the person involved. Death is more likely to show in the charts of the mourners. Diurnal Venus was on her natal Moon. We see that the diurnal Vertex, significant in illness, was within orb of natal (and progressed) Neptune, ruler of the kidneys.

Death of Father

My father survived my mother almost seventeen years. On January 3, 1977, my sister got a cablegram saying he had died. It was limited to ten words, left out the date, the cause, or any notice of final arrangements. It came from the nursing home where he had resided the last eighteen months of his life. The cable was sent as soon as the cable office reopened after the weekend. So when I did the diurnal for the third, not only was it a surprise that nothing showed angular, but one would have had to go back five days, at least, before diurnal Pluto ought have been on the diurnal IC, and maybe the diurnal Moon would have been on the Midheaven. I can see I had just had a lunar return then.

My father was a Scorpio Sun and not an easy man. For a while after mother's death, he lived alone in the family house. First thing he did after her death was to destroy the garden he had built for her, knocked down the gazebo and uprooting the roses. Then he sold the house as is and told his local children that if there was anything there they might want they should come and get it in the next three days. What he wanted went into two suitcases. He then divided his time between two of his daughters and some nieces in the Azores where he lived rather grandly on his American pension and social security. He had made three trips there and was to die there. Wherever he stayed, his stay was limited to when he got angry with his hostesses or felt misunderstood by them.

Even before his first trip there, he had begun having a series of lapses where he would lose twenty or thirty minutes or a couple of hours, during which he did not know where or with whom he was. On his second trip to the Azores, he made a vow that if these incidents stopped, he would buy new gates for his local church cemetery. They stopped, and he did so. This angered a niece who felt it was money better spent on her family. He returned to the States and lived for a time with one of my sisters. But eventually there was the inevitable falling out, and he returned to the Azores. This time he hardly got there before he packed his bag and was headed back to the States. The Azores are a nine island archipelago 900 miles east of Lisbon. From his island, it is a 12 hour boat trip to Sao Miguel where the commercial airport is located. On the streets of Sao Miguel, the police found him wandering around carrying his bag and rather disoriented. They put him in hospital where doctors decided he should not travel by either air or by ship. A nursing home was found for him on an island close to his native island, and that is where died.

Strictly from transits that day, transiting Uranus was on my Sun and transiting Saturn was retrograde on my natal IC. He had diurnal Uranus on my Sun. The diurnal Moon had been coming through Gemini the immediately previous days, and I see a recent Chiron return on which I can speculate. Diurnal Mercury was on my Jupiter. Pluto was square my natal Pluto. Pluto had been on my diurnal IC. Gainful inheritance was not a factor. Any money he had probably went toward his burial.

Birth of First Son

The astrologer never rests. By the time my father died, I had been studying astrology for thirteen years. I then did a diurnal using his November 14, 1893 speculative natal and the event of my own birth to see if that had special meaning in his life, and indeed it did. The diurnal Moon was on the diurnal Ascendant. Diurnal Neptune was on the diurnal IC. Diurnal Sun was in orb of his natal Uranus. Had I had his chart years ago, I would the sooner have had better understanding of how our individualities both meshed or were at odds in our two lives.

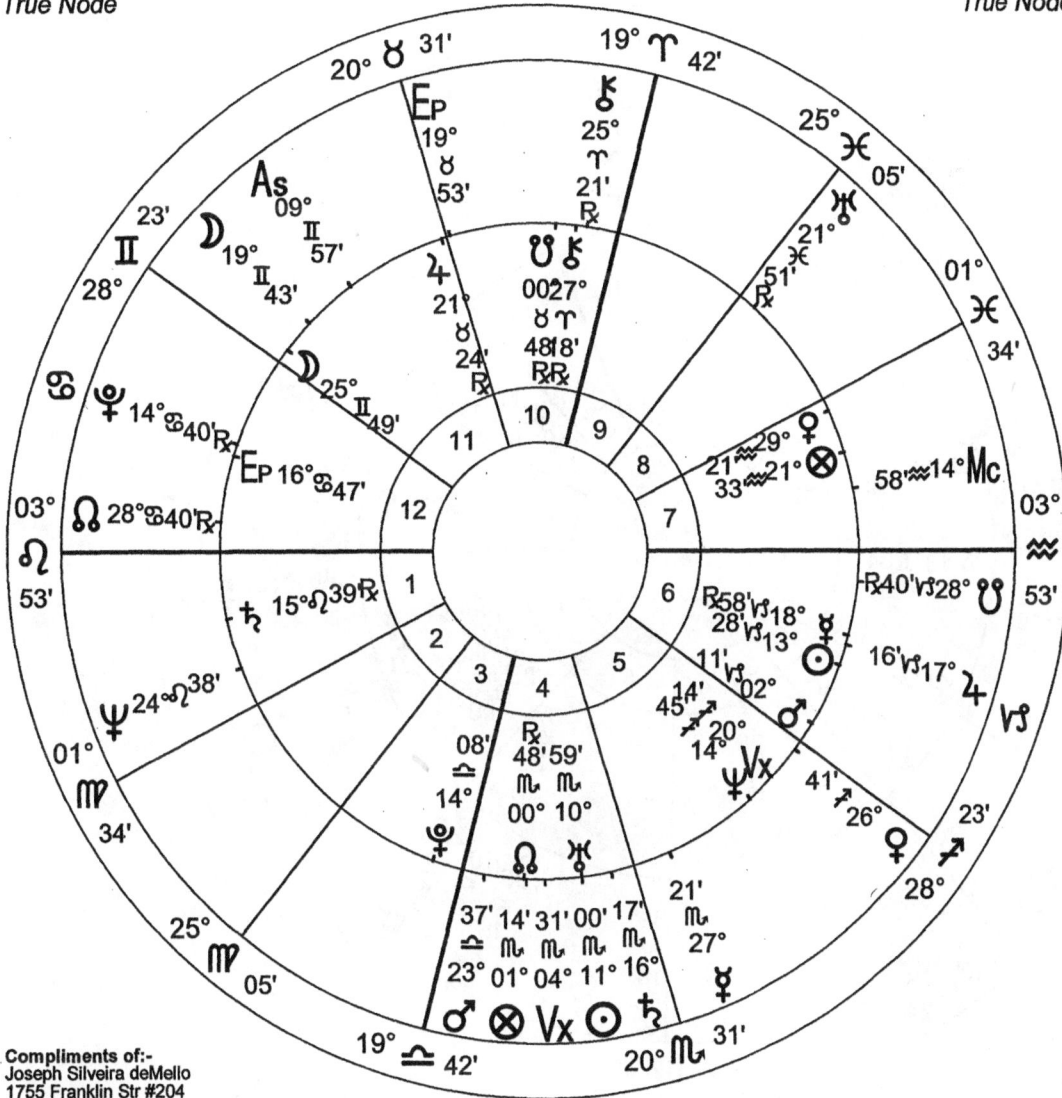

Inner Wheel
170. Death of Father
Natal Chart
Jan 3 1977
6:04:16 PM EST +5:00
Newport RI, USA
41N29 071W19
Geocentric
Tropical
Campanus
True Node

Outer Wheel
Author's Chart
Natal Chart
Nov 3 1925
6:04:16 PM EST +5:00
Newport RI, USA
41N29 071W19
Geocentric
Tropical
Campanus
True Node

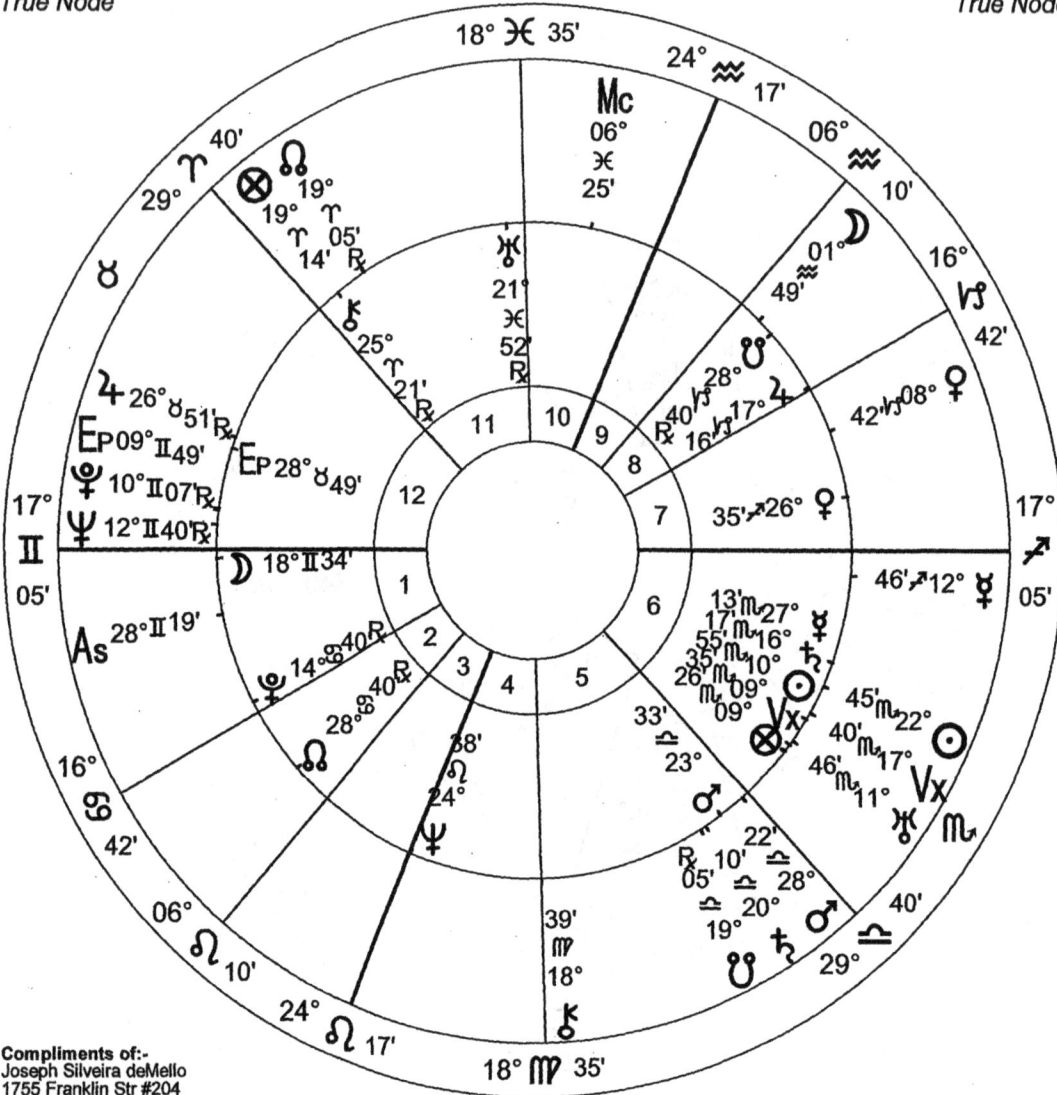

Inner Wheel
171. Birth of 1st Son
Natal Chart
Nov 3 1925
6:56 PM LMT +1:55:16
Isla do Pico
38N16 028W49
Geocentric
Tropical
Campanus
True Node

Outer Wheel
Father
Natal Chart
Nov 14 1893
6:56 PM LMT +1:55:16
Isla do Pico
38N16 028W49
Geocentric
Tropical
Campanus
True Node

Birth of First Daughter

I capped this by doing another diurnal based on his birth chart for the birth of my first sister, and there was nothing in orb of any angle although he was that day having a Mercury return in the fifth house of the diurnal and a Venus return with the diurnal South Node in the sixth house of the chart. In a few days more, the natal nodal axis would be on the diurnal MC/IC of this chart.

Death of Wife

Going one further step onward, I did a diurnal on his chart for the death of my mother, his wife. The only touch is diurnal Fortune on the diurnal Midheaven, and diurnal Uranus on the diurnal Ascendant. His diurnal Moon would have been on the diurnal Midheaven the following day, but we must be aware that Fortune moves at the same speed as the Moon. Father was a late Scorpio rising, Sun in Scorpio and Moon in Aquarius. That day the diurnal Sun was just beyond his natal Moon.

My father was highly competitive. As a mason, he wanted to prove he could lay more stone cleaner and prettier than any coworker. Masons have to work in pairs, one on either side of a wall fitting stone to each other. He worked so fast, no partner would work with him. He was always six feet ahead, forcing any partner to find and fit stone to what he had already laid which additionally slowed down any partner. He never understood that he had worked himself out of a job. He went into working alone as a landscape gardener at which he was also excellent. His lawns were English and weedless, trimmed to precision, his topiary never had a stray sprig, everything he planted came up in great abundance, and everything he pruned severely came back more lushly next season. And it was a pain in the neck for me to work for him (one never worked with him), and I was always made to feel that nothing I did came up to the perfections he would have achieved.

He was a pillar of his church and managed every fund raising event, belonged to every society, and gave up all involvement the minute the church mortgage was paid off. When I grew up, I would happen on older men discussing my grandfather who had several times come to the USA (but never returned here after my father came over). My grandfather was well loved and esteemed, and if I came too near those conversations quickly ended lest they inadvertently revealed what they thought of my father. My father dearly loved to catch anyone in the wrong and was a great practical joker, and his jokes had a nasty turn that was not at all appreciated by his fellows, since they always were made to come out holding the dirty end of the stick. I did my father's natal chart for 6:56 a.m. LMT, November 14, 1893, Pico Azores 38N16, 28W49, and have let that stand.

Astrologer's Illness

Returning from an errand on April 25, 1990, I found a message from the daughter of an astrologer to tell me her mother was hospitalized and wanted me to call her. When I reached her, I found that she had packed so hastily to go to the hospital that she found herself there without an ephemeris, a distracting situation for any astrologer. For four days she had suffered increasingly severe heart pains and her doctor put her in for an emergency angiogram to be done next day, the twenty-sixth. She could not think where the Moon was that day. She did not want the Moon transiting her seventh house (Leo natally), and who can blame her. You don't want to undergo a procedure by a doctor who is bothered by the problems signaled by the Moon in the seventh house. I was able to set her mind at ease about this. The Moon was in Taurus and had just been a New Moon.

After I had chatted with her, I did a diurnal for the day to see under what conditions she had been hospitalized. It would also tell me of next day, the day of the procedure. Because she is born close to Noon, the diurnal Sun is always going to be on the Midheaven, but at that time was showing in the ninth house, three degrees from the angle. Nothing else was specifically on an angle, although that was the time of year when her natal Ascendant came to the diurnal Descendant. And next day, not knowing what time she had the procedure or how much she had to rest after having it, I did not call until evening. A nurse picked up the telephone and there seemed to be a good deal of clamor in the background. The nurse quickly asked me to call back next day. And of course I was not told what was going on when I called.

When I did, I found that the previous evening I called at the very moment my friend went into some shock as an allergic reaction from the procedure, and the room had been full of medical personnel. Usually allergic reactions happen just after the dye is injected and while the dye is circulating in the system prior to such a procedure which was actually done at 3:45 p.m. PST. In the meantime, I had looked more carefully at the chart and its aspects. It can be easily seen that the rough days occurred prior to hospitalization.

Diurnal Mercury in the tenth was retrograde and opposite diurnal retrograde Pluto in the fourth, while diurnal Uranus was exactly trine the diurnal Midheaven and making a grand trine to natal Saturn. The day of the procedure, the day after this chart the diurnal Ascendant would have been at 16 Leo in orb of natal Jupiter. The diurnal South Node was on natal Neptune in the diurnal twelfth house. The diurnal Moon which had been at 13 Taurus the day before the procedure would have gone on past diurnal Mercury and square the diurnal Ascendant. Diurnal Neptune was on the cusp of the sixth house, an even more telling feature to say that an unknown factor was involved. Neptune was also retrograde. Diurnal Saturn, ruler of the diurnal sixth house, was also in the sixth house. Great hindsight.

Checking a Past Event

For my same astrologer friend, since I had a computer and her own was not working, she asked me to check an event from her past. She has, all her life, suffered from hereditary myasthenia gravis. This is an ailment which manifests to afflict various parts of the body almost by turn. and in various ways, and she was sure

Inner Wheel
172. Birth of 1st Daughter
Natal Chart
Dec 22 1926
6:56 PM LMT +1:55:16
Isla do Pico
38N16 028W49
Geocentric
Tropical
Campanus
True Node

Outer Wheel
Father
Natal Chart
Nov 14 1893
6:56 PM LMT +1:55:16
Isla do Pico
38N16 028W49
Geocentric
Tropical
Campanus
True Node

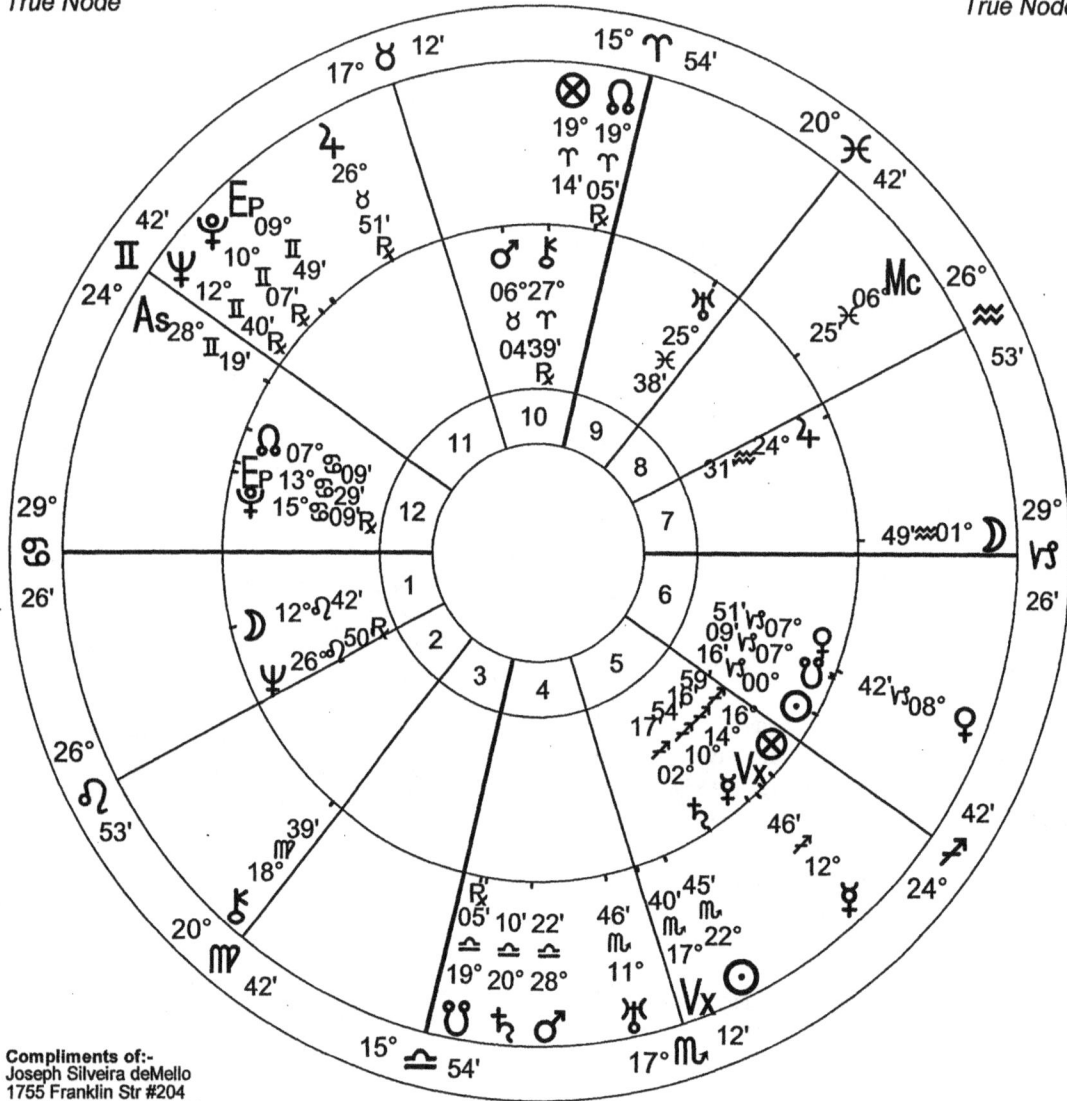

Compliments of:-
Joseph Silveira deMello
1755 Franklin Str #204
San Francisco CA 94109
Tel (415) 775-8939
email jsmgemscorp@juno.com

Inner Wheel
173. Death of Wife
Natal Chart
Jan 23 1961
6:56 PM LMT +1:55:16
Isla do Pico
38N16 028W49
Geocentric
Tropical
Campanus
True Node

Outer Wheel
Father
Natal Chart
Nov 14 1893
6:56 PM LMT +1:55:16
Isla do Pico
38N16 028W49
Geocentric
Tropical
Campanus
True Node

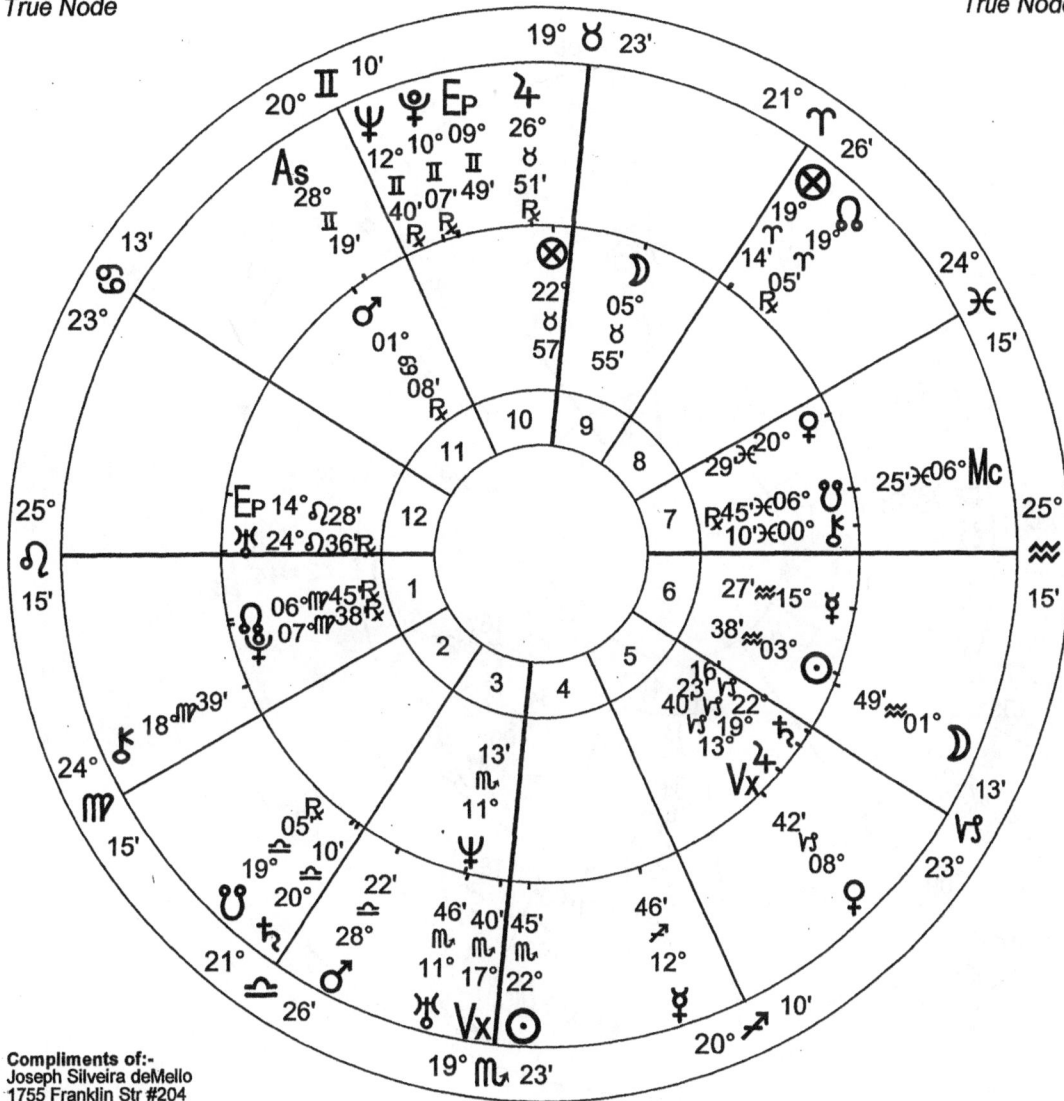

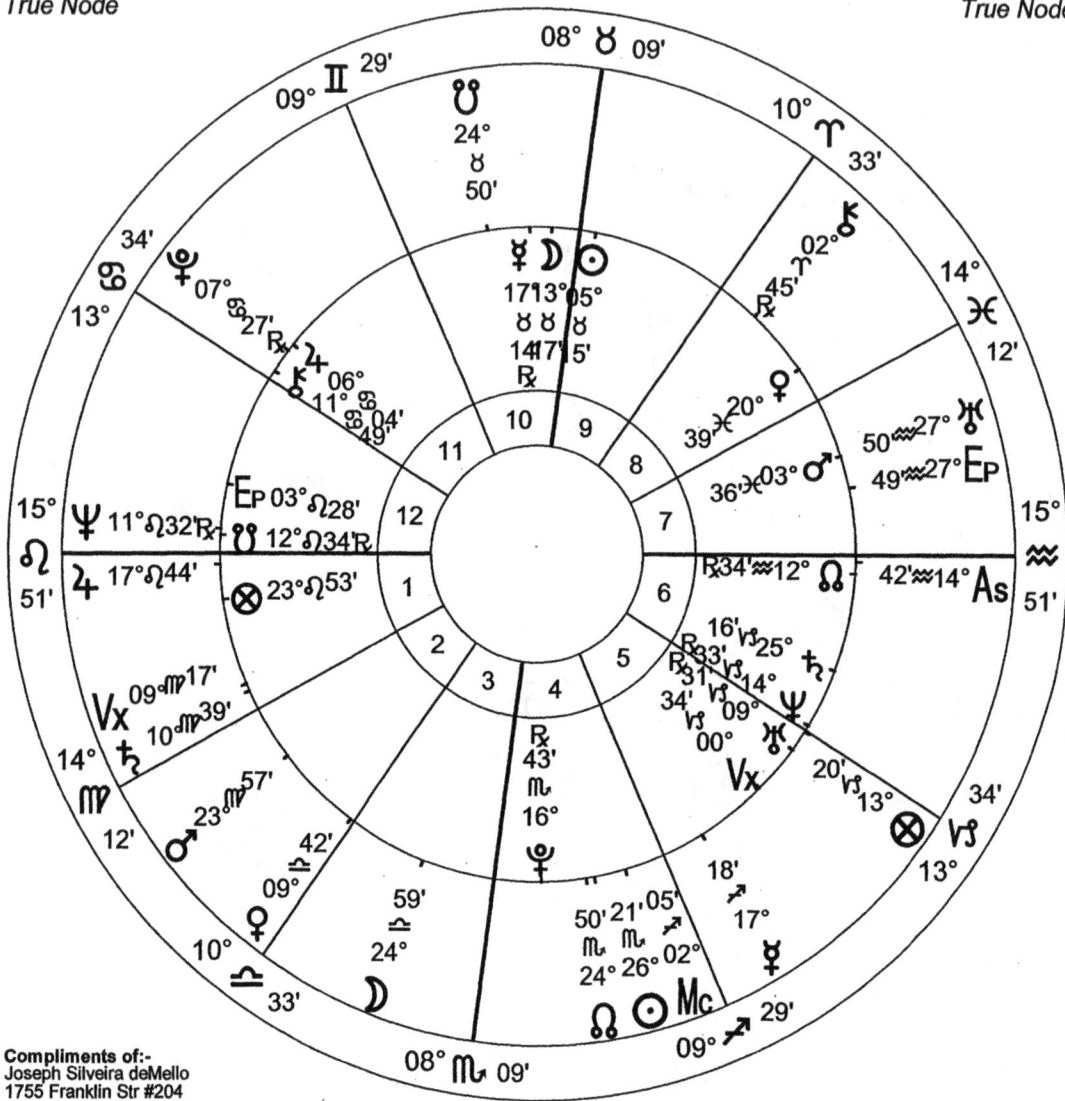

Inner Wheel
174. Astrologer Hospitalized
Natal Chart
Apr 25 1990
11:55 AM CST +6:00
Bowling Green KY
36N59 086W27
Geocentric
Tropical
Campanus
True Node

Outer Wheel
Lady Astrologer
Natal Chart
Nov 19 1919
11:55 AM CST +6:00
Bowling Green KY
36N59 086W27
Geocentric
Tropical
Campanus
True Node

Compliments of:-
Joseph Silveira deMello
1755 Franklin Str #204
San Francisco CA 94109
Tel (415) 775-8939
email jsmgemscorp@juno.com

Inner Wheel
175. Past Event
Natal Chart
Jul 15 1935
11:55 AM CST +6:00
Bowling Green KY
36N59 086W27
Geocentric
Tropical
Campanus
True Node

Outer Wheel
Lady Astrologer
Natal Chart
Nov 19 1919
11:55 AM CST +6:00
Bowling Green KY
36N59 086W27
Geocentric
Tropical
Campanus
True Node

Compliments of:-
Joseph Silveira deMello
1755 Franklin Str #204
San Francisco CA 94109
Tel (415) 775-8939
email jsmgemscorp@juno.com

there had been a landmark change in how it manifested on July 15, 1935. She was in fact not quite sure if it was 1934 or 1935, so I did a diurnal for both dates based on her natal chart and found that, indeed, it had to have been 1935. Again the Sun highest in the chart but now within a one degree orb of the diurnal Midheaven, and with the North Node exactly on the diurnal IC, the diurnal South Node was on the diurnal Sun. This opposition was part of a cardinal square to diurnal Mars which was not on the diurnal Ascendant and natal Moon and involved diurnal Fortune which had within the day passed over diurnal Descendant. I must stress again that Fortune moves equally with the diurnal Moon. Here we see that day the diurnal Moon was to go over the South Node and the fourth house cusp. On that date, she had a significant change in that her ailment began to affect her control of her limbs. Note also that the diurnal Ascendant is going to immediately pass over diurnal Mars and natal Moon. The final thing we do with diurnals is to check the movement of the diurnal placements to the natal chart positions. We begin here by noting that diurnal Venus is coming to a conjunction with natal Vertex and Saturn and diurnal Neptune.

Diurnal of a Cure

Perhaps one of the more spectacular diurnals I have ever done for myself was done for July 19, 1989. I was vacationing on the East Coast. I had taken the Red Eye to Boston and, of course, not slept a wink the whole trip. When I got to Boston, I rented a car and drove up to visit an old friend and client on the mid-Vermont and New Hampshire border. It was a lovely drive up through the mountains, and I got there just as she was setting out to work. I told her I would just lie around and see if I could nap as my back was bothering me. I knew my back problem had been aggravated by the lack of sleep. But it was to persist during my stay in a lovely house she had built on a forested hilltop. There were a number of things I could not do, walking was difficult and painful, and I was still having problems when I left and drove down to visit my sister in Rhode Island.

There I had trouble climbing her steps and she wondered what was wrong with me. However I spent a few days with her and was off to New Haven to visit an old friend and editor who was at Yale. I was very interested in catching up with his progress because he had much talent and potential but had never done well on the West Coast. He had returned to his natal place in the Midwest, finished school, and then gone on East to New York where he did very well at further schooling at Union Theological and at Yale, and was now about to do embark on doctoral work in theology at Oxford University.

My back was still bothering me annoyingly, but he had some people to luncheon that he wanted me to meet. One was a psychiatrist interest in astrology and who had just finishing writing a book on horary. The other friend was a woman bent upon becoming a rabbi, and she was also the wife of a chiropractor who had been trained at Palmer Institute and was a kinesiologist. She gave me his phone number, and I found he could see me as his final patient of the day. When he saw me, he stood me up to a plumb line, had me reach my hands over my head, and we found I could not make my palms match each other. Unlike other chiropractors, he did not knead or

massage or go anywhere near my source of pain. My spine was out of line. He took a small punch no longer than a chalk holder and punched me twice at various spots on my body. Then he had me dress and walk up and down his hall, always turning to the right at the ends of the hallway, and half an hour and a credit card payment, I walked out of there entirely relieved of pain.

The diurnal I later did for July 19, 1989 was amazing. Natal Vertex was on the diurnal Midheaven. Diurnal Saturn and Neptune were on the diurnal Ascendant. Diurnal Chiron was on the diurnal Descendant. Diurnal Sun and Mercury were one degree either side of my natal North Node. Diurnal Venus was conjunct natal Neptune, and both were opposite the diurnal North Node. Diurnal North Node was sextile to my natal Chiron which in turn was trine to diurnal Venus and South Node and natal Neptune. In the diurnal tenth house, diurnal Pluto was backing retrograde to my natal Sun. And the diurnal Moon was that day going over natal Midheaven. But how amazing that Saturn of bones should be with Neptune on the Ascendant. This is as close as I have ever come to seeing Chiron on the seventh as the healing doctor who treated me. I did in fact view this placement of Chiron as an indicator of the simplicity with which the cure was effected. But I should not have given up on Chiron as the fly in the ointment, the impish factor for overlooking the obvious. It was to be some further time in the future before a cyst was discovered by an elderly doctor who, bored with retirement, had returned to practice. This cyst, about a ping pong ball in size but well below the skin surface was to the right of my upper lumbar spine, as a matter of fact at belt line, and this cyst, when aggravated, was secreting noxious fluid to my sciatic nerve which caused pain to radiate from cyst location to, somehow, manifest in the calf of my right leg.

The above were the charts with which I illustrated my first presentation of diurnal charts at the Seven Hills Conference of 1991. We should tie up with the end of that trip. Only five days have elapsed, and you will see that the Midheaven did advance five degrees. However, the Ascendant has only moved less than four degrees. When you notice this seasonal motion in your charts, especially when you are arriving at a moment where several positions either natal or diurnal are going to be hit, it really becomes essential to follow your diurnals more closely. See here how we have ended just at a Full Moon period. No one needs diurnals to tell them when Full or New Moons are in evidence.

You also note that this Full Moon is incidentally quincunx my natal Ascendant and two degrees from natal Sun. So we know this diurnal Moon, as usual, is moving and bringing with it Fortune. So diurnal Fortune is on the Descendant and natal Fortune is static on the diurnal Ascendant. Indeed, only the Fortunes show up on the angles. Two days earlier when I committed my dietary indiscretion, diurnal Saturn was at the bottom of the chart. The Vertex was on my natal Ascendant. For me, the Vertex is always significant of health problems. Gout pain is a demonic attack of uncountable pins and

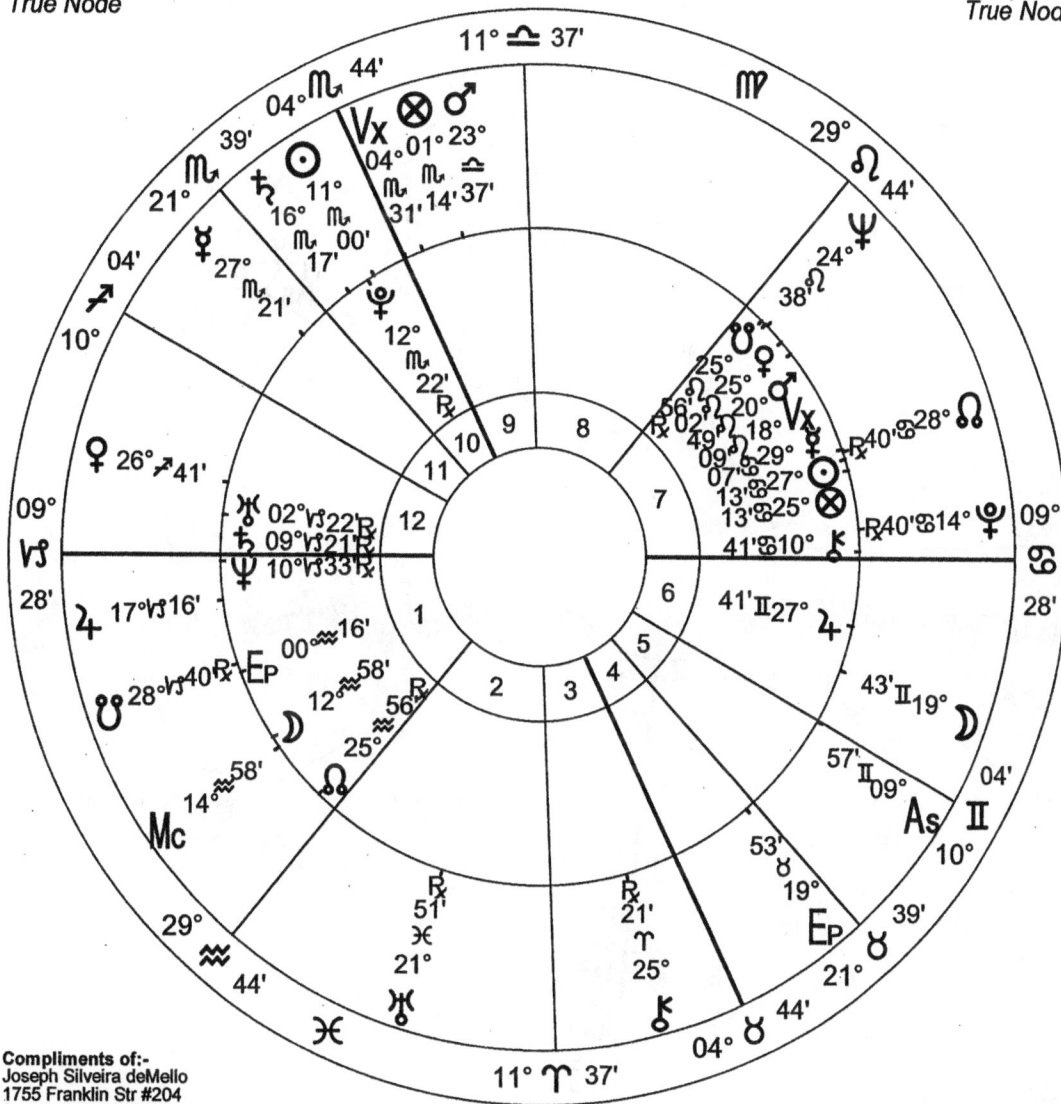

Compliments of:-
Joseph Silveira deMello
1755 Franklin Str #204
San Francisco CA 94109
Tel (415) 775-8939
email jsmgemscorp@juno.com

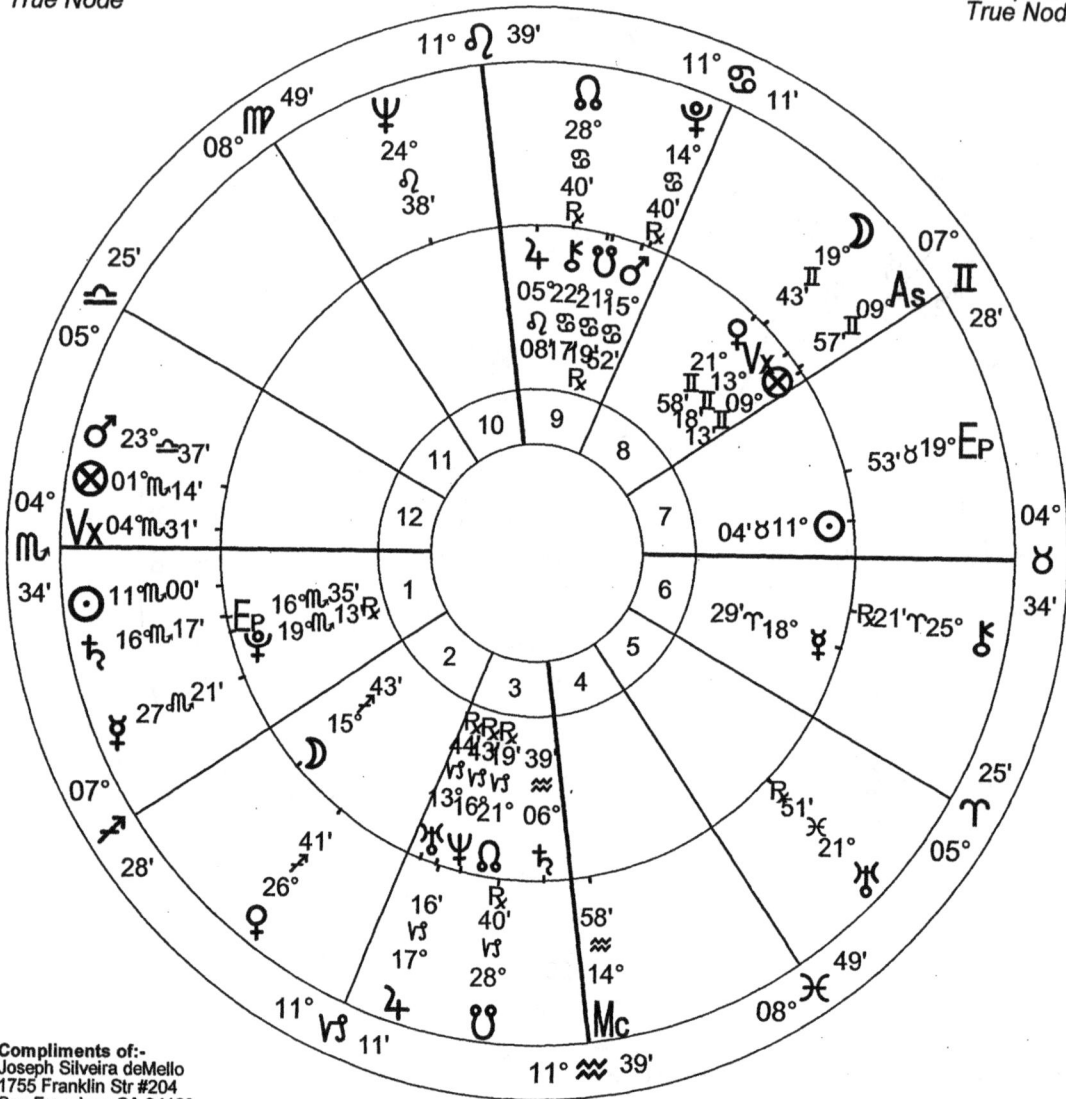

Inner Wheel
178. Flying Home
Natal Chart
May 1 1991
6:04:16 PM EST +5:00
Newport RI, USA
41N29 071W19
Geocentric
Tropical
Campanus
True Node

Outer Wheel
Author's Chart
Natal Chart
Nov 3 1925
6:04:16 PM EST +5:00
Newport RI, USA
41N29 071W19
Geocentric
Tropical
Campanus
True Node

Compliments of:-
Joseph Silveira deMello
1755 Franklin Str #204
San Francisco CA 94109
Tel (415) 775-8939
email jsmgemscorp@juno.com

needles. To this was added a touch of neurasthenia on my right foot. Still, I had a great time at this conference.

The Trip Home

Now, three days later, May 1, having toured Monticello and spent a pleasant six hours at the National Gallery, where I had a sort of airlines meal at what used to be the best cafeteria on the Mall, I had pure ease getting to Dulles International. The diurnal for the day of flight does not go into effect until after six in the evening, so the events of the day should have been on the diurnal of the previous day except that it turned out I got home after the evening time of this chart. The diurnal Ascendant is on my natal Vertex, the diurnal Midheaven is square natal Sun and diurnal Sun, diurnal Neptune is still on natal Jupiter, the diurnal East Point, to be associated with special events is on natal Saturn. diurnal Fortune is on natal Ascendant. I am not quite tickled pink to have diurnal Mars on natal Pluto in the ninth house of the diurnal chart. Not that Mars and Pluto are in any aspect natally and their closeness of the moment should be disregarded, I must confess I was in a testing phase and casting a wary eye to what can be a nasty conjunction. One does sort of bounce back to natal Midheaven in diurnal fourth.

The first happening was that I had filled the car with gas prior to turning it in. When they checked the gas, they said I was returning it with the tank half down. This is because it was a General Motors car, and once you turn off the ignition, the gas gauge goes down, and turning the key on again without starting the car does not raise the gauge to its actual level. I knew that, but I was in no mood to argue about it. I still got to my return flight gate area more than an hour early.

In those days airports still had smoking areas, and there I deposited myself. The first bad news, dear Saturn, was that our flight, originating in New York, would be delayed. I took out a book and lit a cigarette. There was a moment to review that I knew none of my fellow passengers. I am not complaining. As a Scorpio I enjoy being a private person in a public place.

I had been an hour early, and it was now delayed an hour. I did keep an ear open to public announcements, but, suddenly I was amazed to be rousted by a woman shouting at me. She was an older woman, modish in a tweed suit, rather well turned out for a virago. She demanded to know why I was smoking when the signs on the doors leading outside all said "no smoking." I told her I was smoking because I was sitting here, and I had no intention of going through those doors. I pointed to the sign right overhead which designated this as the smoking area in large red letters. I also noticed others around me were hiding their own cigarettes and pretending not to notice our altercation. The lady was not the least mollified by the smoking area sign. I pointed out that I had already been there for three hours waiting for a delayed flight and no one else had objected. Nothing I said penetrated her consciousness. I asked her why she went around airports shouting at men, suggested she find a woman to attack, called her a biddy and a flake, and off she marched to find someone in authority. I saw her complaining to a pilot far across the area, and he was having no success explaining to her about the doors and the smoking area, and she came past me without

glance or apology. Don't ask me why I expected civil behavior.

I was not feeling poorly that day though the waiting was tedious. Diurnal Moon will doubtless reach natal Venus in the next 24-hour period. Diurnal Neptune is on natal Jupiter in the diurnal third house, and diurnal Mars is not yet far enough away from natal Pluto in the ninth house. I bowed to Saturn on East Point as the delay we were having, but I was a little uneasy about the ninth house. The flight, once in the air, was uneventful. The food was dreadful, as the complaining person said, and to which someone added that the portions were also quite small. I landed in San Francisco with the usual ear problems. One would think that after almost a century of passenger flight, someone would learn how to land an aircraft without killing the passengers ear drums.

Gout and Earthquake

The next two charts are for events in my life five days apart. We all live our lives at a normal pace. We have eventful times, and we have much down time during which we recharge our energies, attend to routines. In one of these periods of somnolence, I was doing a great deal of astrology, and I had a full time job in the public sector. We had gone through the usual San Francisco summer (like, said Mark Twain, being the coldest winter elsewhere), which means the autumn gets rather pleasant, usually with a couple or three heat spells. I felt flush and after a cocktail, I crossed the street to a fine French restaurant on Thursday, October 12, 1989. I was just in the mood to indulge in a specialty, *Ris de Veau*, and I proceeded to enjoy every bite. Even sopped up the extra sauce with bits of our local famous sourdough bread.

Notice the gout diurnal. I should have been warned. The diurnal is for less than a month to my birthday, so notice the speed of Midheaven and Ascendant. And by now with the shortness of days, the Sun has dipped beneath the horizon, though natal Sun is in orb of the Descendant. Diurnal Moon has just come over the IC and is approaching the natal North Node. Yes, those do count as two touches. Diurnal Jupiter is backing from natal Uranus. The East Point of special events is opposite diurnal Chiron in Snakebite (19 Scorpio). Diurnal Mercury is on natal Fortune. Degrees of positions do seem a bit active. I was enjoying life in pure oblivion and gourmet indulgence. Nobody is kinder to his needs than Scorpio.

Friday passed well, attended by the usual "Thank God It's Friday" or, in my own humor, "It's Friday, let's get fried." Of course I could see touches ahead, sort of in four days, so I was not quite prepared for Saturday the fourteenth, when I woke in the morning with horrendous pain in my right foot which was somewhat swollen and an angry red. It did seem as if a thousand million pins were sticking into it as if I had walked among cactus. It was no better when I raised my foot on pillows. As an early riser, I hobbled down to the lobby to pick up my paper and into my kitchen for juice and coffee. I had

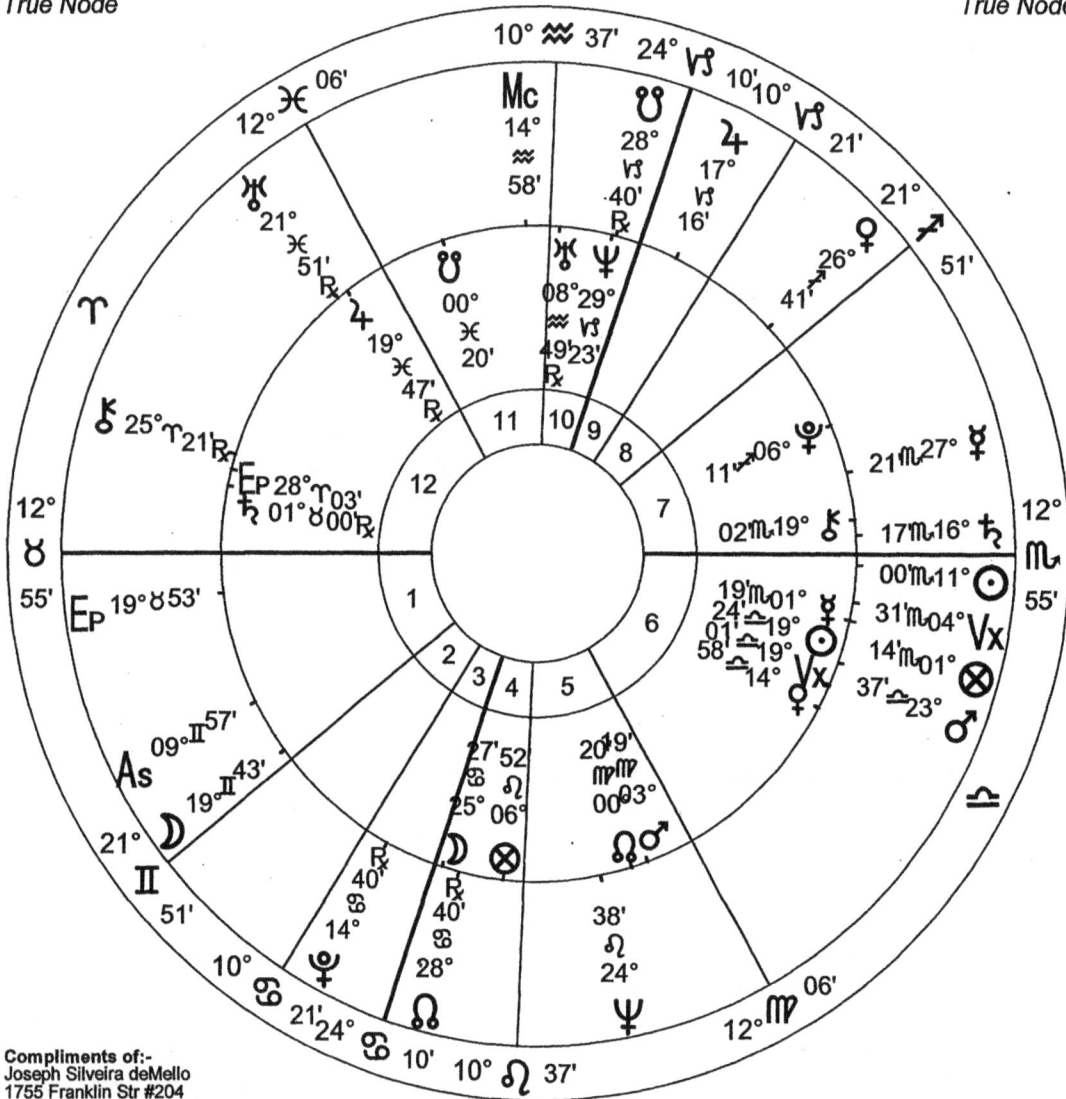

Inner Wheel
179. Gout Attack
Natal Chart
Oct 12 1998
6:04:16 PM EST +5:00
Newport RI, USA
41N29 071W19
Geocentric
Tropical
Campanus
True Node

Outer Wheel
Author's Chart
Natal Chart
Nov 3 1925
6:04:16 PM EST +5:00
Newport RI, USA
41N29 071W19
Geocentric
Tropical
Campanus
True Node

Compliments of:-
Joseph Silveira deMello
1755 Franklin Str #204
San Francisco CA 94109
Tel (415) 775-8939
email jsmgemscorp@juno.com

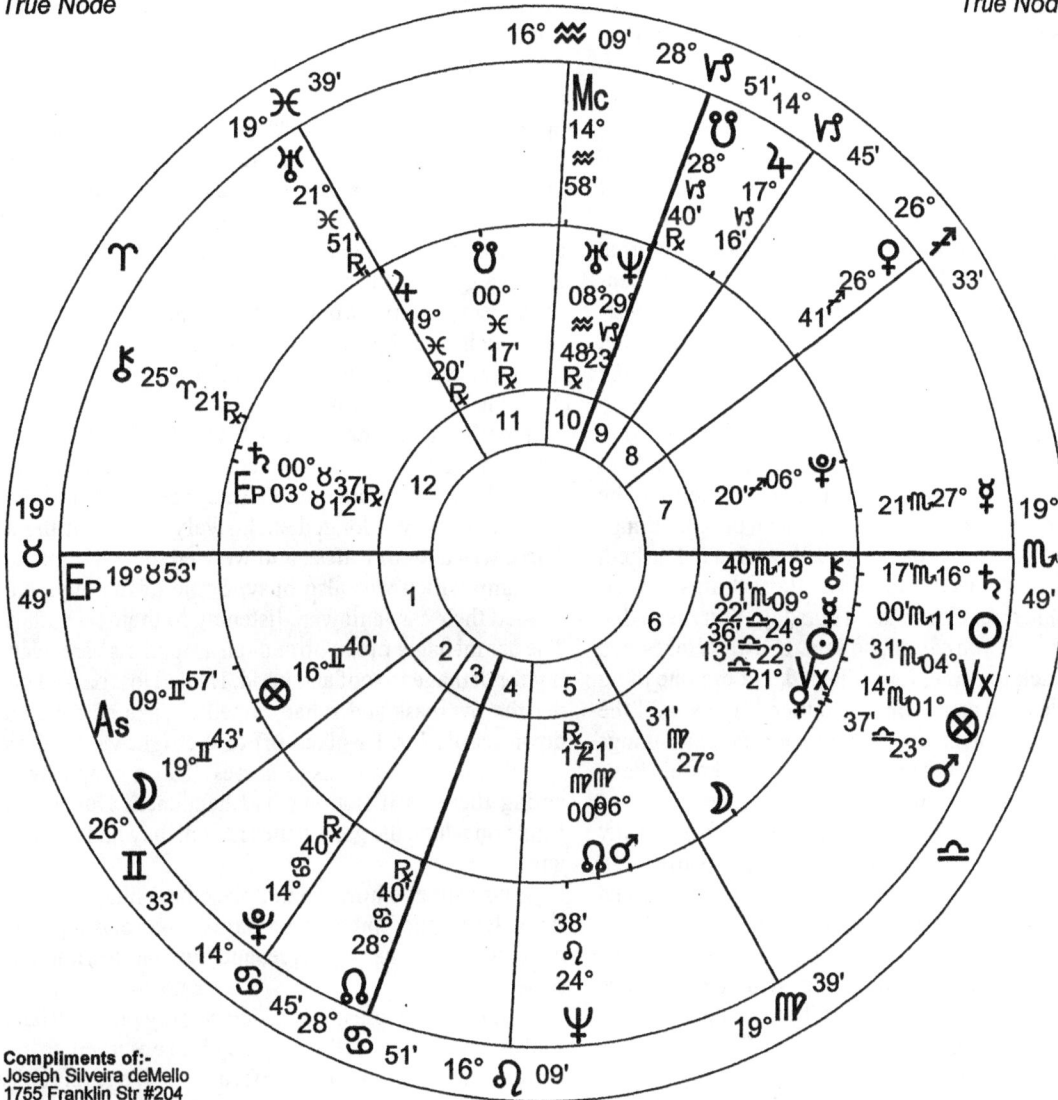

Compliments of:-
Joseph Silveira deMello
1755 Franklin Str #204
San Francisco CA 94109
Tel (415) 775-8939
email jsmgemscorp@juno.com

never had such a pain previously. Putting my foot up on a chair was no good. I had to get up and wait on myself, but the pain did not lessen one bit. And it would be a Saturday. My doctor does not come in on weekends. Finally I got into some gym clothes and soft shoes and called a taxi to take me to my hospital emergency room. The doctor who saw me knew instantly. He pronounced that I had an attack of the gout. He went away and came back with a very small vial of four little pills. He gave me one pill and a glass of water and told me to make an appointment to see my regular doctor as soon as possible. It was nothing short of standard HMO care, and the pain began to ease up as if miraculously.

Scorpios usually follow medical directions. I luckily got another patient's cancellation on the following Tuesday afternoon, October 17. It surprised me to get in so soon, and on the day I was also scheduled to pick up a new pair of eyeglasses just around the corner from my doctor's office. My doctor looked at me with the widest of grins. This doctor was the man who years ago was highly skeptical of astrology and kidney disease until I gave him the maternal family history of four generations of various kidney ailments. He did allow me to say why I was there. Diurnal Neptune was on diurnal Midheaven, and diurnal Chiron was on the diurnal Descendant. The natal East Point was on diurnal rising. Diurnal Vertex and Sun were on natal Mars. His nurse brought in a diet sheet which he handed me with unconcealed delight as he told me that I could no longer indulge in the life I had been living. There was one column of things I could eat, the other column of things which were now forbidden. No veal, beef only in moderation, no pork, no organ meats. Like liver, he explained. No more *pate de fois gras* and a lot of other things normal people don't eat anyway. Like what? I asked. Tongue, sweetbreads, tripe. But I eat all those things. Sweetbreads is what I had for dinner last Thursday. You mean that caused the attack? If you say so, he said. It always takes two days for the attack to come, he explained, but the one thing about gout is that the pain comes and then it goes until the next time you do yourself in. Some of my favorite things were on the list, like spinach and asparagus. But I could have chicken, fish or lamb, and lots of other vegetables.

Now the bad news, he said, is that I'm not giving you any pills because you have had an ulcer and this medication will reactivate your old ulcer. Oh great, the ulcer had not troubled me in thirty years. I want you to control it strictly by diet. I looked at the list. It said no peas or any beans that can be dried. He told me that meant no menu items described as tempura, no soy sauce, and no peanut butter as peanuts are not nuts; they are goobers, therefore beans. So I folded my new diet sheet and with misgivings put it away in my pocket. My doctor was so pleased he had his say. He had told me my kidneys were the problem just as if I had not told him when I first went to him that my chart sixth house is ruled by Libra and my maternal inheritance is one of kidney ailments.

I went to the oculist and got fitted with my new eyeglasses surprised that they were such an improvement over the previous specks. It was now four o'clock, and I had an hour to join the gang to watch the World Series game at a bar. I had also been cautioned to go lightly on alcoholic beverages. Luckily the early five o'clock cocktail group had in it a number of people with whom I drank ginger ale with soda water, and I had been doing that for some time, saving my cut down alcoholic intake for the last two drinks of the evening. It was a lovely day with an almost deadly quiet atmosphere, what we call earthquake weather and that should have clued us all. There are other signs, too, cats make themselves scarce and birds do not sing. Birds don't sing in the afternoon, they sing in the morning. Any Scientist will tell you these are all superstitions.

The bar to which I went had been opened since four o'clock, so some of the jolly bunch were already in place. Such nice people, they all took their usual seats. The televisions were on to some pre-game sports pundits. We were waiting for the game to come on, yacking it up over the TV announcer, elbows on bar. In my elbows I felt a rumbling from the east like I was sitting in a boat on choppy water. Earthquake, I said, and everybody but I jumped up and dashed out to the street. The rumbling continued briefly and then gave three hard north to south shakes. Not a bottle fell over, not a glass. One idiot tripped over a barstool and overturned it. I continued to sit at the bar while the bartender who had observe quake cautions by bracing himself in a doorway, were the only two to stay in the bar, a frame building which would give easily against the quake motion. The television stopped dead at 5:04 p.m. PDT, and all the lights had gone out.

Finally, the bartender and I wandered out into the street to see if the world had come to and end. All the traffic lights were out, and drivers were behaving like the right of way belonged exclusively to each of them. There was a lot of traffic, and we were near a highway off ramp which was also busy. Some of the guys had opened their cars and were listening to their car radios. The bar manager drove up and ran around his car checking for damage to roof and hood. He had just passed under the overpass and it had rained chunks of concrete down on his car. I walked off to the right where there was a glazier's business premises. Those people were sitting there as if nothing had happened. Due to the forms on which the glass panes rested, they had no damage.

It was strange how we got piecemeal bits of revelations. It was the Loma Prieta Earthquake, and opinions differed on its location, force, and how far down it happened.

One of the people in our group was my printer friend. I joked about how well everybody had observed proper earthquake cautions and procedures. We eventually went inside resigned to the lack of television. The game itself, we learned, from car radios, had been called. About twenty minutes later, my printer's business partner came around from two blocks away to say that the front door up to their apartment above their business was jammed shut. The front windows which had never been open had opened on their own from the force of the quake. All the surrounding area where we were was very old creek bottom land long ago filled in and paved over. So we walked the two blocks to the print shop building.

Yes, the door would have to be removed, taken off its hinges. The bolt was bent in the lock. They also had a hatch up to the apartment from the press room, more like climbing a ladder. But after they took the door off the hinges, the problem was going to be how they should live through the night with their street door wide open. Other friends had come with us, so I left them to see about making my way home. By that time we knew that a couple of brick buildings had lost their facades. The whole front fell off a nearby building just as employees were leaving the building, and they and some cars were buried under a mountain of bricks.

Since electricity was out, I had to take a line which used motorized coaches. As I stood waiting in the bus stop, I looked at a building I had just walked past where there had been bits of glass and brick dust on the sidewalk. It had a tower on its corner, and I saw two wide open gashes to the sides of the windows on the fifth and sixth floors of the tower. It took long for the bus to come, and when it did come it was not the least crowded. But everybody was very talkative, had all sorts of reports. The normal fifteen minute ride home took forty minutes. There was no one directing traffic, so there was gridlock at each corner.

It was dusk when I got home. A bookshelf on my north wall had toppled, and stuff had fallen out of the bookcase on the south wall, but the double stacks of book- shelves on the east and west walls were intact. Of course there was no electricity, and the manager came around and turned off the gas in all apartments. I was totally unprepared. I had no transistor radio, only one candle. I decided to go down the street to see what was going on at my neighborhood bar. I met them just as they were locking up. The police had come by and suggested all shops selling alcoholic beverages be closed in case of crime sprees. The chimney of a building across the street had fallen but no one was hurt.

Someone suggested going shopping downtown since a number of shop windows had fallen out. By now the people at the football game were trying to get home. It was on radio that one end of an upper deck sections of the Bay Bridge had fallen onto the lower east bound deck. All the crowd at the ball park south of the city would have to go to either of two bridges well south of them or come north and use the Golden Gate Bridge and go around the north end of the bay to their homes in places like Berkeley and Oakland. Of all the main streets which lead to the Golden Gate Bridge, the drivers got fixated on only one street to the point that there was no traffic on the streets either side of divided Van Ness Avenue. Civilians were trying to direct traffic to the consternation of drivers who wanted to get over the bridge before authorities closed it. It did seem as if everybody was in carnival spirit out on the streets. Some had flashlights, some had candles. A woman who had broke a fingernail insisted a man who was doing volunteer traffic duty call her an ambulance. Otherwise it was like a big party. There were of course fires a mile away in the Marina where the subsoil was mostly sand and water. I went home, felt my way up to my apartment and simply went to bed.

Of course I was then up at five in the morning and down the street trying to see if there were any newspapers. I found one and returned home, called my sister in Florida to tell her I was okay, and she was listening to her own television which reported that I did not have to go to work that morning. So I had a day off and went to work the following day only to discover I need not have shown up until Noon. For my boss, getting to work was particularly pesky since the bridge she normally uses was the one that was closed, and she had to go all around by Charlie's barn to get into town.

This diurnal chart shows something of the transits of the day, but its angles are derived strictly as a progression of my natal angles. For someone else the angles would have been due to their own charts. Diurnals are always done for the time of birth. This is not an event chart but a chart for my next 24 hours. I was present at an eventful day. It surprised me my natal nodes were on the diurnal vertical axis with diurnal Neptune, and though reality was perhaps nebulous, the importance was as practical as it came to be earth shaking, I proceeded cautiously. This is astrology at work.

Buying a Car

Coming into 1992, I had been working for over a decade as a civil servant and had a job I liked so much that I had stayed with it a year longer than retirement age. I would have liked to stay with it, but the system decided to rid itself of older workers often in the upper salary brackets. They made an offer, a gift package we could not refuse. I joined others who accepted retirement and grand plans began to unfold for a date in late March. There were to be two astrology conventions in 1992, and I would be able to go to both. I would have the time to drive cross-country and, if I had a car, I could stop to visit relatives and old friends. I thought it a clever idea to give myself a car as a "graduation" present.

Jim Haynes, sidereal astrologer in Los Angeles, suggested that a good day to do so would be when transiting Sun would go over my natal Jupiter, and, although that sounds astrologically reasonable, it really only amounts to a bit of astrological generality. The Sun and Jupiter may be the two most benefic planets in the heavens, and in my natal chart Sun and Jupiter are sextile at a six degree orb. I had lived with my Sun and Jupiter and knew that what could be expected of either had often been as nebulous as clouds. I also recalled sitting down with Lee Lehman and Maggie Meister when they did an election to replace the car Lee had just had totalled by a semi rig. Although all of us had worked with horary astrology, elections are a part of horary which is rather ticklish to tackle. It does require one to be especially alert to every possible nuance. For buying a car is the great American activity, usually known as car fever, and it almost should be in the books alongside diseases and ailments. The considerations are myriad. When is the showroom open? When can I go to the showroom to shop and try out? What about the date I accept delivery? Will it have parking karma? What color do I want? What style? What accessories? These are only some of the questions. And when you have car fever you might just forget half the stuff you should determine ahead of time.

Inner Wheel
181. Possible Car Purchase
Natal Chart
Jan 8 1992
6:04:16 PM EST +5:00
Newport RI, USA
41N29 071W19
Geocentric
Tropical
Campanus
True Node

Outer Wheel
Author's Chart
Natal Chart
Nov 3 1925
6:04:16 PM EST +5:00
Newport RI, USA
41N29 071W19
Geocentric
Tropical
Campanus
True Node

Compliments of:-
Joseph Silveira deMello
1755 Franklin Str #204
San Francisco CA 94109
Tel (415) 775-8939
email jsmgemscorp@juno.com

I decided to simplify election techniques by using the diurnal technique. Diurnals are a technique which teaches us trenchantly how our planets work in our own charts. I had long knowledge of the weight of my natal Jupiter in Capricorn in the eighth house and almost exactly sextile Saturn in Scorpio in the sixth house. The Saturn influence was such I could not avoid it. My gains from Jupiter always came when it was in aspect to Saturn. These had been small gains arriving perhaps later than earlier. Jupiter was then sextile my natal Sun, and both those were in a very wide sextile in my natal chart. Jupiter had always brought me feedback and lots of help from fellow astrologers. So I did a diurnal for the date when the Sun would be on natal Jupiter, January 8, 1992. There were further considerations, I might add, a Mercury retrograde period was coming and I did not want to buy a Pisces automobile.

See this lovely chart. The transiting Sun is indeed on natal Jupiter, but I was not at all prepared to have that Sun so closely with Neptune and Uranus. Although Saturn is further away, it happens to be in orb of the Descendant. Its buddy Chiron is in the diurnal Ascendant, and natal Chiron is on diurnal Midheaven. No one looking at this chart would buy a car with such a chart.

As it happened, a co-worker suggested we go to a auto-mart showroom that had many different makes of cars. My co-worker, a family man, got very interested in vans and it was that day that the seed idea was planted and he eventually did buy a van. But to everything at which I looked, I had some objection. Even opening and closing the door of one model, I saw the whole side of the car tremble.

The best remedy when you have car fever is to look at everything. I wanted a four door sedan of conservative color, gas economy, a good radio, and air-conditioning. I also wanted a car I would drive, meaning a manual transmission, and that put me into foreign cars. I did think of lessening the load by buying a well kept second hard car, but that did not last long as an idea. I remember my brother-in-law saying that when you buy second hand you buy some other fellow's discarded problem. Also foreign cars do not depreciate enough to make a second hand car an economic concern. I looked at Toyotas, Nissans, Chevrolet and Geo Metros, and always had the back of my mind on Honda.

Actual Car Purchase

So, with a lot of astrological gymnastics, I arrived at February 12-13, 1992, as a good day to make up my mind. I did event charts and felt I had as good a day as I was ever going to get. I had been to a Honda showroom and looked at and tested some of their secondhand vehicles. A new car would cost very little more than a used car. I was impressed by the Honda sedans on display and surprised that this model seemed to have more leg room for back seat passengers than other economy cars. The model that impressed me was a gray so dark as to almost be black. But I determined not to be in a hurry. To the model in which I was interested, the dealer was going to have to add air conditioning and a radio, and that would be done next day. I would pick up the car on Thursday around 4:30 p.m. But then the salesman was going to sit with me and go over the features of the car to familiarize me with

them enough so I could drive from the showroom to home without problems. So I signed the purchase papers the early evening of Wednesday the twelfth. The diurnal for that day does not have the best degree of Taurus on the Midheaven, but that would change next day. Diurnal Jupiter is retrograde in the first house and sextile my natal Sun. I did not notice it was also quincunx diurnal Saturn, but I do not believe that would have worried me. The angles were free of malefics. The Moon was on my natal Ascendant, the East Point was on natal Neptune, and diurnal Neptune was on natal Jupiter. These were not angular touches. The Moon for next day would have been past my natal Moon. I felt quite comfortable with what I was doing. And next day I got the keys at 4:30 p.m. and drove out of the showroom one hour later.

Retirement Luncheon

My final day of work was supposed to be Friday, March 27, 1992, so a retirement luncheon was scheduled for noon of the twenty-sixth. It was a well catered affair. The day was lovely. The diurnal Sun was in orb of my Descendant, and the diurnal Moon would earlier than this chart have gone over my IC or fourth house cusp. Diurnal Moon and Uranus would be coming to my natal Jupiter, with diurnal Neptune another degree away. Saturn was on my natal Midheaven, a fitting indicator of retirement, I would not be at any loss for things like astrology to do in the future. When we got back from the luncheon, my boss announced that, since I had not taken a lot of time off during the previous three months when she had much needed me, that she was going to let me have the rest of the day off and give me the following day. So I cleaned out my desk, squared things away, gave my coworkers a rundown of my files, and said my good-byes.

Set Off on First Big Trip

I had it all thought out. By this time I had broken in the car, having quickly put 600 miles on it, easy to do in California. I would be making two big trips, the first across the South to the Washington convention and then to Florida and back. I had written letters giving people and idea of my schedule. I would head down the coast starting Wednesday the first of April, and the date did not bother me, visit a nephew in Los Angeles for two days, and then go on to San Diego to visit a friend there for the weekend. Monday I would set out across Interstate Ten with my next stop at Las Cruces where my niece and her family lived on an Army post high in the mountains where I stayed only overnight. The big drag was going to be from El Paso to Corpus Christi, and there was no way I was going to do that in under two days.

The chart for the start off is done for the day but not yet specifically in place, as far as the Moon was concerned, until that evening. So actually we have to think of the diurnal Moon in Pisces going over natal Uranus and diurnal Venus. The main thing is that natal Pluto is exactly on the Midheaven, so I am going to have to be

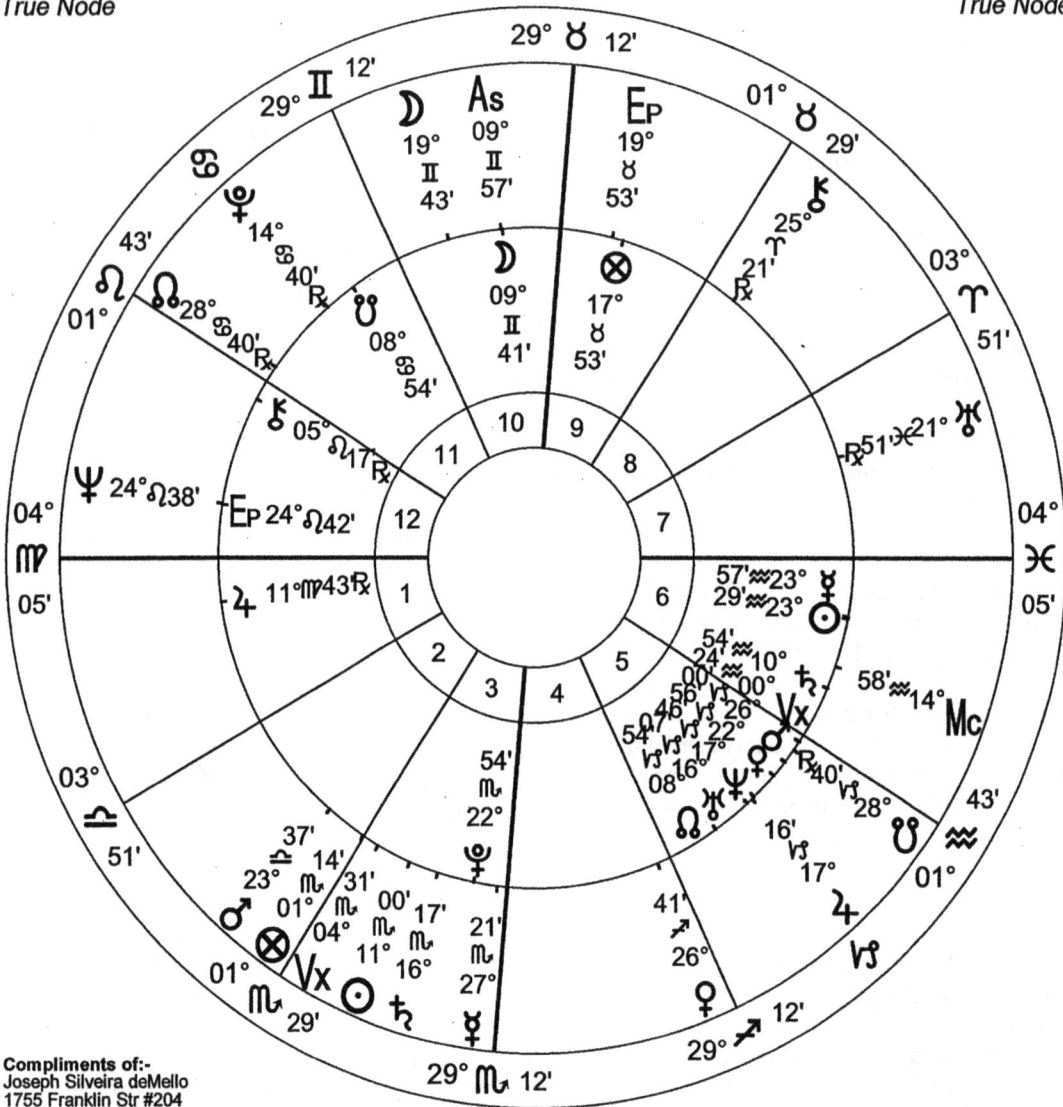

Compliments of:-
Joseph Silveira deMello
1755 Franklin Str #204
San Francisco CA 94109
Tel (415) 775-8939
email jsmgemscorp@juno.com

184. Set off on 1st Trip
Natal Chart
Apr 1 1992
6:04:16 PM EST +5:00
Newport RI, USA
41N29 071W19
Geocentric
Tropical
Campanus
True Node

Author's Chart
Natal Chart
Nov 3 1925
6:04:16 PM EST +5:00
Newport RI, USA
41N29 071W19
Geocentric
Tropical
Campanus
True Node

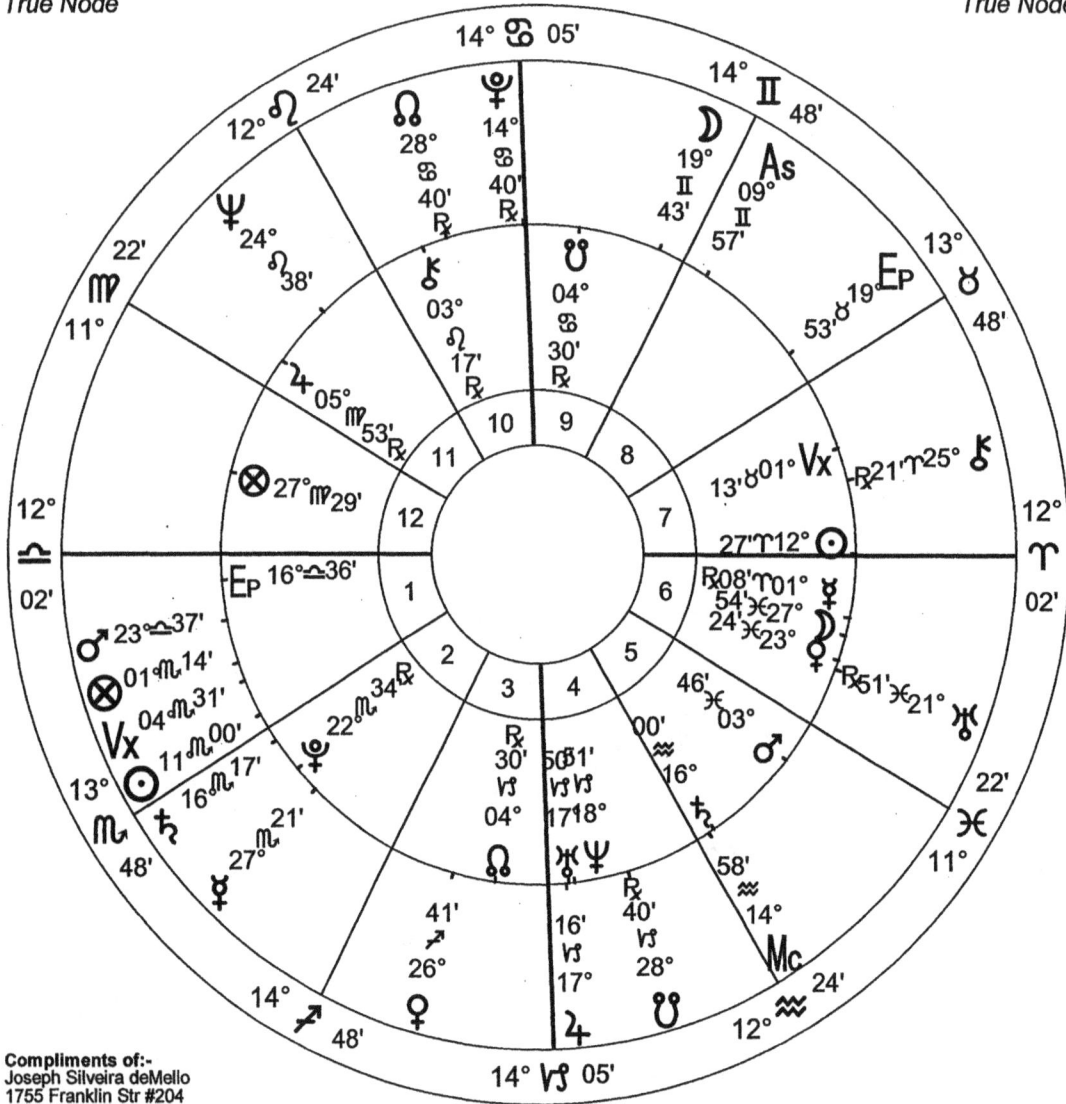

cautious and not be my own undoing. After all, natal Sun and Pluto are trine in my natal chart. Looking around the chart, natal Jupiter is on diurnal Uranus, and they will be in effect in two days, and stay in effect for three or four with the added touch to diurnal Neptune. Now that is going to cover most of the time I am in San Diego. I did not see myself having a problem with Interstate 5 to Los Angeles, but I knew from the past the road from Los Angeles to San Diego is literally a race track. I am glad to see that diurnal Saturn is past my natal MC. But some flexibility is called for with the Sun these few days lingering on my Descendant. Just about this time of year the days start growing longer, and my normally sixth house Sun creeps up to stay in the seventh house of diurnal charts until September. But nothing else is touching any other sensitive spots on the chart. I had plenty of time to look at this chart, so I did check for exact aspects of things in the diurnal to each other and then to things in the natal chart.

In fact the trip went swimmingly. I remember stopping in west Texas to get gas and saw a Wal-mart where I could go replenish my stock of cigarettes. When I arrived at the door of the store, I found there a big black wreath, and it turned out that Sam Walton the founder of the store had died that day. I did not stop in Austin which would have involved making a dog leg in my route, but I was not quite prepared for coming to the city limits of Corpus Christi at what I would call thirty-five miles from downtown. Of course the speed limits are immediately curtailed so you are sure not to miss one of the many electrical transformers to the north side of the road. I had all the directions I needed to drive up to the house of the couple I was visiting there, arriving the eighth and leaving on April 12. As a matter of fact, the long trip was uneventful. In good time I got to the UAC convention site in Crystal City across the river from Washington, DC. The convention was delightful and very lively. I had meant to go south via Charleston, but I decided not to do so. I drove south all the way to Savannah, where I spent the night and as I left next day, a Mercedes ahead of me threw some gravel into my windshield and pocked it. It sped away. I went on down to spend a few days with friends in central Florida. From there I went to Fort Lauderdale where I spent two weeks. I then followed the roads around the Gulf of Mexico to visit an old client in Gulfport and go back to Corpus Christi for a week with my friends there. Driving through Houston in mid-afternoon, natal Neptune on the diurnal Midheaven, diurnal Venus on the Descendant, traffic came to a standstill. I resigned myself to the delay. We soon had a five lane bottleneck.

As we came close to what caused all this I had to laugh out loud. A very old plumbing truck had broken an axle and spill plumbing supplies, pipes, sinks, a toilet, joints of all sorts, some of them if not exactly antique were definitely used, scattered over three of the five highway lanes. I crossed Texas back to New Mexico and in Arizona made a detour to the Grand Canyon. I did get sick of a luncheon I had at a roadhouse on my detour. I spent the next night in Palm Springs. I thought I might call a friend there, but I was so tired I abandoned the idea, and the following day, I drove home to San Francisco on May 22. The first thing I found upon arrival was that the friend I almost tried to look up in Palm Springs had in fact committed suicide by shooting him-

self a month previously. On Sunday, June 21, I would leave on my second and northern cross-country trip.

In the meantime I was very busy between the two trips. I decided to re-write one of my presentations at the coming AFA Convention in Chicago. Of course I had also to make sure I had all the handouts photocopied and collated. There was also a great number of client problems, which surprised me. The most important client event is next.

Business Opportunity

I have a client who is a printer, partner in firm of quality printers, and I had been following the charts of the partners for ten years. The partner whom I saw most often and regularly was a Taurus Sun with Aries rising and Moon in Pisces. This partner ran the front office, furnished estimates for print jobs and made sales, and took care of the books.

His partner, eleven years younger and an Aquarius Sun with Capricorn rising and Moon in Leo, ran the printshop. My friend has always been interested in astrology, but his partner declared he did not believe in astrology. Yet all staff in the printshop were air signs, or as his partner calls them, the airheads. Coincidence, his partner said.

The partner who was my friend was rather difficult in several ways. He had gone to an astrologer many years earlier when an elderly lady astrologer achieved publicity for helping local police find a murderer. Full page newspaper stories had gained her many well to do clients. The astrologer was "of the old school," did charts by hand, never corrected house cusps, rounded out degrees and was casual about minutes. Yet she had given him a more direct reading than he might have wished. She had picked up that he had been twice successful and lost, but did not say whether he would succeed or lose in his present endeavor. As he put it, she flattered him when she could but was "hard as nails" when it came to the bad stuff. I took his data and did his chart on computer and brought it back to show him. Positions and cusps of the chart were quite a few minutes off from those of his first chart, and I had an incredibly hard time explaining to him that I had used the Campanus house system where his previous astrologer had used Placidus. To understand that the angles were the same (but minutes off) was a concept he could not understand no matter how progressively technical and computer smart he professed to be. Then it came out that he had shown the other astrologer's chart to another friend who told him that his astrologer had miscalculated his Pluto. Incredibly, as only an Aries rising with Taurus Sun could do, he took the chart back to the lady and told her what his friend had said. She refused to look at the chart, told him that she had not made a mistake, the chart she had done was correct. She dismissively refused to discuss it further. Just the sort of treatment he deserved, I smiled to myself. She was right.

He is devoted to *Horoscope* magazine, buys it every month. He had picked up on Void of Course Moons, and

Inner Wheel
185. Business Opportunity #1
Natal Chart
Apr 28 1993
4:30 AM CST +6:00
Gadsden AL, USA
34N01 086W01
Geocentric
Tropical
Campanus
True Node

Outer Wheel
Printer #1
Natal Chart
Apr 26 1938
4:30 AM CST +6:00
Gadsden AL, USA
34N01 086W01
Geocentric
Tropical
Campanus
True Node

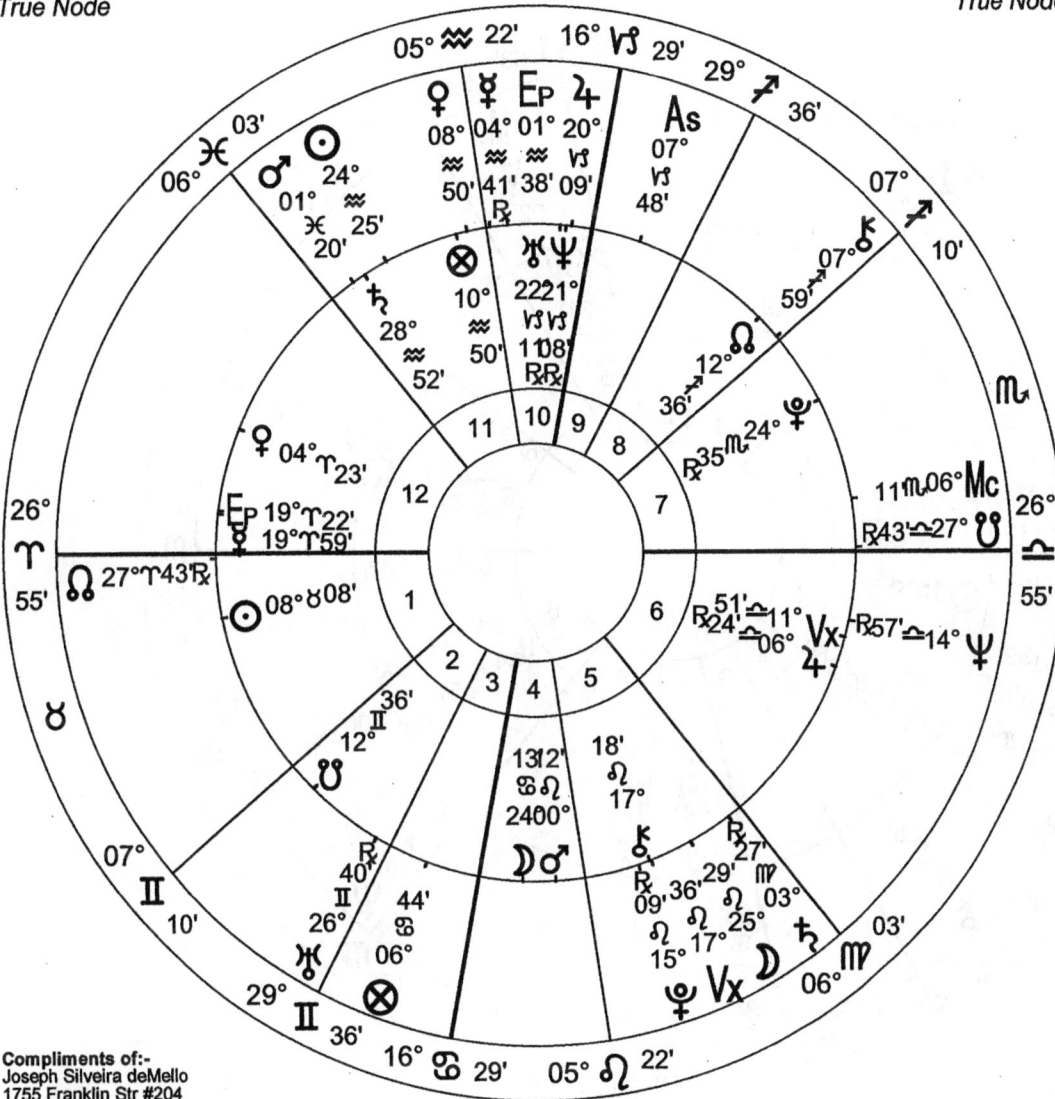

Inner Wheel
185. Business Opportunity #1
Natal Chart
Apr 28 1993
4:30 AM CST +6:00
Gadsden AL, USA
34N01 086W01
Geocentric
Tropical
Campanus
True Node

Outer Wheel
Printer #2
Natal Chart
Feb 13 1949
4:56 AM CST +6:00
Minneapolis MN
44N59 093W16
Geocentric
Tropical
Campanus
True Node

Inner Wheel
185. Business Opportunity #3
Natal Chart
May 6 1993
4:30 AM CST +6:00
Gadsden AL, USA
34N01 086W01
Geocentric
Tropical
Campanus
True Node

Outer Wheel
Printer #1
Natal Chart
Apr 26 1938
4:30 AM CST +6:00
Gadsden AL, USA
34N01 086W01
Geocentric
Tropical
Campanus
True Node

Inner Wheel
185. Business Opportunity #3
Natal Chart
May 6 1993
4:30 AM CST +6:00
Gadsden AL, USA
34N01 086W01
Geocentric
Tropical
Campanus
True Node

Outer Wheel
Printer #2
Natal Chart
Feb 13 1949
4:56 AM CST +6:00
Minneapolis MN
44N59 093W16
Geocentric
Tropical
Campanus
True Node

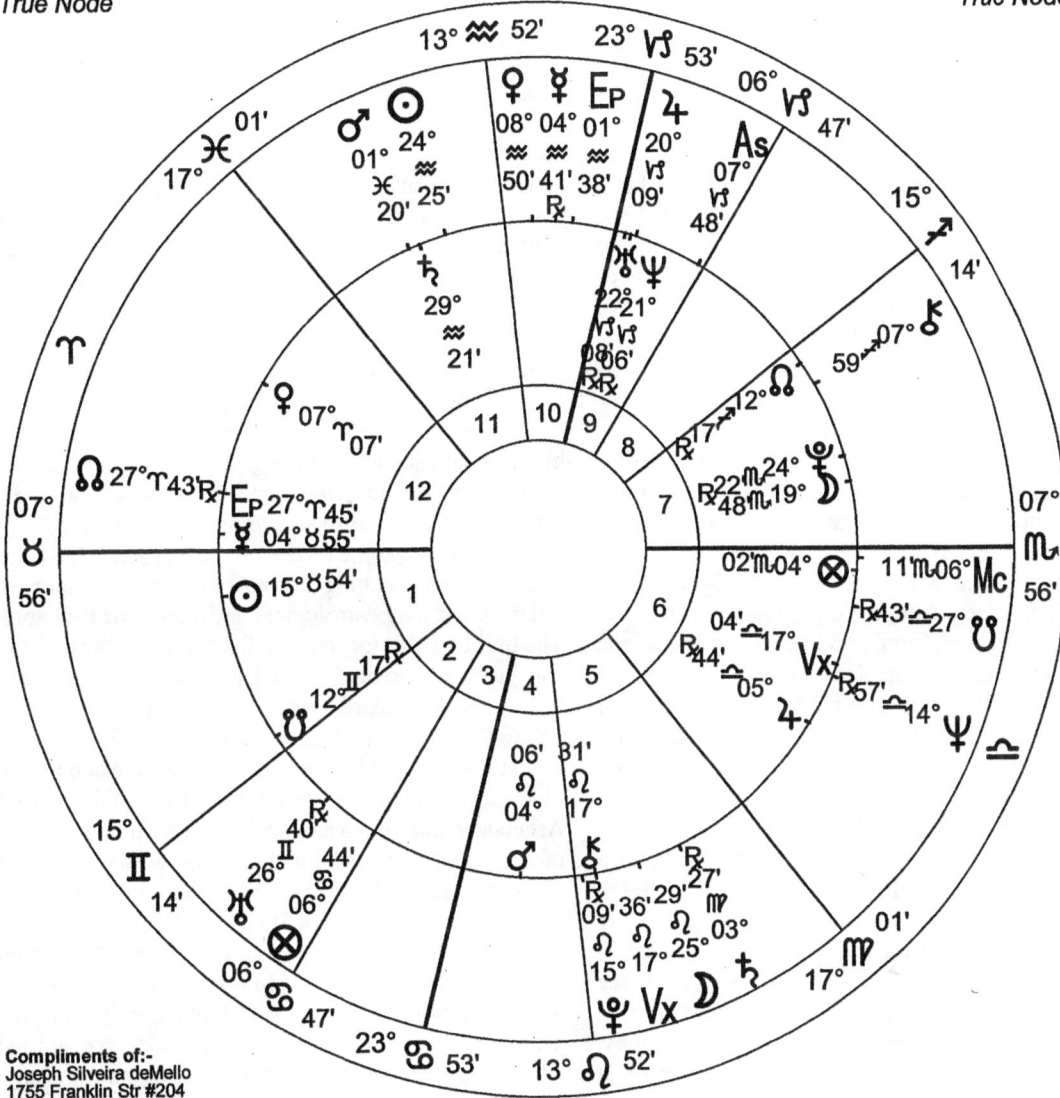

Compliments of:-
Joseph Silveira deMello
1755 Franklin Str #204
San Francisco CA 94109
Tel (415) 775-8939
email jsmgemscorp@juno.com

nothing I could say could shake him from what he had read. He had a strange belief was that the printed word was always correct, otherwise it would not have been printed. On the one hand he is quite cynical, and on the other, he is inclined to believe anything published in newspapers. When published reports turn out to be wrong, he very typically refuses to discuss the subject at all. I assured him that he had brought in his biggest contracts on void of course Moons, and eventually showed him a copy of Bonatus' aphorism (#64) on void of course Moons, pointing out that his biggest contracts had all been landed when the Moon was void of course in Taurus, Cancer, Sagittarius or Pisces. Only an Aries would fail to be impressed by his own experience. But by that time, I had filled in part time work to help him with his office work, and another of his shibboleths had made itself known. Information from an employee, past or present, is always inferior to what he chooses to think. No one ever worked with him, always for him.

In the spring of 1993, the long expected event occurred. The landlord decided to sell the building which had been retrofitted after the Loma Prieta earthquake of 1989. He gave them first choice as he had long promised, told them he wanted top dollar for the property and, at my friend's request, I checked their charts, and what the timing would be for the process to go through successfully. I sat down and really updated with secondary progressions and solar returns and finally did a series of diurnal charts for both of them for the first of every subsequent month through the summer.

It was then I got the surprise of my life. I could hardly credit the strange similarity of the diurnal charts I had done. First, I had to check if my work had been correctly done, whether or not I had mixed up the charts of one partner with those of the other partner. When I held up any two pairs of diurnal charts for the same date, the diurnal angles were exactly the same for both of them, and being diurnals, all the diurnal planets were in the same places around the chart. My friend was born in late April, and his partner was born in mid-February. In the period between their birthdays, the angles were two degrees off, but for the rest of the year, they marched together exactly. Of course the natals around each chart were different. I had never been in the way of seeing anything like this, and the next time we met, I had with me a sheaf of papers and placed pairs of them together up to the light for him to see.

To my amazement, the reaction was skeptical and somewhat wary. I told him that I would have only expected to see this sort of thing in the charts of people who had been married fifty years. Never would I expect it in the charts of business partners. Suddenly I noticed that he was also displeased. It took away some of his uniqueness. I had done enough work with both their charts that I was aware of their karmic ties and I had no doubt but they were meant to be business partners.

Now the secret of how this similarity had been achieved was that I had done the whole series by changing the latitude of where they were born to where they were living. Done that way, naturally the angular similarities were going to be the same. I began to be suspicious of my method of work. Doing these charts with the latitude of San Francisco, the latitudes of their natal places are halved. Having produced such a batch of work, I had at hand study references to use to check actual serious event days. I was soon able to conclude that these charts were not correct. As it happened, these were the charts which brought me to scuttle this way of doing diurnals. At the same time, astrologers were reporting to me on their work with the diurnal technique. Using charts done based on natal time and zone left intact, the Midheavens of these two men were one degree apart, while the Ascendants of individual latitudes of birth, varied by five degrees. And a batch of new charts proved to be more effective for prediction.

Over the years, I have learned to be unbothered by the strange attitudes of clients who have been unaware they were showing me their warts. There was much I simply overlooked. Let the client have some privacy, combined with the realistic sense that one rarely can make a difference or rarely influence the lives of those clients. I sat down and discussed with him what these charts showed me month by month. At least he was aware that this was not going to come off in a week or two. They were going to have a mortgage, and take out a loan, and go through a mountain of paper work and a period of escrow, and both their charts demonstrated remarkable improvement in the months ahead. I even did a horary on the loan in late April 1993 which showed the loan would come through. Of course in the times and considering the frugality in which they had started out, they should buy the building. No other course was viable. If someone else had bought it, the alternative was going to be not only relocation of the business but relocation of living premises. Owning the whole building, they were living at the lowest possible rent and have the luxury of just walking downstairs to work. Point by point I went over astrological and economical factors. The building was located in a light industry area which had just been granted special tax breaks. It had been retrofitted, seismically enhanced by steel girders, repainted, and entirely brought up to code.

In the first chart I did for each partner, the one for the older partner does not have anything in orb of the diurnal Ascendant, but it has a neat split between diurnal and natal Mercurys. Note that this chart is for two days after the older man's birthday. While the diurnal Ascendant will not catch up to the diurnal Sun, it would in less than ten days come to the natal Sun. Just watching the diurnal Ascendant and thinking of May and June, the diurnal Ascendant will, along with the diurnal Sun, go through Taurus and Gemini. By the same token, the diurnal Midheaven is going to move from Capricorn through Aquarius and into Pisces. Looking at this movement in the second chart for the younger Aquarian partner, the touches become much more interesting. The Descendant will rise through Scorpio and Sagittarius. At the bottom of the chart, the diurnal IC is going to be moving through Cancer and Leo, and here we find the very telling Moon, we are brought up sharply with the realization that, in two months, that diurnal Moon is going to make two complete revolutions around the whole of the two charts. My suggestion was that they have meetings

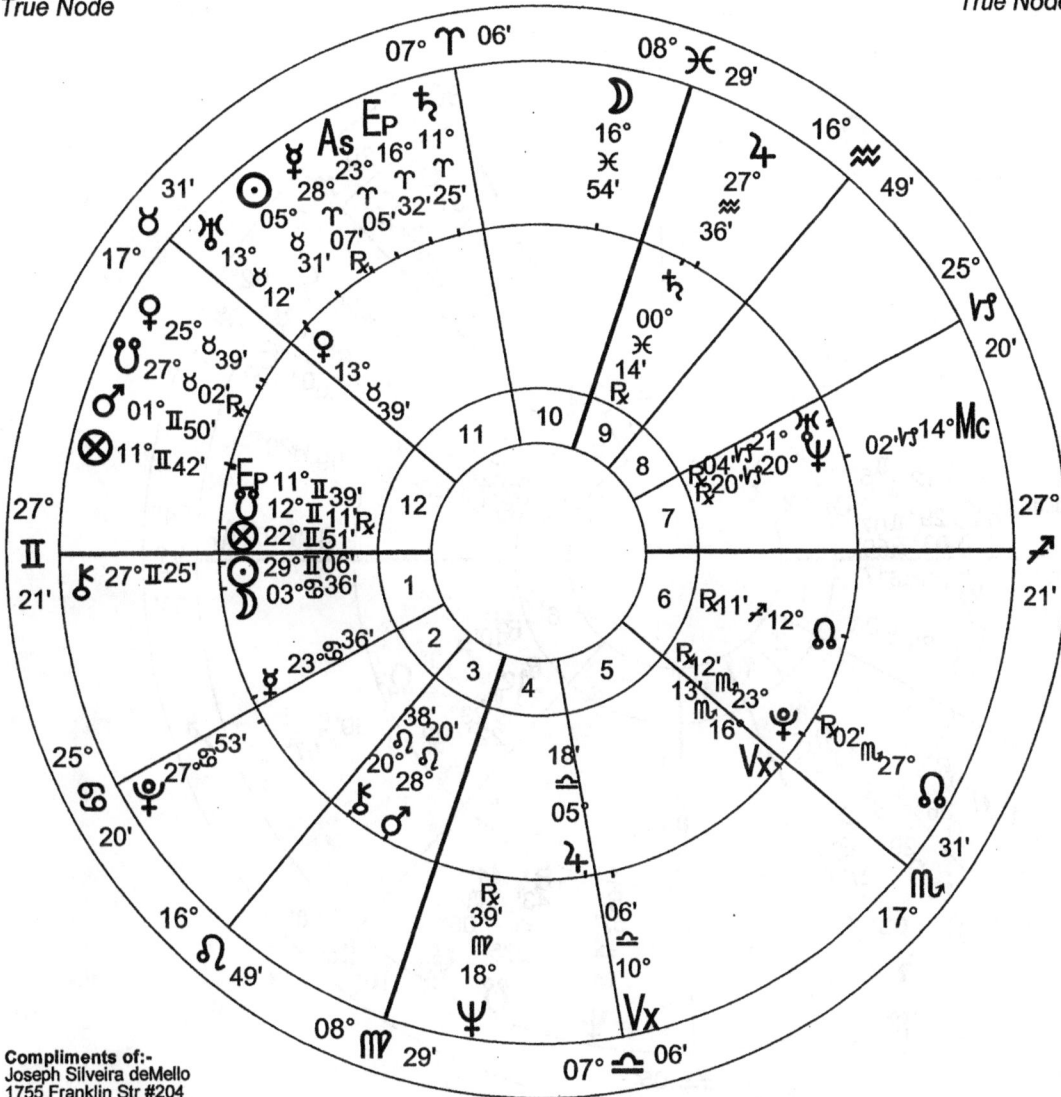

Compliments of:-
Joseph Silveira deMello
1755 Franklin Str #204
San Francisco CA 94109
Tel (415) 775-8939
email jsmgemscorp@juno.com

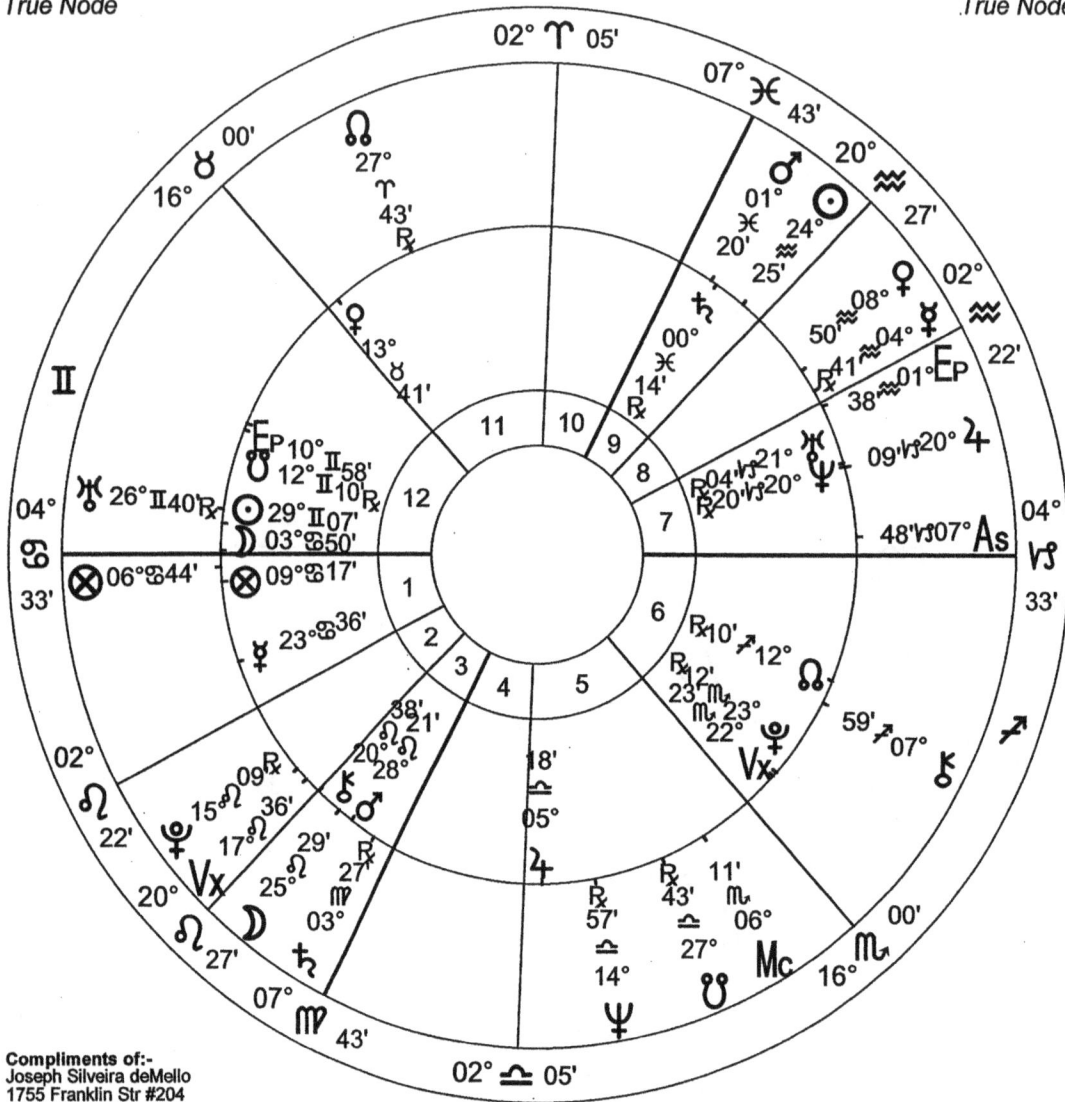

Inner Wheel
185. Business Opportunity #6
Natal Chart
Jun 20 1993
4:56 AM CST +6:00
Minneapolis MN
44N59 093W16
Geocentric
Tropical
Campanus
True Node

Outer Wheel
Printer #2
Natal Chart
Feb 13 1949
4:56 AM CST +6:00
Minneapolis MN
44N59 093W16
Geocentric
Tropical
Campanus
True Node

Compliments of:-
Joseph Silveira deMello
1755 Franklin Str #204
San Francisco CA 94109
Tel (415) 775-8939
email jsmgemscorp@juno.com

with their bankers and accountants leading to the most favorable period which was in the latter half of June 1993.

O.J. Simpson

It was not the crime of the century, but it certainly was front page news for a couple of years. From the days when television too thoroughly covered the McCarthy hearings, we were now satiated with day to day Simpson case coverage. We saw a murder trial hinge less on murder than it did on a very old history of spousal abuse. By the time the first trial ended, most television viewers were substantially convinced that this was a badly handled criminal investigation and prosecution. And all of this spilled over into the world of astrology. We had excellent birth certificate data for Simpson. But we also had data for everyone from the judge to the most minor witness called to testify. Astrologers pointed to Simpson's Mars-Pluto to prove him a murderer despite the fact that this aspect was shared by non-murderers. Astrologers jumped on the feminist bandwagon. Little attention was paid to Simpson's transits for the day of murder or whether he would have the time to rush over there and use commando tactics on his ex-wife and a waiter running an errand without getting himself covered in blood and gore.

This diurnal is for the day he was found not guilty in the criminal trial. Diurnals need only two placements from either diurnal or natal chart to fall upon a diurnal angle. Here we find that all four angles are spectacularly covered. But first a note on the natal chart. Simpson is a Leo rising, Sun in Cancer, with what I have been calling an unfortunate Pisces Moon. He even had Mars in Gemini. After a career as a sport's hero, he was a celebrity who's every appearance was dynamic. Whatever his other faults of ego and self-dramatization, he always was a family oriented person. He contributed financially to the support of his own extended families, some of whom turned out to be unable to forget his good deeds and want him publicly flayed. His Pisces Moon very viably contributes to his personality and behavior. In football, he had an almost amusing record for not allowing himself to be sacked. He would sooner run offside than allow himself to be tackled. Mars in Gemini (while it might make the swinger, hardly makes him a murderer), and that the Sun in Cancer was his chart significator.

Astrologers had more than enough material. A whole astrology book could be written about this collection of charts. The media spared us no details of the lives of all concerned in this affair. Some of the charts at which we looked were of people far more reprehensible than Simpson's chart. You could hardly open an astrological publication without finding an article on any of those people. Out of rags to riches, we had a saga of modern moralities and highlights of cafe society living to damn him. The whole scenario was a made for television event and fodder for every grocery store tabloid.

This chart was done for October 3, 1995, the day the verdict of the jury was read in court. The jury had come to this verdict the previous day, so we are prepared to note that the Moon of this chart has come through the degrees of the previous twenty-four hours to bring the diurnal Moon closer to the IC of the chart almost to the very minute the verdict was going to be read in court, and the natal Part of Fortune right up to the Descendant to show us where he would be protected. Natal Saturn is on the diurnal Midheaven, and Saturn in this position often brings rewards and responsibilities. Natal Chiron is on the Ascendant to, perhaps, indicate the obvious verdict we failed to see coming. Note now that in the previous 24 hours, the Moon had come over diurnal Neptune and Uranus, sextiled the natal Moon, squared diurnal Venus and North Node and diurnal Ascendant. There are other touches. Diurnal Sun was on natal Neptune, diurnal Mars on natal Jupiter. And then note that in the next few days there are single touches to the Midheaven of natal Pluto and natal East Point.

Having produced this diurnal prior to the verdict being read, it struck me that I had not done a diurnal of the date of the murder itself, June 12, 1994, a month prior to his birthday. Now doing so, there is but one touch, the diurnal Moon coming to the diurnal Ascendant in roughly eight hours after the birth time which would have given some poor vibrations around four in the afternoon, about the time after his daughter's dance recital. With the Moon, one expects some action from a woman against the man of the chart, and that was when his ex-wife played the bitch card and refused to let him take part in the party after the recital. The Moon beleaguers him with doubts, hits at his assurance, dares him to make a stupid public scene (which he did not do). Looking at the diurnal Ascendant we find all occupants of the twelfth house as moving with or faster than the Ascendant. There is nothing in the past, and it will be six days to natal Saturn, and nine days to natal Pluto, so ten days to natal East Point, and catch up with natal Ascendant on his next birthday. On the diurnal IC, the touch to natal Neptune was fourteen days prior to this date, and the IC will not reach natal Chiron for ten more days. On the Descendant, 11 days earlier diurnal Neptune was on the Descendant, and eight days earlier on diurnal Uranus, but the next touch to his Descendant will be diurnal Saturn, and the Moon will have got there earlier. The same may be said for the Midheaven, almost a month since touching natal Moon, and 11 days to get to natal Fortune. I cannot believe a man can commit murder with so blank a diurnal chart. The diurnal Moon would touch natal Saturn twenty hours after his time of birth, by which time he was already in Chicago. In six more hours the Moon would get to natal Pluto near natal East Point, and the impact of the news should surely have hit him badly. Or do it with the diurnal Sun moving a degree a day, the Sun is two days from natal Uranus, ten days from natal Venus. It had been fifteen days since the Sun had touched his natal Mars.

After the criminal trial Simpson found himself besieged by his in-laws to whom he had given liberal monetary assistance. Did they suppose they would be cut off now that their connection to Simpson had died? And along came the Goldmans wanting to be recompensed for the early death of a son who lived independent of his father who could never have expected a dime from his son, and a mother with whom he had no contact for eons.

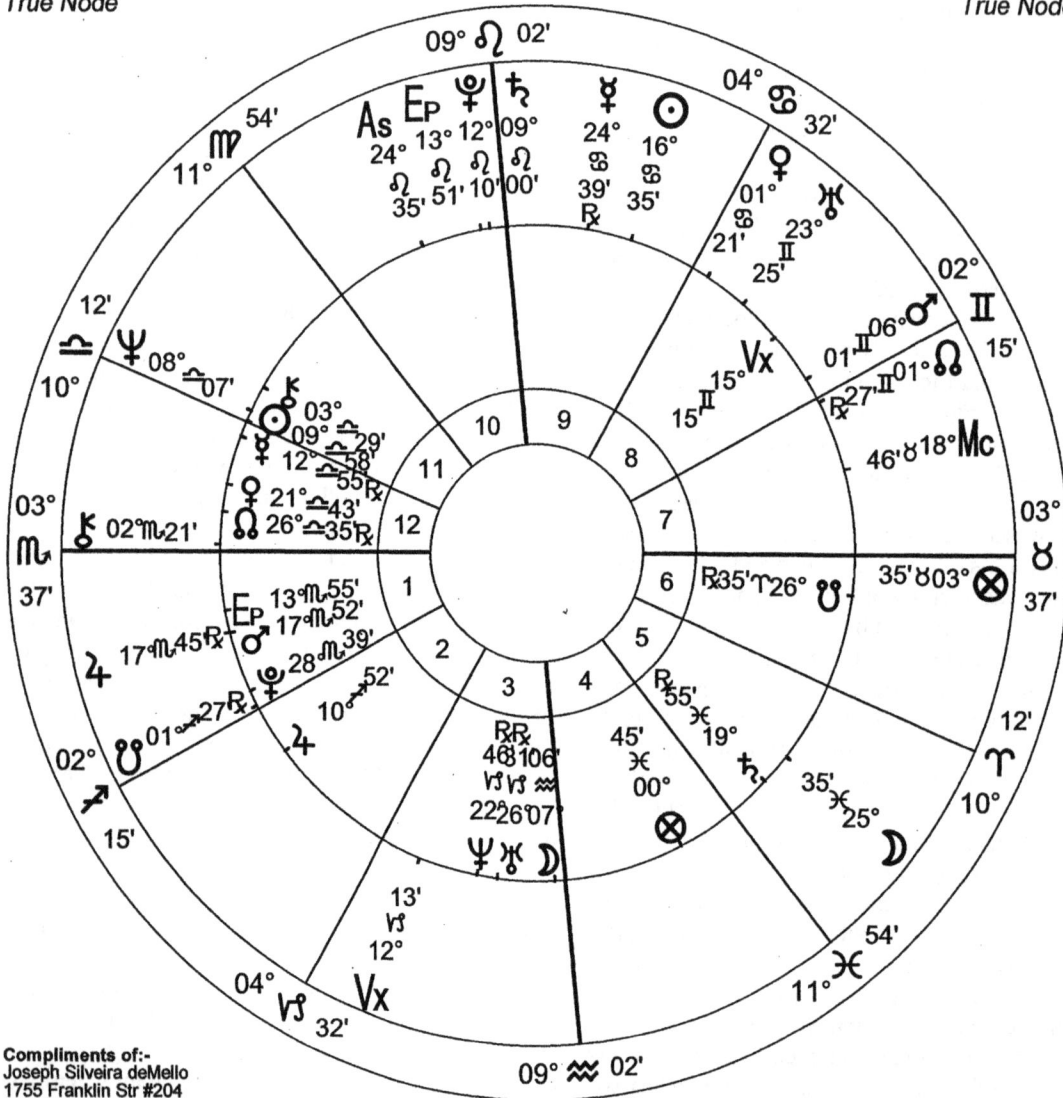

Compliments of:-
Joseph Silveira deMello
1755 Franklin Str #204
San Francisco CA 94109
Tel (415) 775-8939
email jsmgemscorp@juno.com

Inner Wheel
188. Simpson murder diurnal
Natal Chart
Jun 12 1994
8:08 AM PST +8:00
San Francisco
37N46 30 122W25 06
Geocentric
Tropical
Placidus
True Node

Outer Wheel
O J Simpson
Natal Chart
Jul 9 1947
8:08 AM PST +8:00
San Francisco CA
37N45 122W26
Geocentric
Tropical
Campanus
True Node

Compliments of:-
Joseph Silveira deMello
1755 Franklin Str #204
San Francisco CA 94109
Tel (415) 775-8939
email jsmgemscorp@juno.com

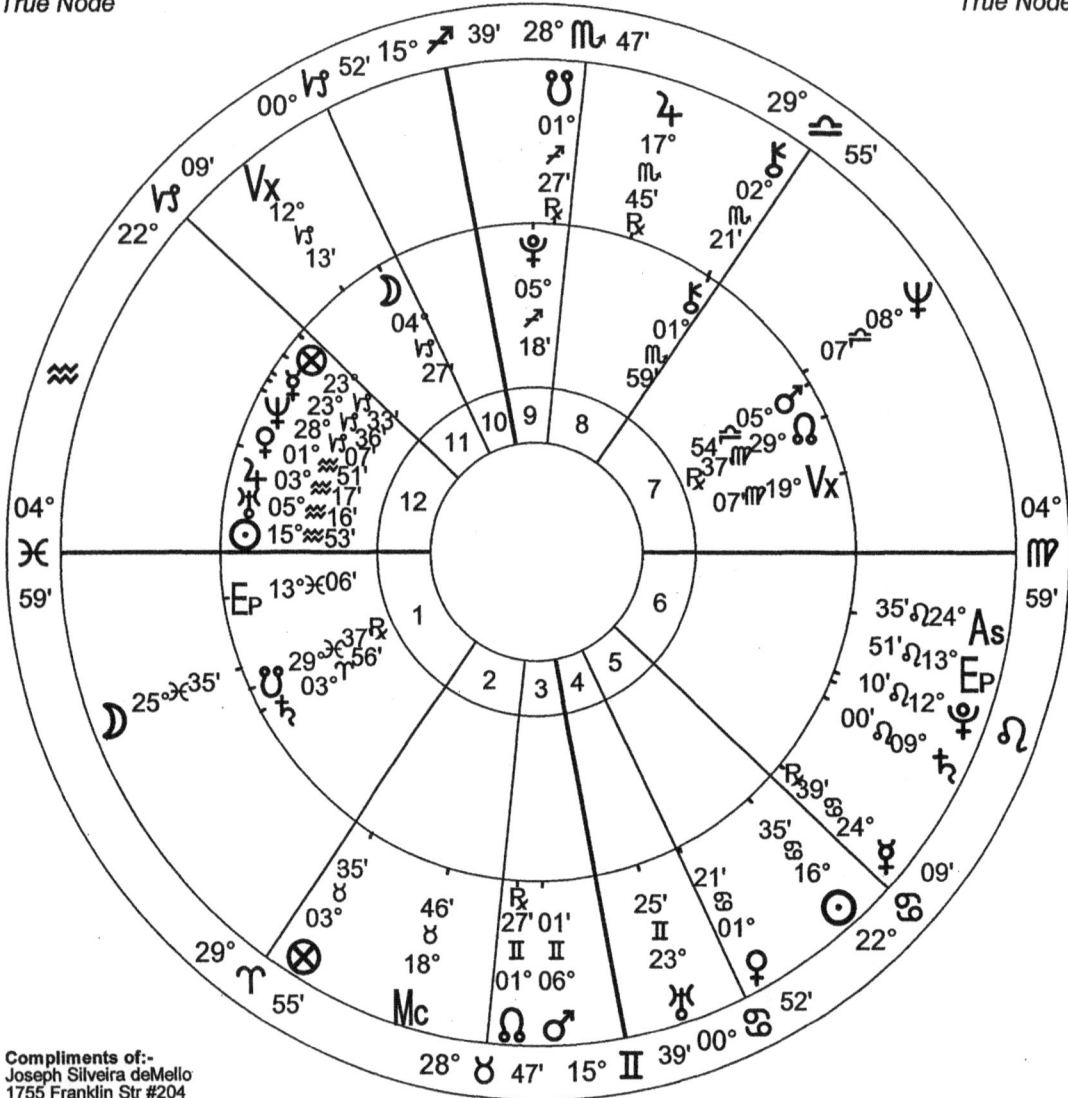

Inner Wheel
189 Simpson civil verdict
Natal Chart
Feb 4 1997
8:08 AM PST +8:00
San Francisco CA
37N45 122W26
Geocentric
Tropical
Campanus
True Node

Outer Wheel
O J Simpson
Natal Chart
Jul 9 1947
8:08 AM PST +8:00
San Francisco CA
37N45 122W26
Geocentric
Tropical
Campanus
True Node

Compliments of:-
Joseph Silveira deMello
1755 Franklin Str #204
San Francisco CA 94109
Tel (415) 775-8939
email jsmgemscorp@juno.com

Was the public ready for a class action suit? Clearly this was a case of Christianity showing its worse face. Such litigation was just a tad from frivolous. O.J. had been criminally exonerated and was now, on February 4, 1997, found guilty of contributing to his ex-wife's murder, possibly for giving her the house in which she lived. The diurnal done for this new trial's end reveals no touches to any of the angles. The diurnal Sun is fully twenty degrees back of the diurnal Ascendant, and one would have to do other charts to see if it would ever catch up to the East Point. There are a certain number of days since the IC was on natal Mars or would be on natal Uranus. And the same for the Descendant and the Midheaven. The results of the first trial were obviously important to him. Can we say the latter trial had no importance for him? He must have felt that he could surmount whatever happened that day though the damages were excessive. We seem not to have come far from an eye for an eye, a tooth for a tooth.

In the diurnal for February 4, 1997, the civil guilty verdict came at 7:15:20 p.m. PST, or for nineteen hours after the time of this diurnal chart. Although nothing is angular, there are two interesting touches. At the average movement of the diurnal eleventh house Moon, the Moon would have moved to conjunct natal Vertex. Was this verdict sick-making for him? Notice diurnal Chiron doing a Chiron return in the eighth house. After these two touches, the diurnal Sun is within orb of a quincunx to his natal Sun and a sextile to diurnal Midheaven. The diurnal Ascendant is square natal Mars and diurnal Pluto, while diurnal Ascendant is also widely quincunx his natal Saturn and natal Neptune, as well as diurnal Mars. Although we may have puzzled over the lack of conjunctions to diurnal angles in this chart, there is still a great deal any astrologer can read in it.

Ronald Goldman

The birth data for Ronald Goldman was found by an astrologer on the Internet and is rectified or speculative data. The time given was 12:27 p.m. CDT, July 2, 1968, Chicago, Illinois. Lois Rodden gives it bad marks as dirty data. No documentation has ever appeared to verify it. His murder was June 12, 1994, just weeks before his twenty-sixth birthday. He met his death on the front steps of a condo in the Brentwood subdivision of Los Angeles just west of Beverly Hills. When I did this chart, I was still keeping an open mind about whether death would show by two or more touches to the diurnal angles. Here I was to get a surprise. The diurnal East Point and Vertex axis, spoken of as secondary Ascendant-Descendant indicators, are exactly with the latter, and all four angles are in an exact mutable grand cross. I would classify grand crosses as cardinal for action, absolutely set for fixed, and phasing out for mutable. I regard the East Point as indicative of a special event and the Vertex as indicative of a health problem, so it irks me to see it involved in a murder scene.

So the next devastating thing is to find other placements in the diurnal or natal to echo these angles, and there we find only the diurnal Moon and natal Moon at the first degree of Leo and Libra respectively. We see diurnal Mercury between diurnal Sun with the diurnal Midheaven as midpoint, diurnal Sun almost conjunct natal Mercury, and these are all part of a grand trine to diurnal Jupiter and Saturn. The reason I did this chart was because he died violently, and his role in this event remains ambiguous. Was he merely running an errand and got to be in the wrong place at the wrong time, or was there any other scenario being played. It would seem to me to be no reason to further rectify this chart, even by use of diurnals, though we would need data of other serious dates in his life.

Indeed the natal chart proffered for Ronald Goldman, Libra rising, Sun in Cancer, and Moon in Libra is not one of the best charts we have ever seen. Both Mars and Venus are rather too close to the Sun. These planets are combust his ego needs. Mars rules his seventh and is in tenth. Venus rules his eighth and is in the ambitious ninth. As a waiter, Pisces rules his sixth, which fits, but Neptune is in his second to speak of an unreal way of making money (waiters do make money, so maybe the unreal thing is the opinion he has of himself). Mars debilitated in Cancer but still ambitious in the ninth, ruling the seventh gives us a more avid insight to his interest in intimate acquaintance. Possibly that evening everything was conspiring against him.

End of Second Cross-Country Trip

I made my second trip across country, and it was filled with much pleasure and a few minor troublesome incidents, a bit of trouble leaving Chicago after a fine convention there. That is, I found myself driving in the wrong direction on a road I should not have taken. There was a bit of driving through rain at night in New England, followed by a minor fender bender that caused to replace my left front directional blinker light, and the job was done poorly. They also rotated my tires while I was there. After I left the garage, I went to a bank, and did some other errands and found myself attracting a lot of attention. I got out to see what passersby were pointing at and noted the new blinker light was hanging by its wires. I took it back to the garage which disbelieved they could have done such a job, and they had no idea why my car was pulling left. And mind you, this was a dealership for my car make. They balanced the tires, a thing I later learned was not necessary, and it was miles later that the answer occurred to me that they had not checked the tire pressure. The car was pulling left because the left front tire was down to almost too soft to drive easily. After more visits, I turned further northward to see the Black Hills Monument where four presidents were carved on a mountain. Driving through Montana was an incredible experience as sometimes driving at sunset through west Texas can be. Short of Missoula, Montana, I found myself one of a half dozen cars which had gotten tire punctures from a nail spill on the road just before a crossroads settlement. We all stood in line when AAA came out. I must say I was amazed we were all so nice about the incident, not laying any supposed blame for the nail spill. I did suggest to the tow truck driver that he wait around as there were bound to be more drivers needing his services.

Of course I had done diurnals for intervals of time all

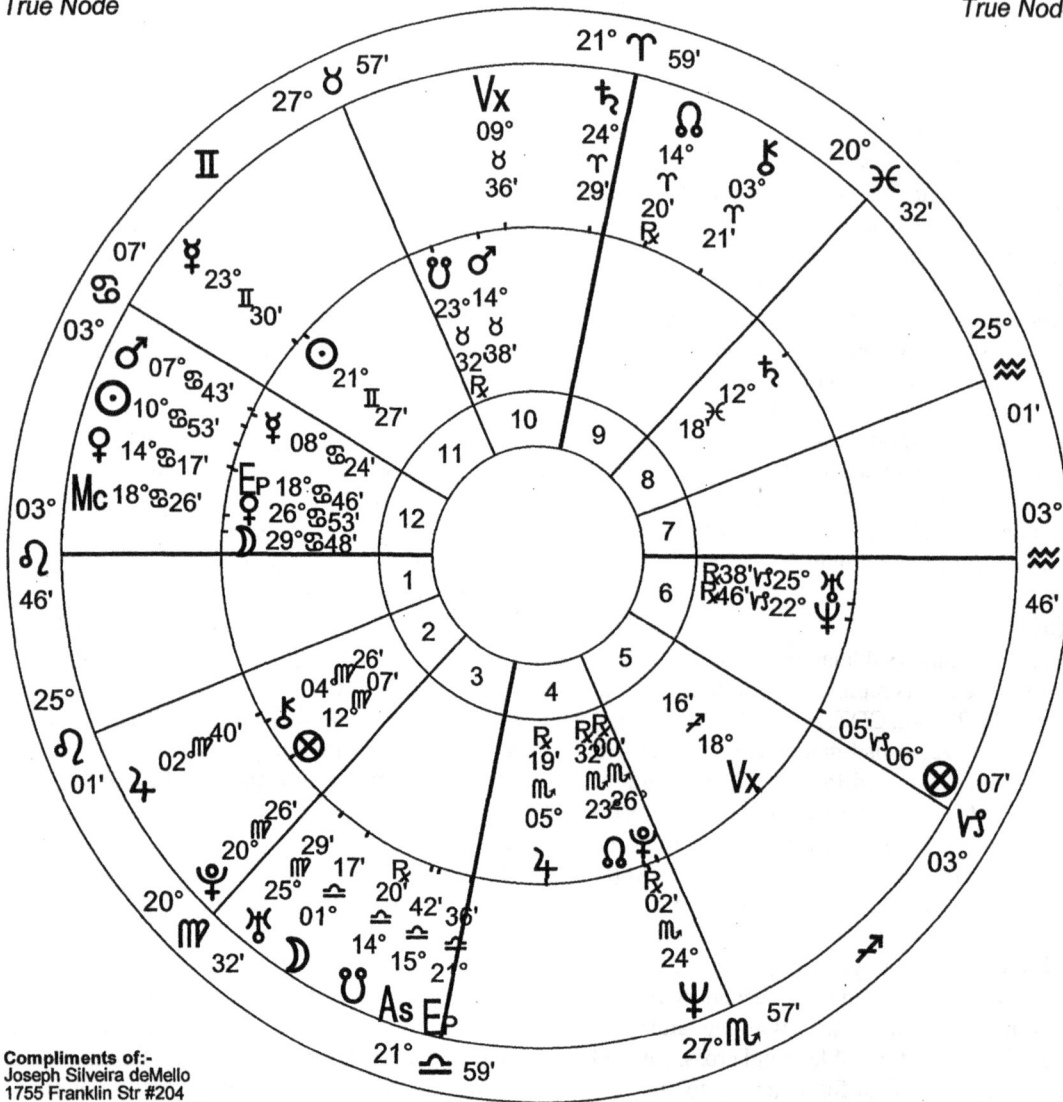

Inner Wheel
188. Simpson murder diurnal
Natal Chart
Jun 12 1994
8:08 AM PST +8:00
San Francisco
37N46 30 122W25 06
Geocentric
Tropical
Placidus
True Node

Outer Wheel
Ronald Lyle Goldman
Natal Chart
Jul 2 1968
12:27 PM CST +6:00
Chicago IL, USA
41N30 087W38
Geocentric
Tropical
Campanus
True Node

Compliments of:-
Joseph Silveira deMello
1755 Franklin Str #204
San Francisco CA 94109
Tel (415) 775-8939
email jsmgemscorp@juno.com

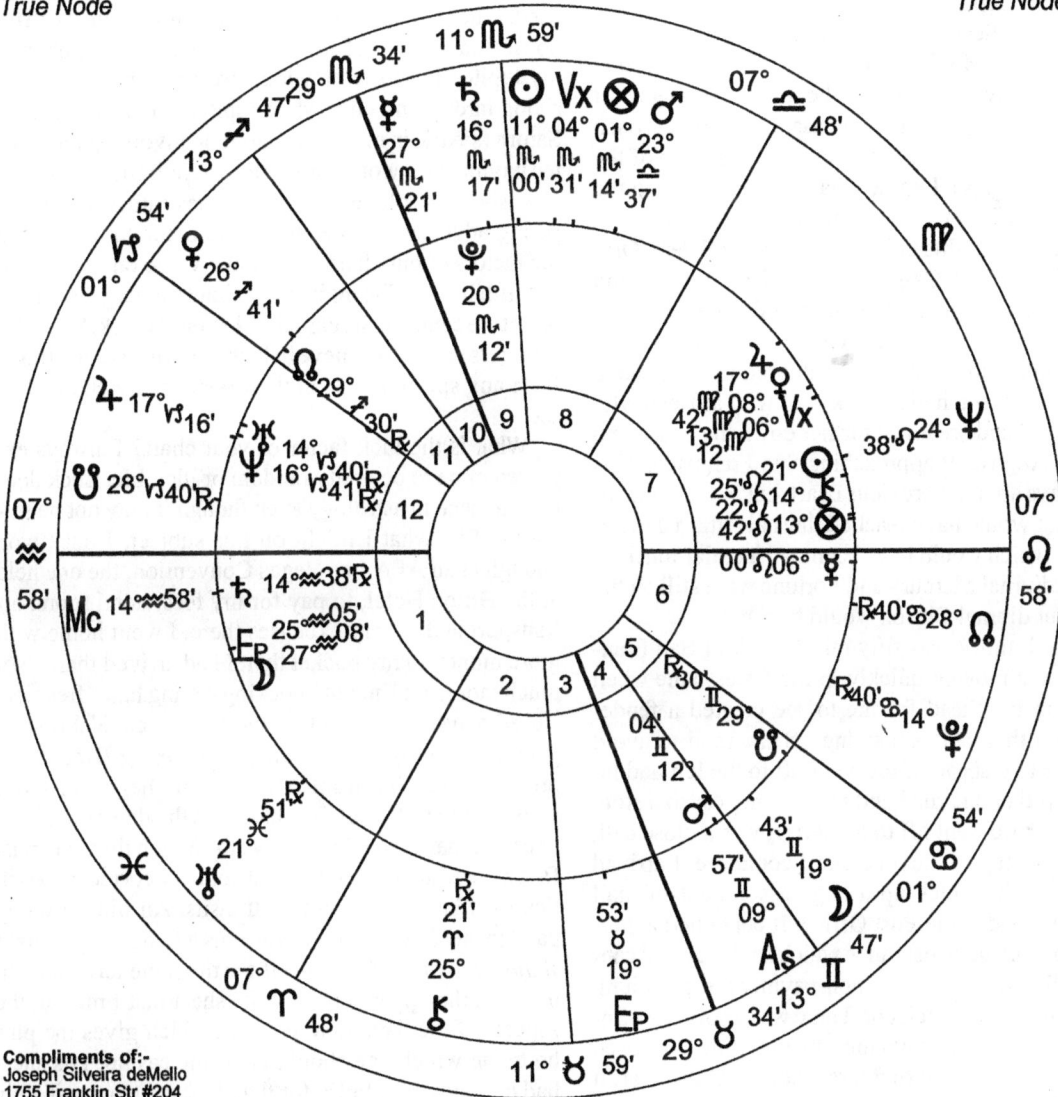

Compliments of:-
Joseph Silveira deMello
1755 Franklin Str #204
San Francisco CA 94109
Tel (415) 775-8939
email jsmgemscorp@juno.com

along that trip and studied them as carefully as I studied my route maps. I have a chart for the 13th August 1992. This is the chart for the end of the day when I reached Missoula. Events happening during this day should more properly be on a diurnal for the previous day's twenty-four hour period. In my motel room I noted the position of the diurnal Moon after seeing diurnal Mercury on the Descendant and natal Mercury two degrees from the diurnal Midheaven. A chart for the previous day would have those Mercurys in more exact orb. But later that evening the diurnal Moon would be square natal Mercury. I pulled into a motel in Missoula and made the discovery that city has the purest and tastiest and coldest drinking water I have ever got out of a faucet. In the morning I took the tire to be repaired and changed, had breakfast and proceeded toward Seattle. In Spokane I encountered a scorching heat wave which was not even a record. But that changed dramatically when I got to the mountain range east of Seattle. Seattle proved to be a pleasant city to approach from the east in the evening. At no time did the glare of the Sun impede my progress. I know what I was smelling in the air was not the Pacific, but it certainly was refreshing.

I spent a couple of nights in Seattle, a night in Salem, Oregon, and a night in Orick, California in the Humboldt Sound area where I actually spent my last night on the road in a very old motel cabin which had a kitchenette and a carport and was only ten dollars for the night. I detoured to Ferndale, a Danish dairy settlement, had a quick visit with a friend who was running a bed and breakfast further down the coast, and was finally on August 19 approaching San Francisco. This was only six days after the previous chart, but in that time diurnal Ascendant would have reached diurnal Saturn and natal Midheaven which would have been two angular touches. I did not think diurnal Mercury and Fortune were still on the Descendant, but diurnal Chiron would be there.

All went well until I was fifty miles north of San Francisco. Traffic was moving quickly in the fastest lane when some driver too far ahead for me to see created a fender bender situation that had cars sluing off the road to avoid each other. The two ahead of me went off to the left and hit bumpers. I stayed on the road and brought my car to a stop. Two cars behind me went off to the left. It was a close call, but no serious damage to anyone that I could see. I arrived home early enough to pick up a huge assortment of mail which had been held at the Post Office. It contained a dunning notice from my auto insurance which said they had canceled me the first of August for non-payment of premium. Good thing I escaped the accident. There was a note from Social Security dunning me for having paid me while I had been still gainfully employed the first three months of the year. It was entirely their fault; I had asked not to have payments start until after my retirement. Of course they acted as if it was entirely my fault. That was difficult and annoying to settle. And there were two checks which should have been wire-transferred directly to my bank account but had instead been lolling in the held mail at the post office. Moreover, as I drove home August 19, Joe Miller of the Theosophical Society had died, and a few days earlier another close friend had died and I returned just in time to attend his funeral, and good thing I did, as many old friends turned up.

Lottery Win

The lotteries which have become so popular in the last ten years are a snare and a delusion. Yet they appeal to everyone who might so easily descend to greed and avarice and the glorious potential for becoming fabulously rich. Yes, we may know that the odds are higher than having a safe dropped on us from a high window. It keeps no one from mulling over the numbers and buying lottery tickets. As astrologers, we are aware that there are types who should never gamble, most notably those with Gemini or Virgo (Mercury) ruling the fifth house of the natal chart. Such people feel that there is a system for winning, if only the right system could be found and used. There is the type born with Uranus in the fifth house, the position of the born gambler. I have spoken of my Jupiter in Capricorn which gives me small gains arriving tardily and only when Jupiter is in any aspect to Saturn (sextile in my natal chart) and involving more often payment for work done or feedback from colleagues. Yes, some astrologers are colleagues rather than competing adversaries. We all have to come to terms with the factors of our chart. I, too have Virgo on the cusp of my fifth house. The main thing about playing the lottery is that we cannot disregard the element of luck. Some astrologers refuse to believe in luck very firmly, deleting it from any speculations on their own or any charts they see.

What is the luck factor of your chart? I always expected mine to be pretty random or illegible. Luck does have a place in astrology even though it may not be scientific. Say what I might on this subject, I once won enough at an AFA Las Vegas Convention, the one held at the Hilton Hotel, to pay for my fees, hotel room, air transport and sundry expenses there. I went home with more money in my pocket than I had arrived there. Not much more, but I'm not knocking having had a free ride. I used a system devised by the late Joyce Wehrmann, gambled for only seventy minutes. *Winning Transits* is a program available from ACS in San Diego, for those who wish to test it out. It is based on the daily transits to your own natal, so I do not have to caution that you must first have a natal chart that is absolutely correct and will tick off like a time bomb to transits. An old astrology pal, the late Jan Muzurus, who was a Leo rising, bought *Winning Transits* for himself for the same day I bought mine. In the upper corner of the sheet that times all the aspects of the day, there is a box which gives the plus hours on which one should enter the casino. His sheet had not one single entry for that day, so he immediately tore it to pieces in disgust. Nevertheless, as he idled around nickel and dime machines, he consistently got catch up drops of coins which kept him even all day. Having stayed up late the previous evening, talking astrology, I dragged myself out of bed at seven in the morning. My only plus times on the transit sheet were from 4:00 a.m. to 8:30 a.m., and one of the times to enter the casino was 7:18 a.m., July 7, 1988. Unshaven and unbathed, I did comb my hair, I got down to the hotel lobby and dawdled so that I would arrive betimes at the

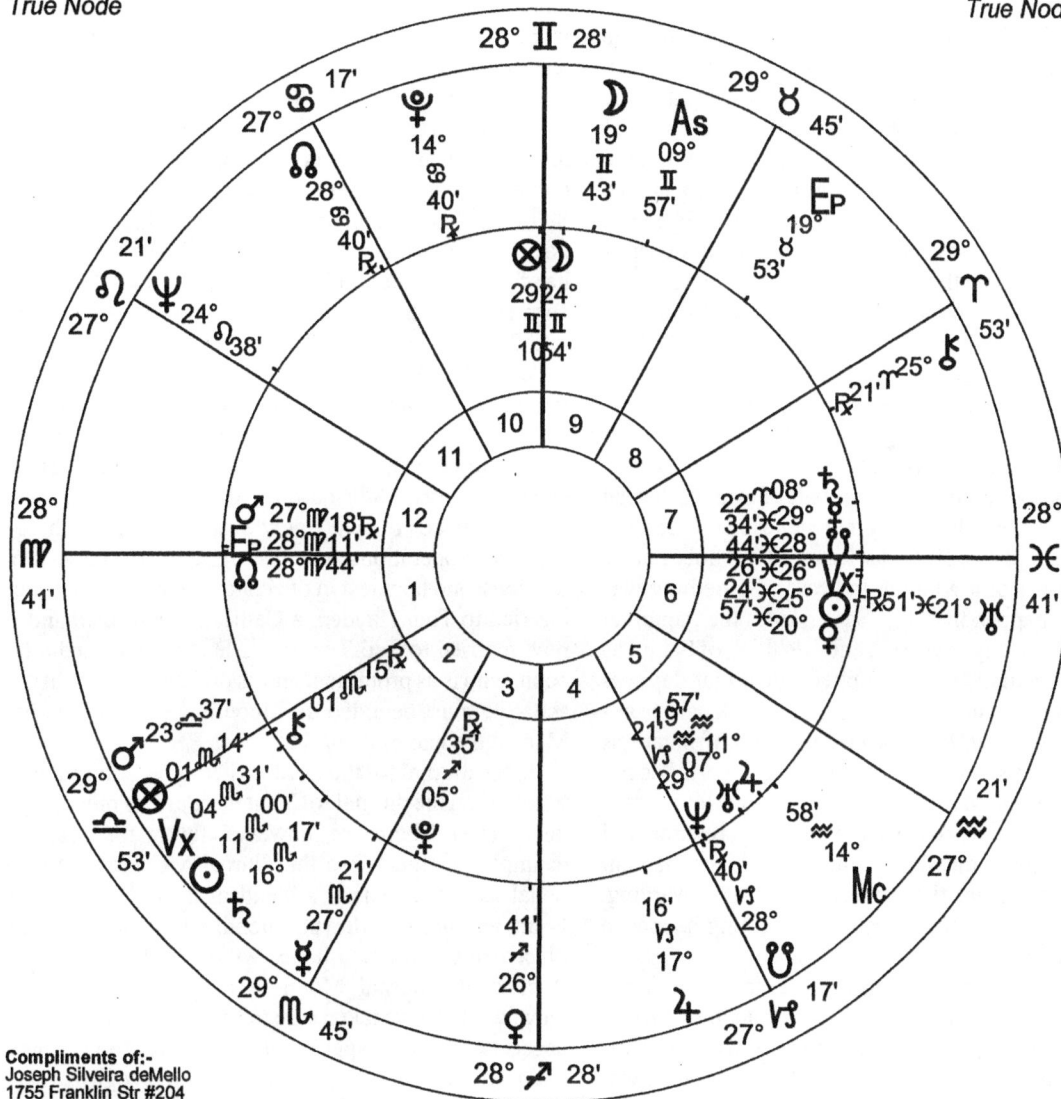

Compliments of:-
Joseph Silveira deMello
1755 Franklin Str #204
San Francisco CA 94109
Tel (415) 775-8939
email jsmgemscorp@juno.com

casino. I began playing a quarter bandits and soon had two big containers full of quarters. The system was working. I shifted to a dollar slot machine and soon was filling plastic racks of silver dollars. On neutral or minus times, I played single coins. On plus times, I played five coins. I played right up to 8:30 a.m., cashed in my chips and went to my room to clean up and change and go start the new round of convention workshop sessions.

I had been systematically watching my diurnals, playing the lottery only on days when I had at least two angular touches. I need not say (or do I?) that this did not always produce more than two out of five which in that game only gets you a free play. The date was March 15, 1997 (chart #194) which you see here, and I won a small three figure amount. The diurnal for this day was going to be a banner day of some sort. Diurnal Moon was in position to go over the top of my chart. That is, the Moon was at almost 25 Gemini and the Midheaven was at 28 Gemini. Where the Moon is involved, I first have to say, the position of the Moon is going to take some time, say eight hours, to hit the diurnal Midheaven. The chart done for my birth time on the East Coast, becomes 3:04:16 p.m. on the West Coast. If you win, much depends on the Moon at the time the of the drawing of the numbers, and it would be an additional six hours before the Moon was in orb. Still the Part of Fortune was on the Midheaven anyway. On the Descendant, that angle we are warned not to read, I had diurnal Mercury above and with the South Node, so that the North Node was on the diurnal Ascendant with the diurnal East Point and diurnal Mars, the latter in retrograde. In addition, I had diurnal Chiron on natal Fortune, diurnal Neptune on natal South Node, diurnal Venus in orb of natal Uranus, and I had just had a Lunar Return. I did not think of this chart as much of a winning indicator. Something was surely going to happen that day. Saturn rules the gambling fifth and was sextile my natal Sun, and I do think of Saturn as more giving of benefits than is Jupiter which that day was square my natal Sun. I dressed warmly, and I took care crossing the streets. I very carefully did not get into confrontations and arguments with strangers. Like most astrologers, I do not give much strength of Mercury, and worry about Mars retrograde. Even so, I won a prize in a low three figure amount. I felt I would like to try for when Saturn came to the Descendant, knowing there are times when Saturn is rewarding. That would have been ten days later, but nothing happened on that single touch.

Short by three days of the diurnal Descendant coming to diurnal Saturn, on March 22, 1997, I had another middle three figure win for again getting three out of five numbers. Now there were no angular touches, but diurnal Mars was opposite diurnal Fortune which was now on my natal Uranus. I had expected nothing on this date due to the diurnal technique has to bow to the astrology of winning prizes. And over subsequent years the transits of March 15 have not repeated themselves.

Jane Fonda Diurnal

Due to the publication of a very superficial and poor delineation of the chart of Jane Fonda, I had devoted some time to the study of her chart with the intention of publishing a re-

buttal to the pop-astrology article. Instead, I presented her chart in a workshop, and I got no further with any intentions to write about this chart. After all, notable people get in the news, but by the time such an article might get published, usually four or five months after whatever event brought her into the public eye, some other notable personality would have replaced her in the news and public eye.

The natal data for Jane Fonda is 9:14 a.m. EST, December 21, 1937, New York City. This is a chart worthy of study by astrologers interested in solstice points or antiscia. She has Jupiter opposite Pluto, but her Jupiter is on the Ascendant. Wouldn't you expect a lady a bit overweight. Perhaps she should be if she were not the maven of exercise and diet. I would be interested to check how the Jupiter-Pluto opposition would work in her chart. Another consideration is that I had come to the conclusion that while death does not always show in the charts of the people to whom death comes, death is best seen in the charts of the survivors. So rather than do a chart for Henry Fonda at his death, I decided to do the chart of Jane Fonda for the death of her father. Her natal chart shows she is a late Capricorn rising with Saturn in the second house and the late Sagittarian Sun in the twelfth house. This presence of a twelfth house Sun gives the lie to the notion that people born with twelfth house Suns are mistrustful of their ego expression. There is nothing of the shrinking violet about Jane Fonda. She is a strong personality, more Capricornian than Sagittarian. She certainly needs to be a *femme sole*, a woman in charge of her own operations, happiest working at her own productions, and happiest in the control seat. She was once married to Tom Hayden, a California politician and is now married to Ted Turner, yachtsman and media tycoon, who is as prominent and as difficult personality as she. She must be aided by Moon in Leo , and she has Mars at the end of Aquarius.

In the diurnal for the death of her father, diurnal Fortune was on the diurnal MC, but there are no other angular touches. There are, however, future touches. For example, in three days the diurnal MC moves to the nodal axis, the diurnal Ascendant moved to the East Point, and in the following month all the other diurnal placements in the first house will be hit by the diurnal Ascendant. Diurnal Moon was square natal Moon. Now, while I have taken care to list and discount current aspects of present aspects not in any aspect in the natal chart, we have to shift gears slightly and recognize that a planet in aspect to itself is an occasion which must be seriously considered. We should consider why there are no other angular positions in this diurnal. Perhaps his death was expected, perhaps she had a bit of time to acclimate herself to this event, and perhaps it was a blessed release to her father and all his family.

Valentino Collapse

Karen Christino, New York astrologer, introduced me to the decumbiture chart done by Evangeline Adams

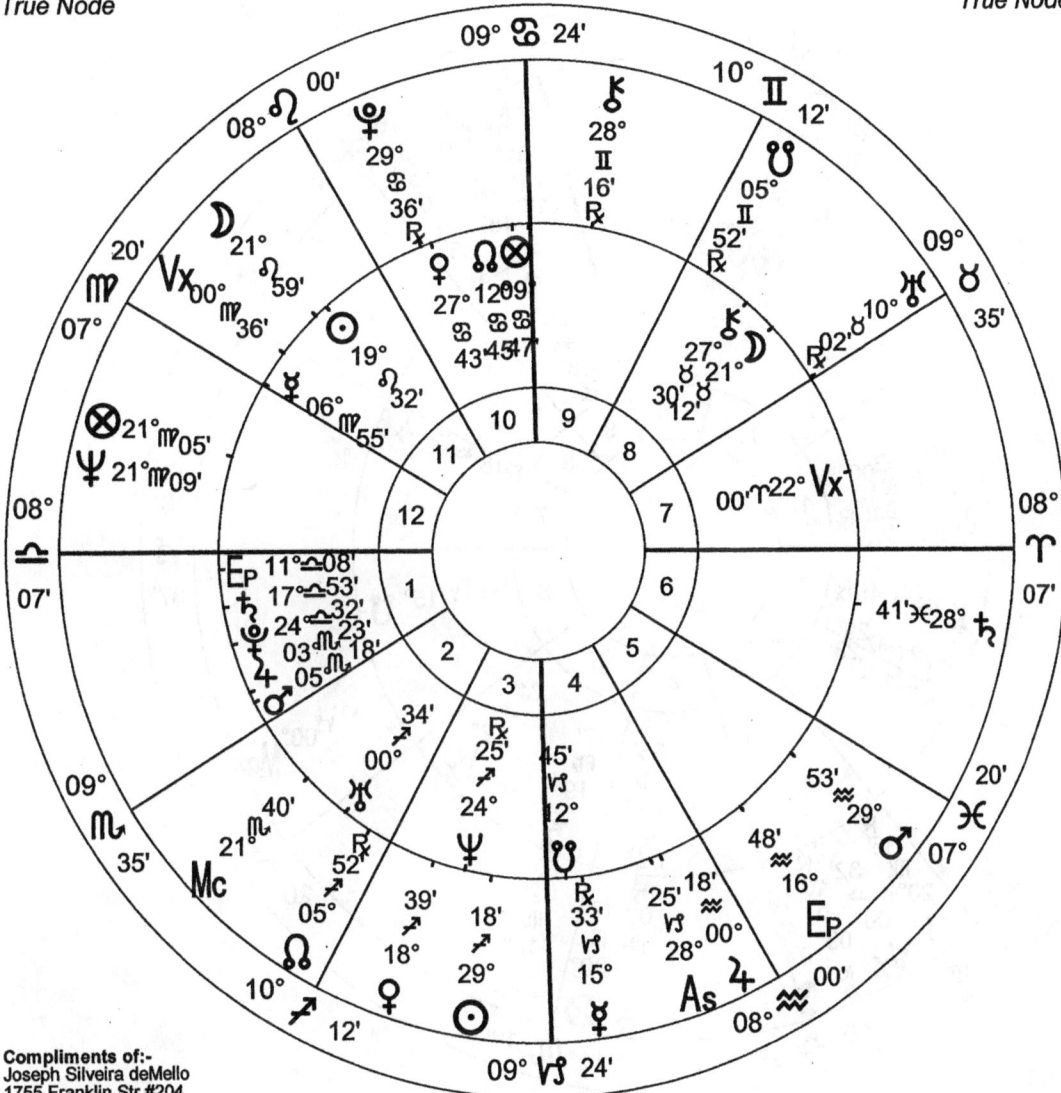

Compliments of:-
Joseph Silveira deMello
1755 Franklin Str #204
San Francisco CA 94109
Tel (415) 775-8939
email jsmgemscorp@juno.com

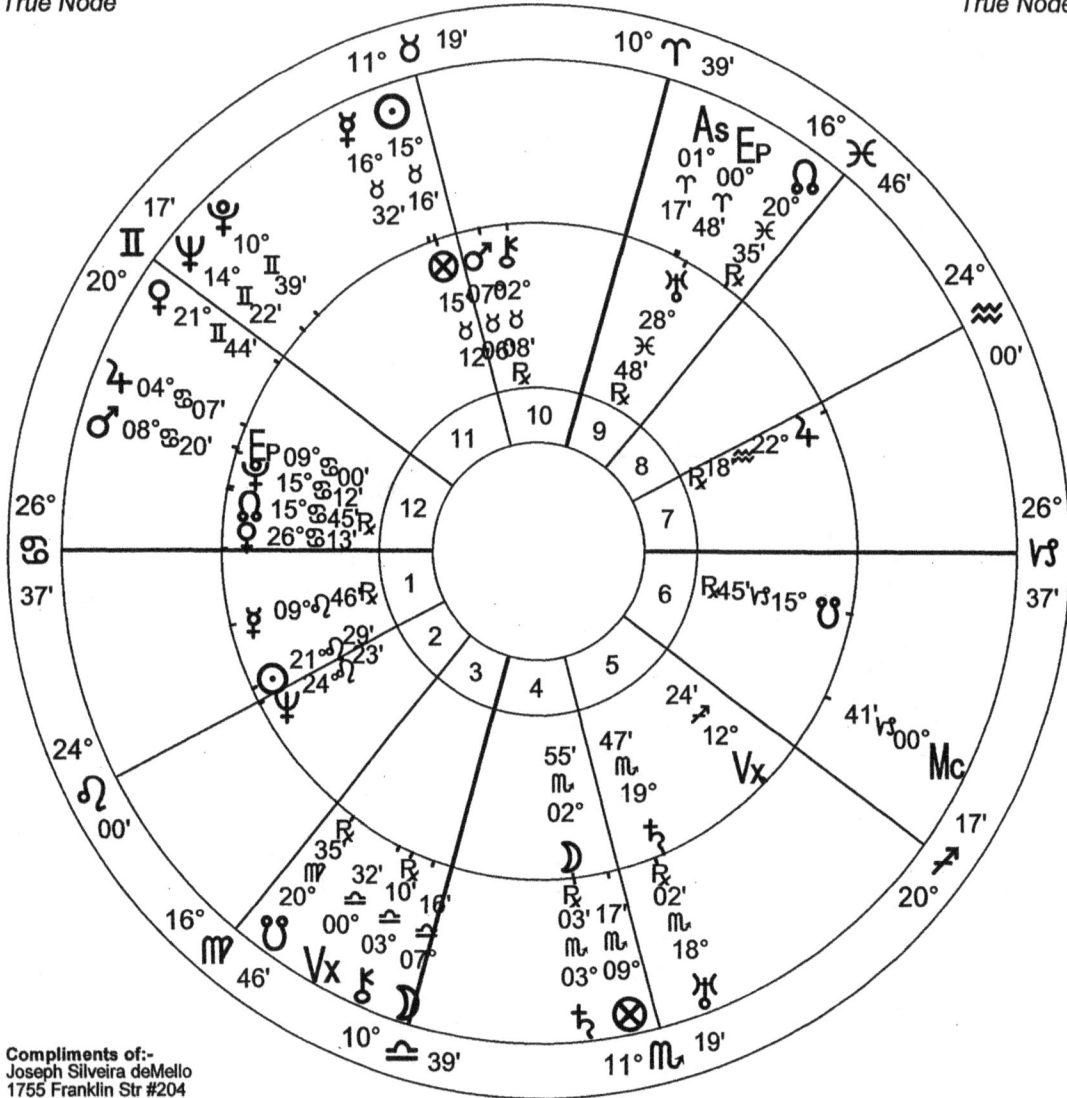

Compliments of:-
Joseph Silveira deMello
1755 Franklin Str #204
San Francisco CA 94109
Tel (415) 775-8939
email jsmgemscorp@juno.com

on the collapse of Rudolph Valentino. This fatal crisis in Valentino's life coincides with a time when I, as a less than one year old infant, was also in peril. Unfortunately I do not have exact date for my illness, but I most certainly looked at this chart with reference to my own chart placements, signs and degrees. Evangeline Adams was prepared if asked by the media for an astrological opinion, and she is said to have predicted his death almost to the minute.

I found data for Valentino's birth in *Sabian Symbols*, and also in the Clifford Data Base. Neither data is sourced. But the earlier data is a.m., while the latter is p.m. This was no great surprise. Much of the movie celebrity data used in the Sabian list was obtained from a Hollywood astrologer who maintained client confidentiality by fudging birth times of his clientele. His usual habit was to fudge the data exactly twelve hours, the Clifford Data might be true, but it had to be checked out.

The next problem was finding latitude and longitude coordinates for his place of birth, a town so small in the arch of the foot of Italy that it is not listed in my Rand-McNally atlas nor in my Solar Fire atlas. I got every coordinate for surrounding towns and came up with 40N38, 17E04, which differs from the latitude given with the Clifford Data. My first chart was done on the 3:00 a.m., and that gave diurnal Venus on the diurnal Ascendant, and the previous day the Moon went over the diurnal IC. The chart for 3:00 p.m. data was no improvement. I have found that diurnals may show up an illness but seldom show the day of death as a special event.

Going around the earlier time collapse diurnal, I was surprised to see that the diurnal Fortune was on natal Sun and Mercury, natal Mars was on diurnal East Point, the diurnal Moon was going from natal Saturn but would not hit diurnal Saturn until the following day (after hitting natal Uranus). Valentino's problem was that he had great pain which his doctors thought was a reactivated stomach ulcer. There had to be a confusion in communications between patient and doctor, and only when he went into peritonitis was he found to have an appendix problem. Note that diurnal Pluto is together with diurnal North Node at 15 Cancer, sextile diurnal Fortune and Natal Sun-Mercury.

The diurnal certainly shows there is something wrong with this time of birth. Had he been born ten degrees or forty minutes earlier, natal EP and Ascendant would have been on the diurnal MC alerting us to the zero Aries point, diurnal Pluto and North Node would have been on the diurnal Ascendant, and natal Vertex and Chiron would have been on the diurnal IC. But on the basis of one event only we cannot "rectify" his natal time to nudge it for astrological significance. We do know his death was on August 23, 1926. But I knew diurnals do not treat death as a special event. Besides which, Barbara Watter's said that finding death is best found using the natal chart itself.

Golda Meir

Since Golda Meir was used in the declinations section, I had several dates of important events in her life. She signed the declaration of Israeli Independence on May 14, 1948. A diurnal for that date shows us diurnal Saturn on the Midheaven. Diurnal Moon was headed from her natal Midheaven, and that day, it went over diurnal Pluto and diurnal Saturn as well as diurnal Midheaven. The diurnal North Node on her natal Sun, and she had just had her fiftieth birthday.

But she succeeded to the position of Prime Minister of Israel on February 15, 1969 and on a chart for that day nothing is angular. Her country was plunged into war, and diurnal Mars and Neptune are at the bottom of the chart as well as natal Chiron. This is an interesting chart for several reasons. The diurnal North Node is as zero Aries and opposite her natal Jupiter. Diurnal Venus is sextile natal Pluto, diurnal Saturn is sextile natal Neptune, and diurnal Moon is traveling to a New Moon, which is strange for a promotion. Diurnal Mercury is approaching her natal IC and is on natal Vertex. This passage of Mercury over her IC would show something of a promotion, but the Vertex would link it to ill health which was going on behind the scenes, not revealed to the public, although when she died, there was a note that she had battled cancer over the last decade of her life.

The diurnal of her final trip to the hospital on October 29, 1978, has natal Venus on the diurnal Ascendant and natal Uranus on the diurnal Descendant. However this event also occurred when she was having a lunar return and the diurnal Vertex was on her natal Ascendant, while diurnal Mars was on her natal Chiron. This particular chart is interesting in the fact that all the diurnal and natal sixth house placements would last have passed the diurnal Descendant, and this chart is for six weeks before her death. When you are watching your own diurnals, you cannot help but get cogent ideas when you see past and future touches to the diurnal angles having happened or about to be happening in a large crowd of difficult days. I look upon the Vertex as a frequent indicator of ill health, while, for me, the east point always signifies a serious even.

She died on December 8, 1978, and I did not expect to find angular touches on the death day. However, from having examined the chart for when she went into the hospital, we now have a good chance to see action continued through November and seeing how the change of angles and placements proceeded from one event to another. At the final event, diurnal East Point, which for me is always of significance in a special event, was on her natal Pluto, while diurnal Venus was on her natal East Point, diurnal Vertex was on her natal Chiron, and diurnal Mercury was on her natal Saturn. Note that Venus was her natal chart significator, so these charts do have a Venus story to tell.

What are we to learn from this series of charts? When we are not seeing at least two angular touches on important dates in a person's life we can only assume that they held no special importance for her, which is very arguable, almost silly, to say or that the natal birth time is incorrect. Should we attempt to rectify such a chart? If such a trial is made, we look to see what planets are close to the angles, check past and future movement, question which planet is evocative of the events we have, attempt to find if we should add to or subtract from the time of

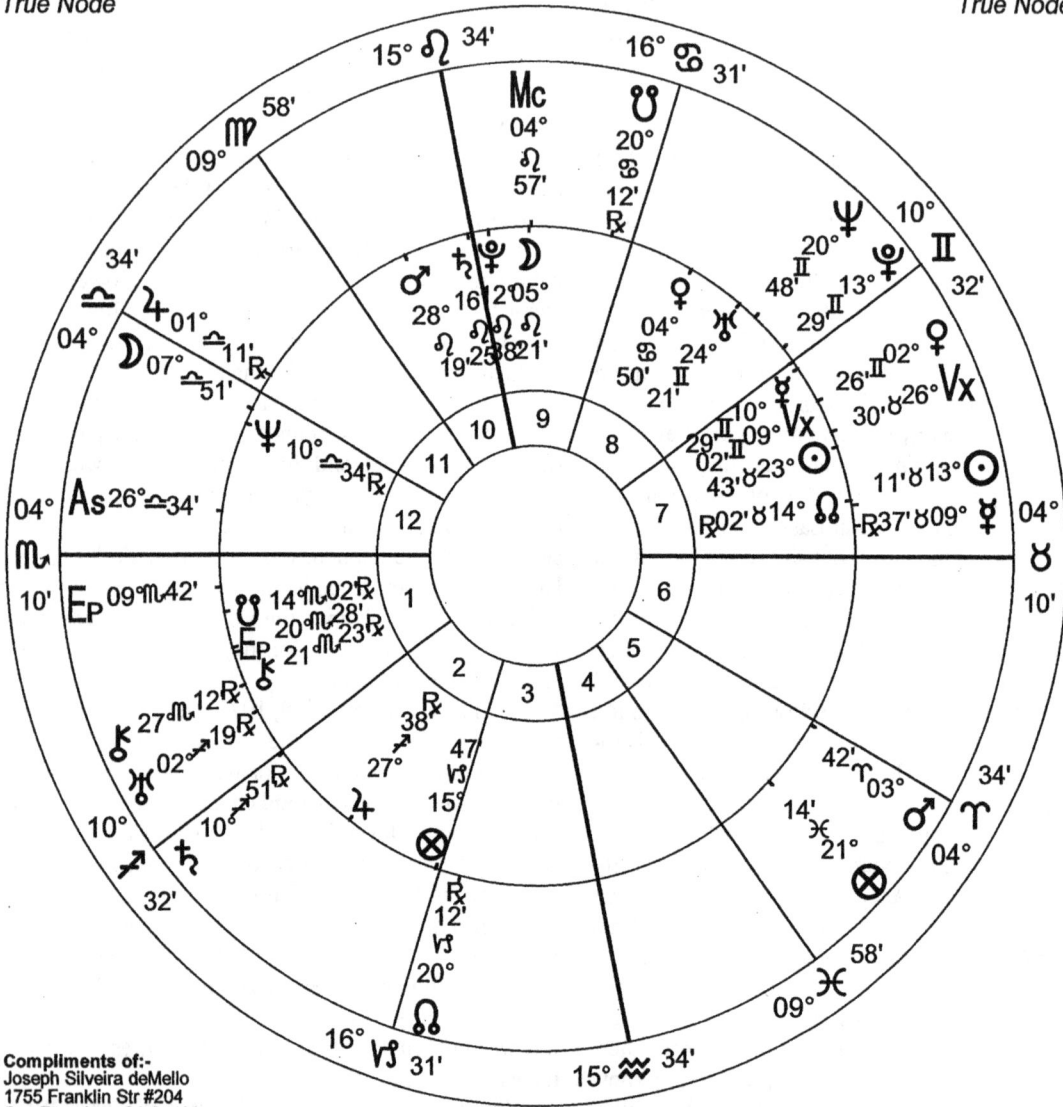

Inner Wheel
198. Independence diurnal
Natal Chart
May 14 1948
5:43 PM LMT -2:02
Kiev, Russia
50N27 030E30
Geocentric
Tropical
Campanus
True Node

Outer Wheel
109. Golda Meir
Natal Chart
May 3 1898
5:43 PM LMT -2:02
Kiev, Russia
50N27 030E30
Geocentric
Tropical
Campanus
True Node

Compliments of:-
Joseph Silveira deMello
1755 Franklin Str #204
San Francisco CA 94109
Tel (415) 775-8939
email jsmgemscorp@juno.com

Inner Wheel
199. Prime Minister diurnal
Natal Chart
Feb 15 1969
5:43 PM LMT -2:02
Kiev, Russia
50N27 030E30
Geocentric
Tropical
Campanus
True Node

Outer Wheel
109. Golda Meir
Natal Chart
May 3 1898
5:43 PM LMT -2:02
Kiev, Russia
50N27 030E30
Geocentric
Tropical
Campanus
True Node

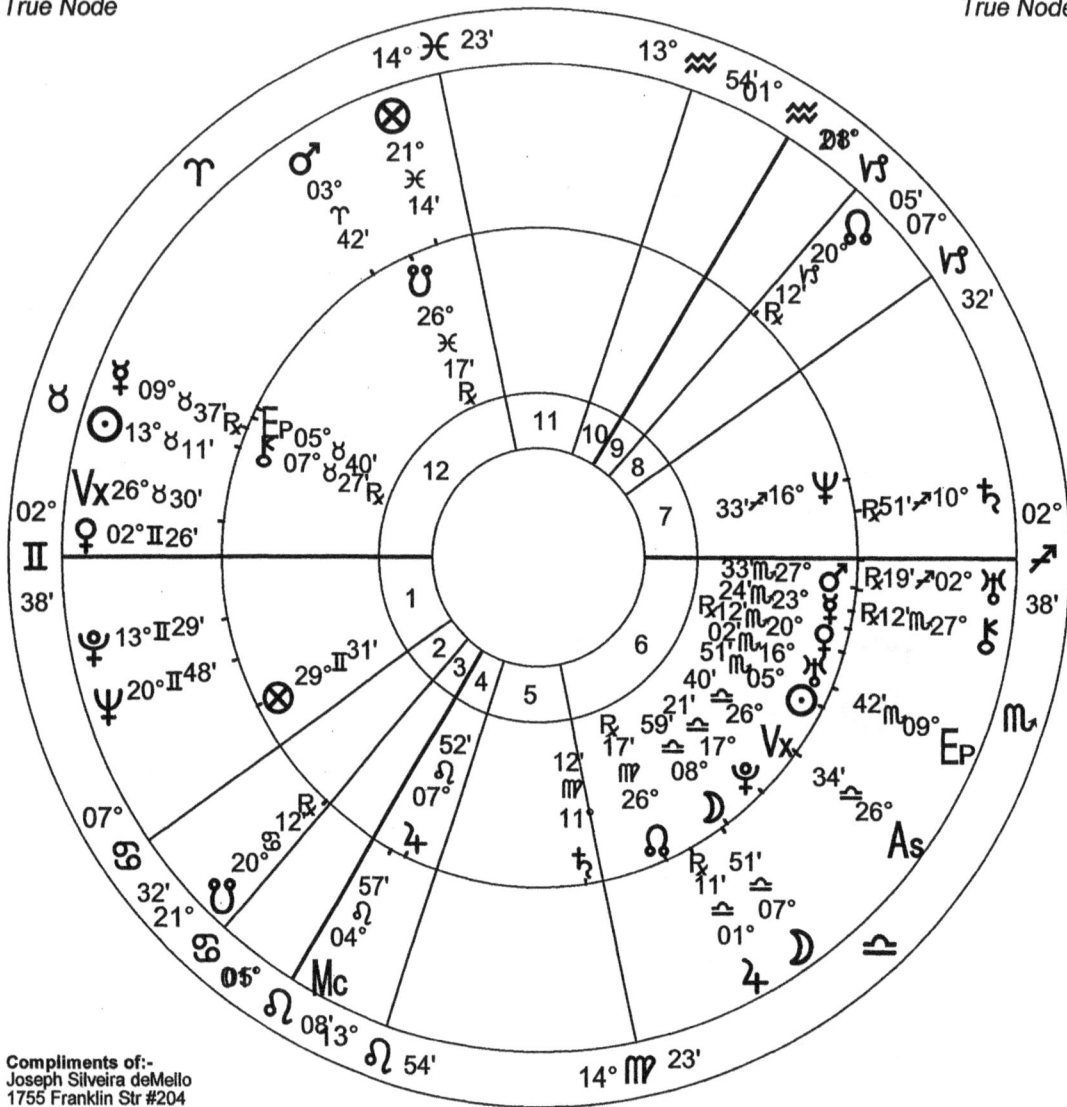

Inner Wheel
200. Hospitalized diurnal
Natal Chart
Oct 29 1978
5:43 PM LMT -2:02
Kiev, Russia
50N27 030E30
Geocentric
Tropical
Campanus
True Node

Outer Wheel
109. Golda Meir
Natal Chart
May 3 1898
5:43 PM LMT -2:02
Kiev, Russia
50N27 030E30
Geocentric
Tropical
Campanus
True Node

Compliments of:-
Joseph Silveira deMello
1755 Franklin Str #204
San Francisco CA 94109
Tel (415) 775-8939
email jsmgemscorp@juno.com

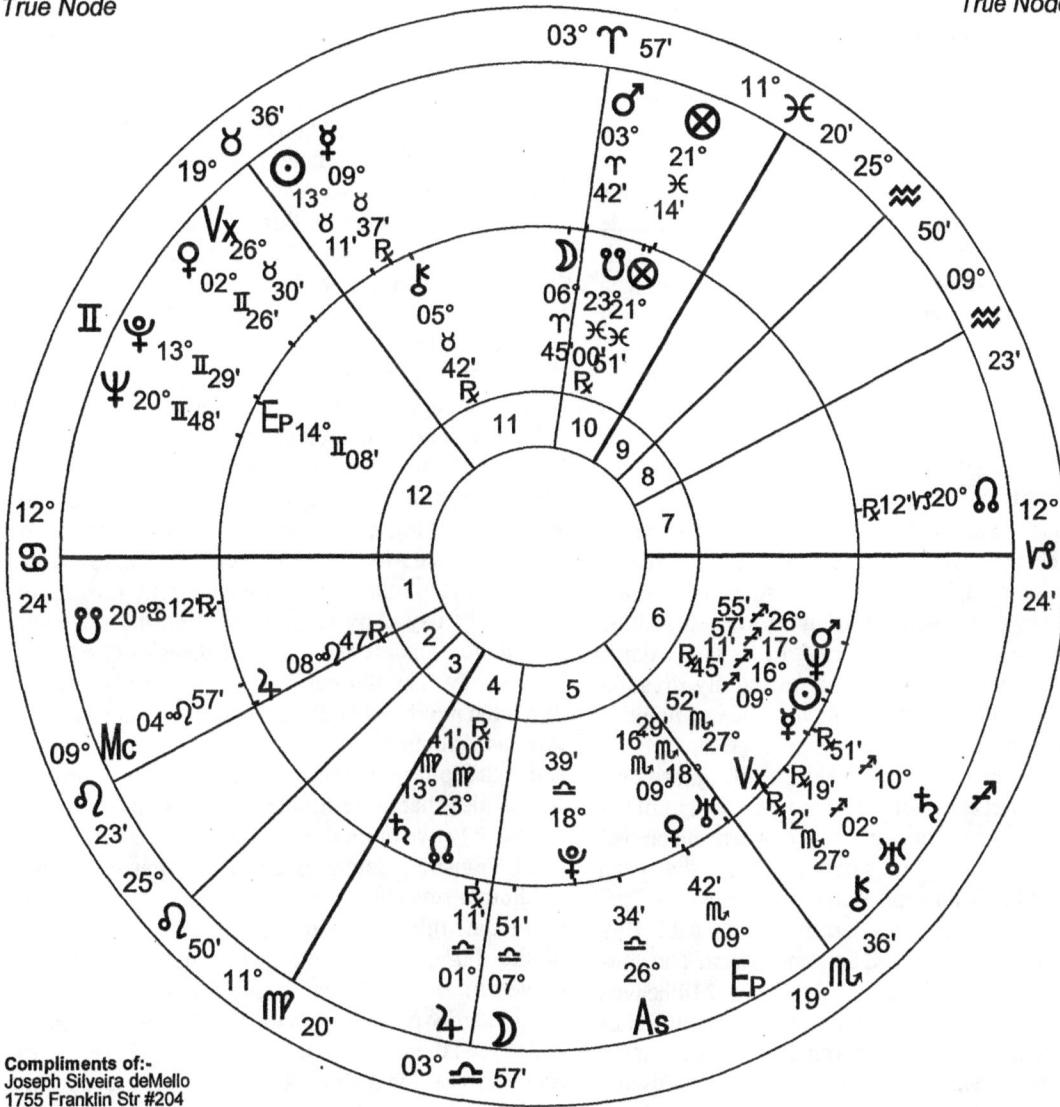

Compliments of:-
Joseph Silveira deMello
1755 Franklin Str #204
San Francisco CA 94109
Tel (415) 775-8939
email jsmgemscorp@juno.com

birth with which we started. It is not fair to use the death date, so that event must be dropped. The signing of the Independence is a viable diurnal, has the touches. To add five degrees or twenty minutes to her birth time would gets us Ascendant-Descendant touches, but would make us loose the Midheaven significance. Nor would it suit well to try to get natal Mars on the diurnal Midheaven, for there would be no touches elsewhere. When she became Prime Minister, surely the Sun should have been involved, or the sign Leo, but subtracting ten degrees or forty minuets from her birth time to put the natal Sun on the diurnal Midheaven hardly aids us with the other angles. Remember once you decide on any time change, the same time change must be suited to all the events. It is best to remember that Golda Meir was an unusual person in that she was not one to aggrandize her status or go about staging media events or photo ops. There was always a vast difference between the private and the public person.

Cancer Cases

When astrologer friends knew I was working on this book, many volunteered chart examples for my use. The late T. Patrick Davis, an Orlando astrologer who was long a advocate of heliocentric astrology, contributed two bits of data for her deceased sister-in-law. She sent this data because it was for her late sister-in-law who had been born two days after I was born. And her data is 3:08 p.m. CST, November 5, 1925, Kansas City, Missouri. So this is going to be as if I were looking at my own natal chart. Some things in this chart are slightly in advance, but many aspects are still there.

It was thought that this data might be used in the decumbitures section of this book, but following strict rules, the lady of this chart was basically in good health, did not feel poorly, did not seek the doctor's care. On August 26, 1982, that early morning, she was dressing to keep a routine checkup at her doctor's office. She might, as any woman making the disturbing discovery of a potentially dreadful breast node, she could only hope that what she has found is not a dreaded omen.

She made the discovery shortly before 6:20 a.m., so bear in mind that this chart does not really go into effect until her birthtime 3:08 p.m. At the doctor's office, when she alerted her doctor to her discovery, he surprised her by the speed with which he put her in hospital. After tests and surgery, the doctor announced that the procedure was successful. But, alas, the tissue excised had indeed been malignant. The diurnal for that day has diurnal Saturn on the diurnal Midheaven and natal Midheaven on the diurnal Ascendant. Natal Venus is another degree away from the Ascendant. Notice that the diurnal Moon had previously gone over diurnal Uranus and was en route to diurnal Neptune and Ascendant. Withal, she did go into remission and confidently went onward with her life. Now, Mrs. Davis also sent me all the heliocentric placements in the hope that I should someday learn and gain the confidence to use these. Some of my readers will also be devoted to helio astrology. In this chart of first finding cancer I was very surprised to find helio Uranus at 24 Pisces 02 exactly on her natal Ascendant and quincunx to her natal geo Mars at 24 Libra, and this position was on that day besieged by the helio placements of diurnal helio Saturn at 23 Aquar-

ius 28 and diurnal helio Pluto at 26 Libra 29.

All seemingly went well until the spring of 1996, at which time she was conscious of depleted energy, tired out for no reason she could fathom, and she complained to her doctor. There were no visible signs as previously. But she suspected that there was a recurrence of cancer. But this time she had to make repeated serious demands for more thorough examinations. Now how things proceeded is a bit sketchy. But on May 21, 1996, she found herself once again on the operating table. Now the story was as bad as it could be. Cancer had metastasized and was now seen to be irreversible. She did submit to chemotherapy and radiation, but these did not help, and she eventually died.

Glancing at the helio placements of the operation diurnal, diurnal helio Jupiter is at 9 Capricorn 21 which is on her natal helio Mercury at 10 Capricorn 21 at the IC of this diurnal. Diurnal helio Neptune is at 26 Capricorn 01 which is on her natal helio Jupiter at 27 Capricorn 30. We still see natal Ascendant with natal helio Uranus now in the sixth house of this diurnal. We can now see that natal geo Moon and Pluto are close to the diurnal Midheaven at this chart, but helio Pluto is also at 13 Cancer 29. Helio Mars is at 14 Libra, while helio diurnal Chiron is at 13 Libra 34.

The diurnal for the operation shows the diurnal Midheaven approaching her natal Moon and her natal and helio Pluto. The diurnal Moon before 3:08 p.m. of the day of the operation had gone over her diurnal Midheaven and natal Moon and Pluto and helio Pluto. What I am trying to say here is that we must remember that the diurnal Moon is the mover here, the fastest traveler, while the diurnal Midheaven is only moving one degree per day. Any astrologer worth his salt would have done a lunar return to see what such a chart would have to say. The diurnal Ascendant had, the previous day, been in orb of her diurnal Chiron. At the bottom of this chart, Jupiter is retrograding from a Jupiter return, and both Jupiter positions were six days from diurnal IC. Notice also that these Jupiter diurnal to natal positions are the only two diurnal conjunct natal pair in this entire chart. Transiting Saturn, five days previously, had been on diurnal seventh house cusp. Having seen the situation at the Midheaven and commented on the movement of the diurnal Moon, we now consider the coming movement of the diurnal Midheaven itself. This chart would hardly present the patient with any reassurance, and indeed there was none to be had. We do see diurnal Sun in opposition to diurnal Fortune and Pluto and natal Mercury. You will remember that diurnal Fortune moves at the same speed as diurnal Moon.

This exploratory surgery had pretty much produced a very negative prognosis, and while all along she had known there was something wrong with her and had to pester the doctors to really examine her, the general feeling after the operation was that by the time she had begun to notice her excessive tiredness, the cancer had been in pernicious growth. Still she went in for extensive therapies, and put herself through the agonies of ra-

Inner Wheel
202. Cancer diagnosis diurnal
Natal Chart
Aug 26 1982
3:08 PM CST +6:00
Kansas City MO
39N06 094W35
Geocentric
Tropical
Campanus
True Node

Outer Wheel
Lila Davis
Natal Chart
Nov 5 1925
3:08 PM CST +6:00
Kansas City MO
39N06 094W35
Geocentric
Tropical
Campanus
True Node

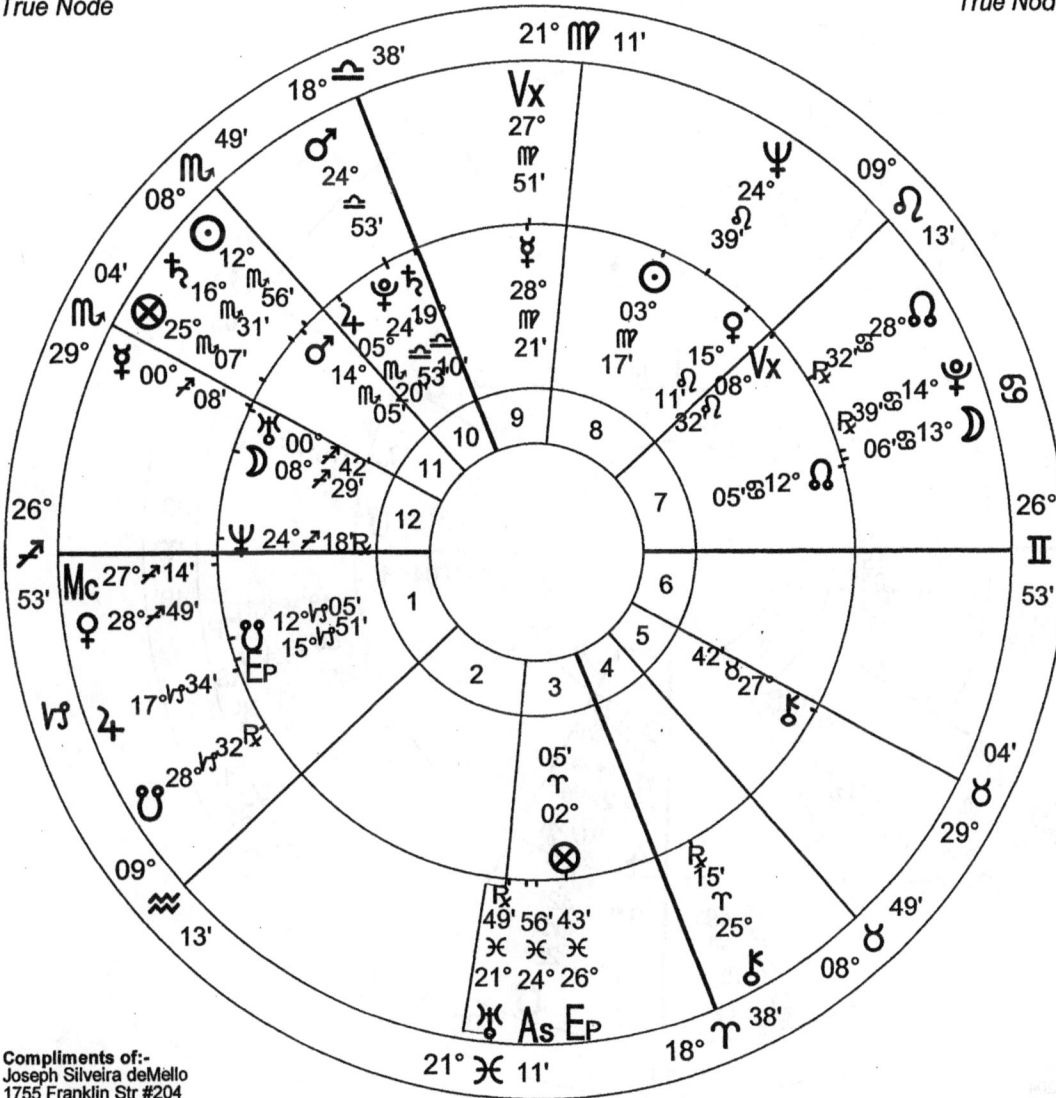

Compliments of:-
Joseph Silveira deMello
1755 Franklin Str #204
San Francisco CA 94109
Tel (415) 775-8939
email jsmgemscorp@juno.com

Outer Wheel
Lila Davis
Natal Chart
Nov 5 1925
3:08 PM CST +6:00
Kansas City MO
39N06 094W35
Geocentric
Tropical
Campanus
True Node

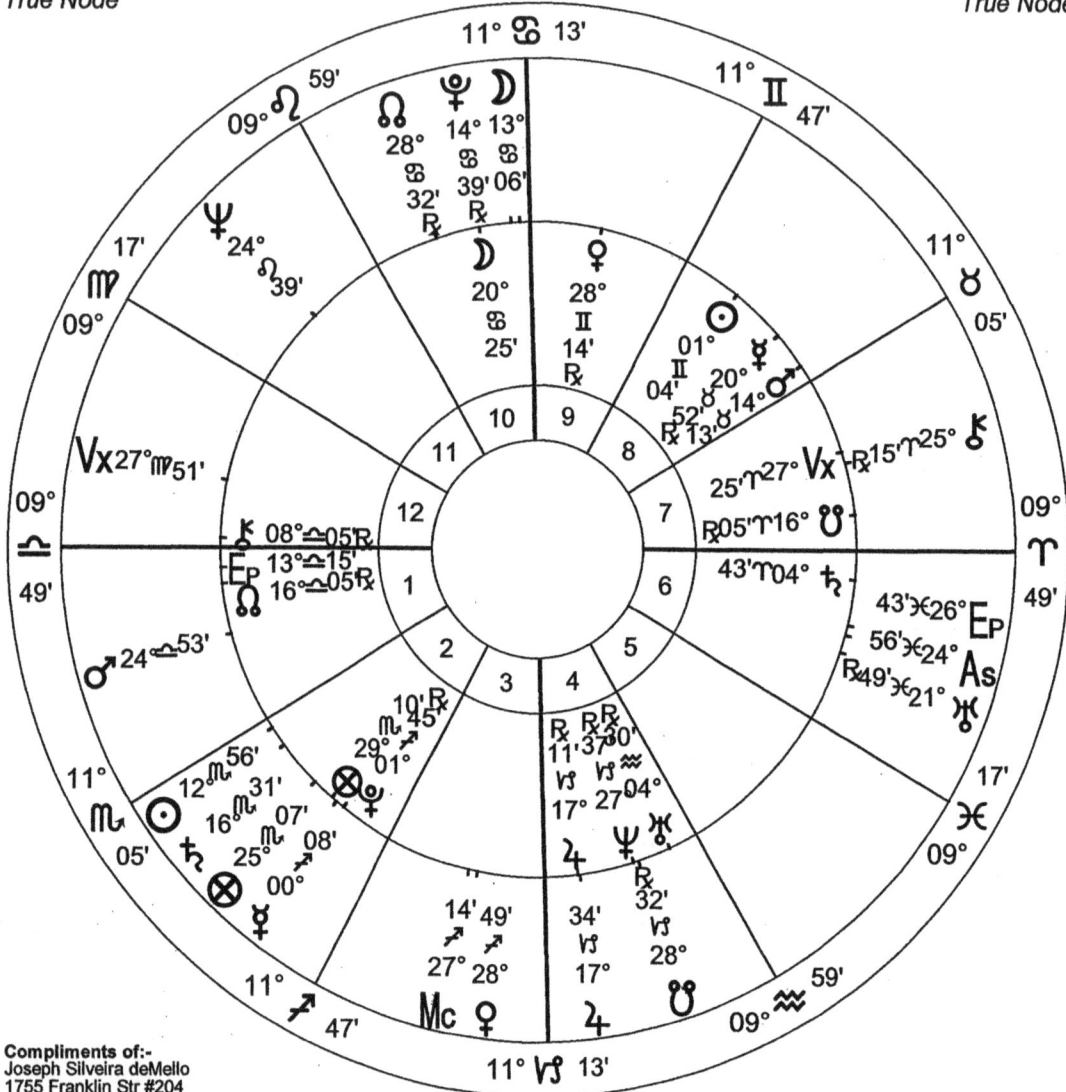

Compliments of:-
Joseph Silveira deMello
1755 Franklin Str #204
San Francisco CA 94109
Tel (415) 775-8939
email jsmgemscorp@juno.com

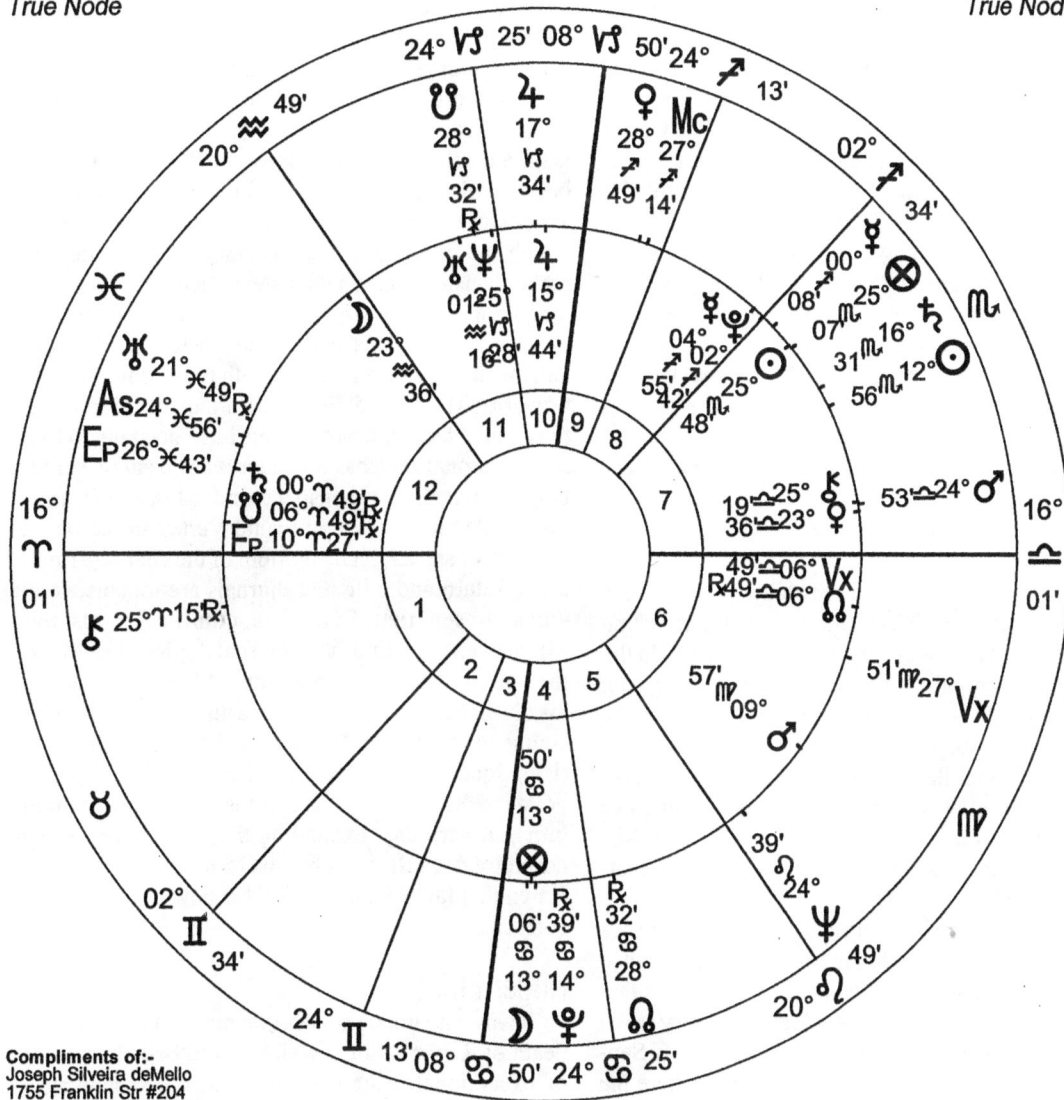

Inner Wheel
204. Day before death diurnal
Natal Chart
Nov 17 1996
3:08 PM CST +6:00
Kansas City MO
39N06 094W35
Geocentric
Tropical
Campanus
True Node

Outer Wheel
Lila Davis
Natal Chart
Nov 5 1925
3:08 PM CST +6:00
Kansas City MO
39N06 094W35
Geocentric
Tropical
Campanus
True Node

Compliments of:-
Joseph Silveira deMello
1755 Franklin Str #204
San Francisco CA 94109
Tel (415) 775-8939
email jsmgemscorp@juno.com

diation and chemo the last six months of her life, for she died on November 18, 1996.

Now the diurnal has been done for the day prior to her death to encompass the period when she actually died. She died November 18, but well prior to her birth time. This matter of the day for which the chart is done is important when we watch the Moon and Fortune movements doing their thing in the twelfth and fourth house. This diurnal has Aries rising, and the Midheaven at 8 Capricorn 47 is close to her natal helio Mercury at 10 Capricorn 21. When Mercury comes to an angle there is always change of status. If we watch transiting Mercury to our natal angles, it is no less true to see change when diurnal geo or helio Mercury are on a diurnal angle, especially when death certainly implies a change of status. In this case she went on to a higher plateau.

Now notice that natal helio Jupiter at 27 Capricorn 10, is on the diurnal geo and helio positions of Neptune. The Aries Ascendant gives 15 Libra descending or on the seventh cusp where we may be surprised to find natal helio Mars at 14 Libra 02. Notice that she was on her way to a Jupiter return. The diurnal Fortune, moving as quickly as the Moon, would have crossed the IC of this chart and was in the act of being at her natal Moon and Pluto conjunction. If we have spoken of helio Mars on the diurnal Descendant, giving a look to natal geo Mars, we find that it is besieged by diurnal Venus and Chiron. Also note that while the natal Midheaven and the diurnal Midheaven are twelve degrees apart, she having died twelve days after her birthday, we have here a really fast diurnal Ascendant which, in those twelve days, traveled 21 degrees.

Collapse Diurnal

Karen Christino is a well known astrology writer. As she got interested in what I was doing, she continued to send me interesting data and events to get my opinions on them. In the course of time, she brought up an event which, following strict guidelines, could not be called a decumbiture for the simple reason that the subject of the chart, her father, made no decision about being ill. He suffered an unexpected collapse and was taken off to hospital unconscious. She also mentioned that there was only birth data for her father, and she confessed that she had never checked out his or attempted to rectify it.

Donald Christino began his career as a motorcycle police patrolman, gradually went into the motorcycle maintenance garage, and after many years, switched to the Sheriff's Department where he became a court bailiff, a job he very much enjoys and from which he has no intention or retiring. In September 1993, his routine was to drop by his club where the bar regularly opened at eight in the evening. He was sitting at the bar after 7:45 p.m. on January 7, and his drink had just been put in front of him. Before he could take a sip, he collapsed in such a way that he broke his nose on the edge of the bar. Since the local fire house was right next door, the time of this event is officially logged, well enough for an event chart, but not so important when we are checking out diurnals.

Mr. Christino's time of birth was a family tradition, 10:00 a.m. EST, March 21, 1924, Brooklyn, New York, so that was the time for which I did the diurnal, and did it for the date of the event. Immediately we notice that we have the diurnal nodal axis on the vertical axis of the diurnal chart, with natal Jupiter exactly on the diurnal Midheaven. Note that the diurnal IC is coming toward his natal Ascendant. How nice for some convivially at his club to have diurnal Mercury, Sun, Uranus and Neptune all in the eleventh house of this chart along with natal Mars, but Sun, Uranus and Neptune are in opposition to diurnal Mars. It is to be noted that Donald Christino had no history of problems with his heart. At the hospital, a pacemaker was installed, and he was eventually released. But he never seemed quite to recover. Over the subsequently months, he was constantly complaining of a series of health and lack of energy problems. Finally his doctors took him seriously, and they decided that he was a candidate for bypass surgery. This was done slightly more than nine months after his original collapse. This lackadaisical attitude of the medical establishment, although now more widely publicized, has been coming down the pike for more than a decade. Where any costly surgery is involved, doctors seem to weigh the probable life expectancy of the patient and make decisions on whether the patient is going to live long enough to benefit from any sort of surgery.

This surgery was performed September 16, 1993, and the diurnal for that date has diurnal Venus on the diurnal Midheaven and diurnal Saturn on the diurnal IC of the chart. Medical professionals have been heard to describe coronary bypass procedures as cosmetic surgery. On the seventh house cusp we find natal Venus, and on diurnal Ascendant we find natal Vertex in the one degree orb of aspect. At the bottom of the chart we find diurnal Saturn and note that diurnals are transits, so that we also see that Saturn is coming to his natal Midheaven. We find both diurnal Jupiter and Mars in the twelfth house square to diurnal Uranus-Neptune in his diurnal second house, but we must not be thrown off course to see diurnal Pluto in the first house of Scorpio rising square to both MC and IC and the planets on those points. Note also that this chart is going into a lunar return that very day, expanding the work any astrologer normally does. It was obvious to me and surprising to Karen that family tradition for his time of birth must be correct.

Roger Elliot

It was with great sadness that many of us heard of the death of Roger Elliot, a well beloved British astrologer of exceptional brightness and wit, on September 29, 1993. I have several particular memories of meeting him at astrological conventions. Note that he is also chart #27 in the declinations section of this book. So I had his chart file ready at hand and noted that I had done a diurnal for him when I learned of his death.

Roger was born June 25, 1937, 3:15 a.m. BST, in or near Torquay, England, according to the data he himself gave me. He sometimes gave out his birth time as 2:15 a.m. GMT. Torquay, incidentally is the city where Alan Leo went to live at the end of his life. Roger died in the

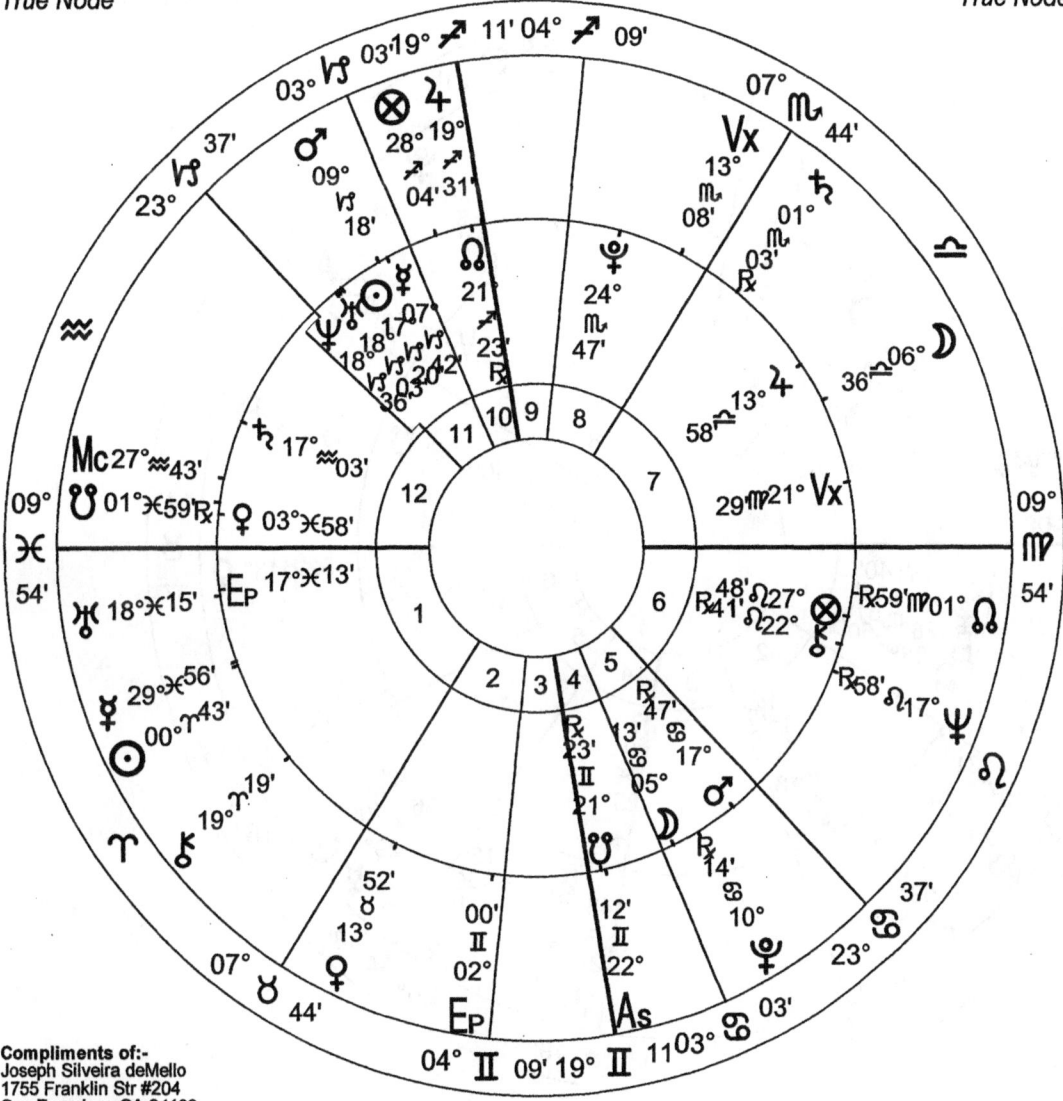

Inner Wheel
205. Collapse diurnal
Natal Chart
Jan 7 1993
10:00 AM EST +5:00
Brooklyn NY, USA
40N38 073W56
Geocentric
Tropical
Campanus
True Node

Outer Wheel
Donald J Christino
Natal Chart
Mar 21 1924
10:00 AM EST +5:00
Brooklyn NY, USA
40N38 073W56
Geocentric
Tropical
Campanus
True Node

Compliments of:-
Joseph Silveira deMello
1755 Franklin Str #204
San Francisco CA 94109
Tel (415) 775-8939
email jsmgemscorp@juno.com

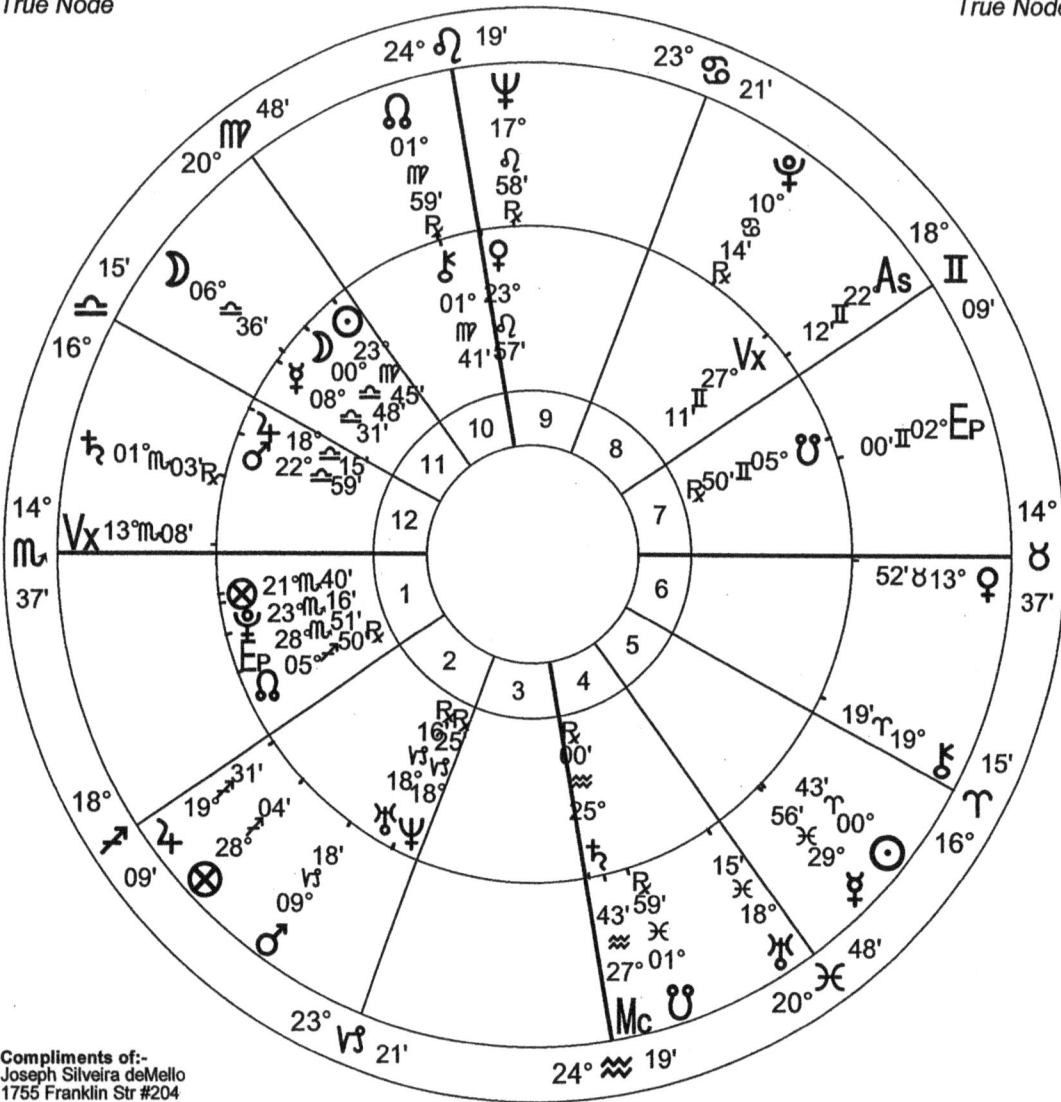

Inner Wheel
206. Surgery diurnal
Natal Chart
Sep 16 1993
10:00 AM EST +5:00
Brooklyn NY, USA
40N38 073W56
Geocentric
Tropical
Campanus
True Node

Outer Wheel
Donald J Christino
Natal Chart
Mar 21 1924
10:00 AM EST +5:00
Brooklyn NY, USA
40N38 073W56
Geocentric
Tropical
Campanus
True Node

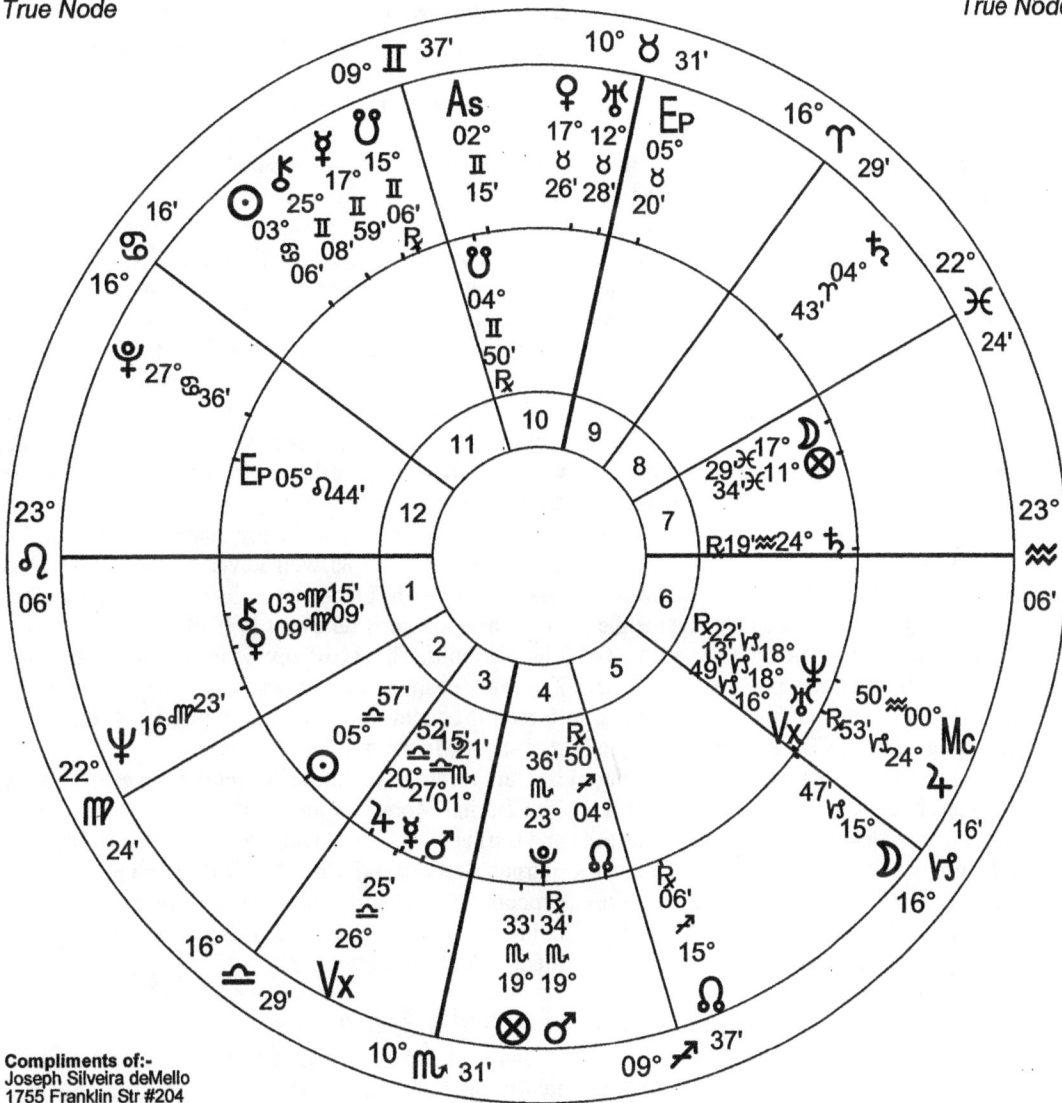

Compliments of:-
Joseph Silveira deMello
1755 Franklin Str #204
San Francisco CA 94109
Tel (415) 775-8939
email jsmgemscorp@juno.com

course of a coronary bypass surgery. Bearing in mind that death seldom shows up in a diurnal chart, I thought I would use his chart and death as an example. Diurnal Leo was rising. There is nothing on the diurnal Ascendant, but diurnal Saturn is on the diurnal Descendant. Natal Uranus is on the diurnal Midheaven but is two degrees away and out of orb.. Because Roger was a Gemini rising, I noted that diurnal Mercury was on his natal Vertex. Diurnal Uranus and Neptune (retrograde) are together with diurnal Vertex on the cusp of the sixth house of this chart where we also find natal Moon. The diurnal Moon is headed for the eighth house of this chart in about ten hours. Note the degree of the Moon and check what natal and diurnal positions it will aspect.

Death Diurnal

Dorian Bagwell was one of three Taurus Sun, Aries rising people I knew at the same time. His chart is also discussed in the declination section of this book as #100. This is another death diurnal in the eternal check to enable me to say that death showing in a diurnal chart is quite rare. Dorian had a small rental house in a quiet cul de sac, and he had a roommate who provided companionship and care. As he was able to, he did only what interested him. He did not want people doing things for him but was available when he was needed by others. From time to time he would put in some part time work with two friends (Charts #185) who operated a neighborhood print shop. Near Christmas, he habitually made himself scarce to avoid receiving gifts. This sort of privacy in the face of an unstable medical condition was very Scorpio, and I was amused to see his natal Mars in Scorpio at that time of year when he had diurnal Scorpio rising. But make no mistake. Dorian was in every way an Aries rising more than he was a Taurus Sun sign person. His natal Sagittarius Moon did not manifest optimistically; he was reluctant to let people get too close, and when asked a serious business or accounting question, he was turned into an instant consultant. Our printer friends were his closest friends and they had carefully picked out a selection of new music CDs and were trying to play it by ear, trying to sense their own moods before taking their gift around the corner. If Dorian felt the gift was exorbitant, he did not hesitate to turn it down. They debated when to deliver the gift and did not want to get too close to the holiday. They could look out their back windows and see Dorian's cottage. On the morning of December 19, 1993, Dorian's roommate telephoned to report that Dorian had died in his sleep prior to 6:00 a.m.

I did a diurnal for Dorian's chart for his 3:12 a.m. birth time, and found natal Mars too far out or orb of his diurnal Ascendant. Diurnal Jupiter was with natal Mars. The diurnal Moon was exactly opposite to diurnal Chiron, and square his natal Moon. Diurnal Saturn was on his natal North Node (instead of on the South Node where the ancients found it more seriously afflictive). A rather telling aspect pattern exists in a sextile from diurnal East Point to diurnal Uranus and Neptune, and the points of this sextile both were quincunx to his diurnal Vertex. The diurnal Moon was trine diurnal Jupiter and Ascendant and natal Mars, all of which are sextile to diurnal Chiron. This is one chart where seen as transits, it might make better predictive sense to most astrologers. Note

that the Neptune- Uranus conjunction was on his natal Sun and diurnal East Point is quincunx diurnal Vertex.

Dorian had only a minor indisposition, thought he was getting a cold, when he died.

Lew Ayres

The interesting Hollywood actor Lew Ayres whose chart was #7 in the declinations section of this book, died on December 30, 1996, two days after his eighty-eighth birthday. I felt obligated to check this diurnal because the event occurred close to the time when the diurnal angles return to their natal positions, as if I were daring something to come up on the angles of a death diurnal which occurred due to natural causes. And there we found diurnal Sun and natal Mercury on his diurnal IC.

Of course the natal East Point is on the diurnal Ascendant, too, but let's just bow nicely and take this as if we must have known this would be the kind of example we would have used if we were loading the deck in our favor. It was interesting to see he was about to have another Saturn return and that the diurnal South Node is neatly between his natal and diurnal Saturn positions. Our astrologer predecessors of not so long ago looked upon "malefic" planets on the South node as a sure indication of death. And in those days they were not bothered to be politically correct or especially tender about striking dread in the hearts of their clients. In our time, we have tended to tone down this sort of thing, a case of misplaced sensitivities. Surely in a busy career and an 88 year life span . . . , but is any man ever ready for his own demise? Even as well keyed to the certainty of death as he might be due to philosophical background, or even when such an event is likely to be more of a blessed relief. This is, of course in contrast to Marlene Dietritch, costumed as a black wigged gypsy, refusing to read the palm of a gangster, impatiently telling the mobster, "Mister, you haf no future."

But to ladle it on, diurnal Mercury is on natal Uranus. The diurnal Moon has just gone into the twelfth house and is trine to the diurnal Sun. Note that Saturn is square diurnal Mercury and trine natal Venus. In looking at the aspects around this chart, there are a number of quincunx aspects. With Libra rising, is not the placement of Venus of interest?

Husband's Stroke

Jan Van Schuyler sent me some chart data for her family. Included in this was the date that her husband suffered a stroke. The intent was to use this data as a decumbiture chart, but this could not qualify since he himself never admitted he was ill.

He got up and had breakfast on January 17, 1997, and announced his intention to go visit a friend in a town some distance away from where they live. Although there was something very different about him that morning, he complained of nothing, and off he went to have luncheon with his old friend. After the luncheon, the friend telephoned Jan and told of how incoherent and

Inner Wheel
213. Diurnal death Lew Ayres
Natal Chart
Dec 30 1996
0:15 AM CST +6:00
Minneapolis MN
44N59 093W16
Geocentric
Tropical
Campanus
True Node

Outer Wheel
7. Lew Ayres
Natal Chart
Dec 28 1908
0:15 AM CST +6:00
Minneapolis MN
44N59 093W16
Geocentric
Tropical
Campanus
True Node

Compliments of:-
Joseph Silveira deMello
1755 Franklin Str #204
San Francisco CA 94109
Tel (415) 775-8939
email jsmgemscorp@juno.com

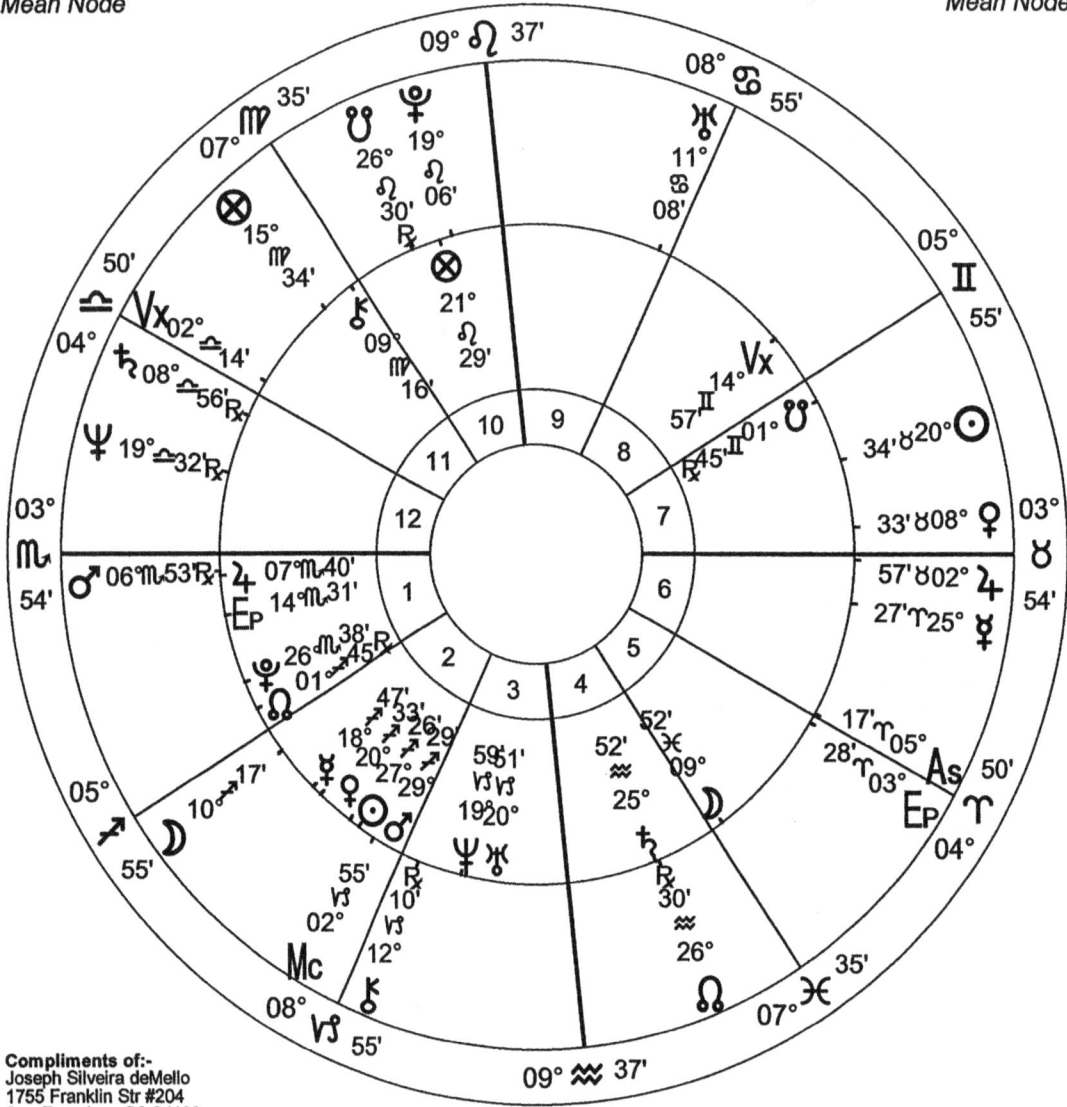

Inner Wheel
208. Death diurnal
Natal Chart
Dec 19 1993
3:12 AM EST +5:00
Harrisonburg VA
38N27 078W52
Geocentric
Tropical
Campanus
Mean Node

Outer Wheel
100. Dorian Bagwell
Natal Chart
May 11 1952
3:12 AM EST +5:00
Harrisonburg VA
38N27 078W52
Geocentric
Tropical
Campanus
Mean Node

Compliments of:-
Joseph Silveira deMello
1755 Franklin Str #204
San Francisco CA 94109
Tel (415) 775-8939
email jsmelscorp@aol.com

uncoordinated her husband had been, and it was obvious to his friend that her husband was having some kind of stroke. Jan called her doctor. Her husband was now driving on his way home. The doctor suggested that she call him on the car telephone and ask him to meet her at the local hospital on his way home.

When he got to the hospital to see what might be wrong with her, they were waiting for him and fell upon him to examine his state of health. He made no objections. He said he knew something was going wrong with him, and he just wanted to get off by himself to think about it. He was hospitalized for further examination and testing. Indeed he had suffered a small stroke. Note that this chart is for an event which was in motion by the time of her birth time. In the diurnal done for her, there is nothing on the angles. But the chart does have some interesting planetary positions.

Bear in mind that we are looking at what was going on in her day while her husband was going through changes. Her diurnal Chiron was on her natal Venus, and diurnal Mars is on her natal Mars-Saturn conjunction which are trine to diurnal Uranus and diurnal Pluto was sextile. Also see that diurnal Saturn is opposite Mars-Saturn and diurnal Mercury, also in four degrees of its sign (Leo) is involved to these other placements. Diurnal Moon is also much involved. She has just had a lunar return, and the Moon to an opposition to her natal Sun, and that means that diurnal Fortune was moving at the same pace. Not having angular indications, this was but a minor indisposition.

The next step was to look at his day using the diurnal technique. Now, quite differently, the importance of the diurnal is instantly seen with diurnal Mercury on the diurnal Midheaven, and the diurnal Venus up there is going to be traveling at quicker speed that the diurnal Midheaven; always check the ephemeris to see if Venus might be going retrograde, which it this case it was not. Natal Pluto is a the bottom of the chart on the fourth house cusp. Note the square from diurnal Vertex to diurnal Mercury and diurnal Uranus as well as to natal Pluto. See this also as a day when diurnal Mars is opposite diurnal Saturn, and that natal Chiron is involved. The diurnal Moon is on natal Mars and Sun. Last, but not least, diurnal Pluto is in orb of natal North Node, so, see also the trine to diurnal Saturn and sextile to diurnal Mars and Vertex, the latter always being a health indicator. As we enumerate all these aspects, we seem to be checking all the same things we checked in the wife's diurnal.

Bill Clinton

Most astrologers have been preoccupied with the chart of the President who, as this material was being collected, suffered a knee tendon injury while on a jaunt to Florida March 13, 1997. The first thing I noticed that it was lunar return time, so naturally I felt I had to look at the lunar return chart. This is how we learn astrology. We have to check whether the event can be seen in all other astrological techniques. Particularly for me as I was involved in how I did returns charts. This took years as I kept seeing that some years a return for my natal place worked far better than one for where I was living. Furthermore I had been using precession and was about to abandon that use. Now, I have finally decided to do all re-

turns for place of birth and without precession.

Descending the stairs from his host's terrace to the path to the guest house, diurnal Neptune is in orb of the diurnal Midheaven, and we have all come to know the significance of Clinton's specific natal arrangement of rising sign, Mars, Neptune and East Point in his life. This is one man who should realize that his sex urges propel him, that he can deceive himself that any sexual experience is not only misguided and not secret, but also becomes a media event. Neptune is not the planet for the presence of reality. And the only adage that any secret between two people is not going to be very secretive at all. Because of only one angular touch, although discomforting for some time to come, for there is another single touch of natal Saturn at the diurnal IC. Our action is going to show by other things that mere angular touches. Diurnal Mars is on diurnal North Node and diurnal Chiron in opposition to diurnal east point. Notice the correlation of diurnal Vertex making an opposition to natal Vertex. See that diurnal Saturn is sextile to diurnal Uranus, this Uranus is trine to the natal Libra placements. Because of the position of diurnal Neptune at the top of this chart we can presume that he was distracted by his usual conviviality upon bidding his host *Good Night*.

I happened on another item in my file. This was the chart of his second Inauguration done for 12:04:30 p.m. EST, January 20, 1997 at Washington, DC, an event chart. If you do this chart, you will see Taurus rising and a Capricorn Midheaven. While event Neptune will be on this Midheaven, it will be followed by Jupiter in Capricorn, Sun and Uranus in Aquarius, all in the tenth house. Event Saturn is on the South Node, not a nice indicator, but also opposite to Mars, and Mars is sextile to Pluto which is trine Saturn. Mars and Saturn in this event chart are contraparallel. Into these charts heliocentric placements are surely going to be a revelation.

Lou's Bad Fall

What a busy spring. My third sister, at this same time, reported a fall in which, to save herself, she managed to break her left wrist. She could kill the doctor who remarked that putting out her hand to save her from hitting her head had certainly worked. She had tripped over a crack in a cement floor which she has known well for ten years and on which she has never previously fallen. The event occurred at 9:50 p.m. EDT Newport, Rhode Island.

Once again we have a chart with only one touch to an angle, natal Neptune to the diurnal seventh house cusp. Even the touch of diurnal Venus to natal Chiron is out of the one degree orb we allow ourselves with diurnals. Yet the chart presents us with an alarming array of T-squares and trines. The diurnal Moon is opposite her natal Mars which are in a four degree quincunx in her natal chart, but I mention this because her natal Moon is also in a three degree orb of a natal quincunx to the natal Midheaven. Diurnal Pluto is square natal Neptune. Notice also that diurnal Jupiter is in quincunx to natal Jupi-

Inner Wheel
214. Husband's Stroke diurnal
Natal Chart
Jan 17 1997
9:25 AM CST +6:00
Chicago IL, USA
41N30 087W38
Geocentric
Tropical
Campanus
True Node

Outer Wheel
11. Jan Van Schuyler
Natal Chart
Nov 14 1921
9:25 AM CST +6:00
Chicago IL, USA
41N52 087W39
Geocentric
Tropical
Campanus
True Node

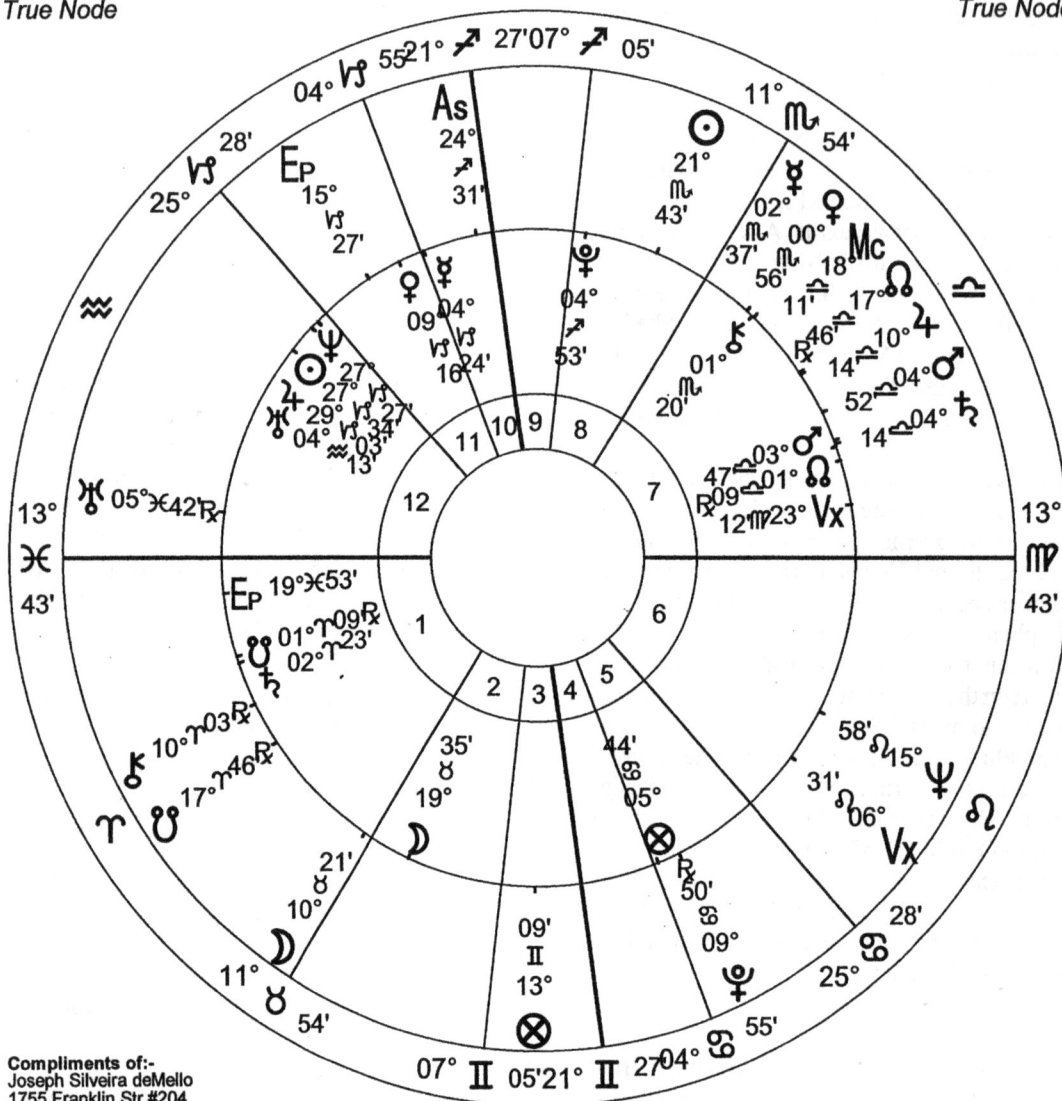

Compliments of:-
Joseph Silveira deMello
1755 Franklin Str #204
San Francisco CA 94109
Tel (415) 775-8939
email jsmgemscorp@juno.com

Inner Wheel
215. Stroke diurnal
Natal Chart
Jan 17 1997
11:35 AM EWT +4:00
Plainfield NJ
40N37 074W25
Geocentric
Tropical
Campanus
True Node

Outer Wheel
Philip Van Schuyler
Natal Chart
May 12 1919
11:35 AM EWT +4:00
Plainfield NJ
40N37 074W25
Geocentric
Tropical
Campanus
True Node

Compliments of:-
Joseph Silveira deMello
1755 Franklin Str #204
San Francisco CA 94109
Tel (415) 775-8939
email jsmgemscorp@juno.com

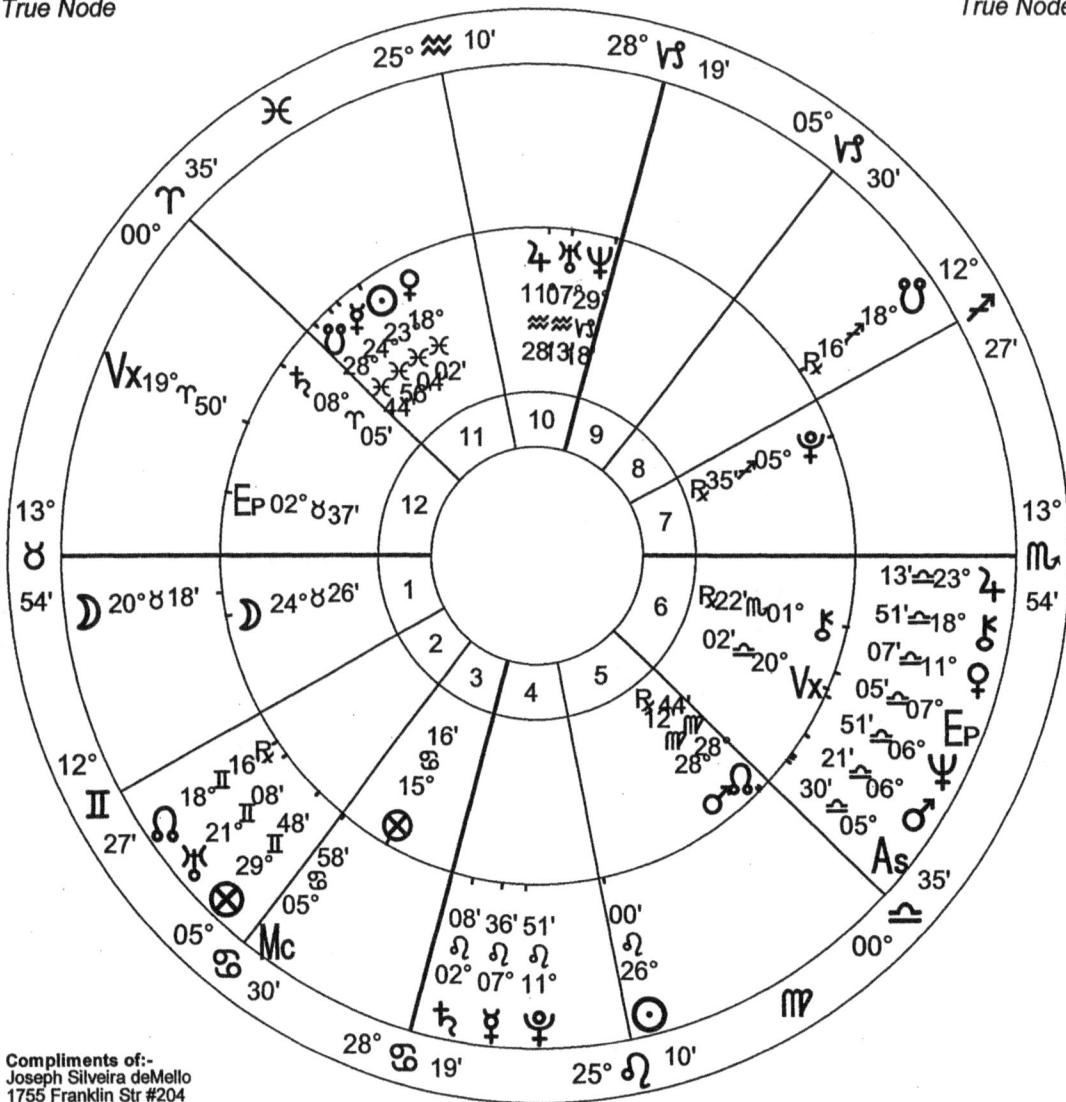

218. Diurnal Serious Fall
Natal Chart
Apr 30 1997
2:17 AM EST +5:00
Newport RI, USA
41N29 071W19
Geocentric
Tropical
Campanus
True Node

Mary Lou Spencer
Natal Chart
Nov 24 1930
2:17 AM EST +5:00
Newport RI, USA
41N29 071W19
Geocentric
Tropical
Campanus
True Node

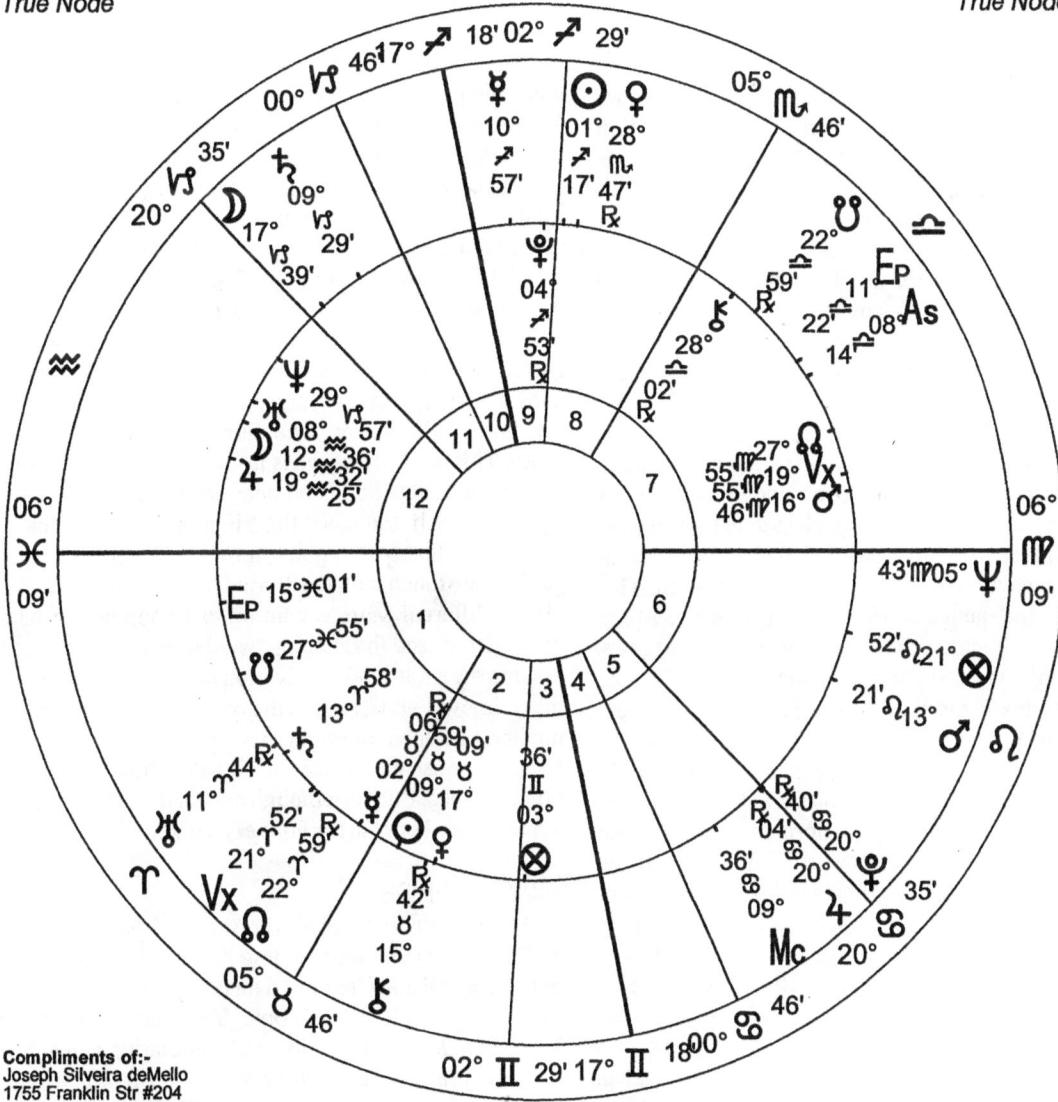

Compliments of:-
Joseph Silveira deMello
1755 Franklin Str #204
San Francisco CA 94109
Tel (415) 775-8939
email jsmgemscorp@juno.com

ter and Pluto. She is one of the most outspoken persons I have ever met, and, indeed, one nephew said of her that she had probably never suffered a shy moment in her entire life. Absolutely no one gets the best of her, but it must be her Mars in Leo, for she has only natal Venus in Scorpio. She was volubly discomforted by a wrist cast, but, never one to sit at home in a sunny window, she lost very little work time.

Death per Misadventure

This is how I would think of the death of Alex Brashier on August 24, 1997 in Palm Springs, California. Such a verdict is well known in British law but not common in the United States. We would be more bound to see this as murder, and only a very good lawyer could mount a defense which would cut any ice with a jury.

When I first knew Alex, he and his partner operated an excellent, popular San Francisco restaurant. He and his partner were briefly clients. Partner Rick, a fan of the great motion picture *Casablanca*, had always wanted to own a place of his own which he would call "Rick's Casablanca," but Rick made the mistake of mentioning this to another restaurateur who proceeded to give that name to his own new place across the street from the space Alex and Rick had just leased and were remodeling. Even if they could not use their name of first choice, I was able to tell them that they had opened under good auspices. They were a homosexual couple, and I was slow to become aware that there was an underlying theme of sado-masochism in their relationship. As sophisticated as I like to think of myself, it never occurred to me to check that out, and I learned that everybody else knew of this. Alex was born with Mars and Sun less than two degrees apart on the Midheaven. Any diurnal done for him is naturally going to have the diurnal Sun on its Midheaven. This conjunction is also quincunx Uranus and trine the Moon which was square Uranus. Sun and Mars were further square the East Point of his natal chart, and Mercury was square Neptune and Vertex in the sixth house. Sun and Moon were also semi-square Venus.

According to the news story, six years prior to his death, the partnership of Alex and Rick had dissolved, and Alex had moved with a new roommate to Palm Springs. Both had been community activists and on the board of directors of the AIDS Emergency Fund. As reported to police, Alex's roommate had returned home at five o'clock of a Sunday morning to find a man leaving their apartment. The man asked to be given a ride home, and the roommate obliged. When he returned to the apartment, he found Alex dead. From the description the roommate gave police, the assailant was recognized as a parolee and was immediately apprehended. The suspect claimed that this was the first time he had met Alex, and the strangulation death was accidental and occurred during sado-masochistic consensual sex, usually referred to as auto-erotic strangulation. There was no media follow-up on this story, whether he was charged or remanded for parole violation.

Two Princes

At the death of Princess Diana of Wales on August 31, 1997, we all had chart data for her, and, more important, we had official records of the birth data of her ex-husband and their two sons. I did diurnals based on the natal charts of her children. In the chart done for Prince William, this event which happened two months after his birthday shows one of the quickest moving Ascendants while the movement of the MC is more normal. Only natal Pluto is on the diurnal Descendant. Diurnal Neptune is on the natal East Point, the diurnal Vertex is on natal Mars, diurnal Chiron is on natal Jupiter, and diurnal Pluto is on natal Uranus. This is what we have, and the reader will perhaps like to see the dirunals as transits around his natal chart to check out the basic house rulers before looking at the chart we use for diurnals. You will note that Prince William is the heir to the throne after his father. His natal Jupiter is so close to his natal Midheaven, note that Jupiter is natally retrograde, that it went direct at age eight and thus will proceed to his Midheaven when he is forty-five years of age. The maternal genes in this family are so strong that as long-lived as have been all the matriarchs, his grandmother and father may both be quite long-lived. Note also that it is quite possible that the impact of his mother's death was more strongly felt getting toward her funeral than at its immediate announcement.

For the younger son, Prince Henry, the event occurred two weeks before his birthday. Diurnal Ascendant is on natal Neptune, and natal Pluto is still in orb of the diurnal Midheaven. The diurnal Chiron is on natal Pluto. This chart shows he is just about to have a Venus return. Diurnal Moon is on natal Vertex and just past a square to itself and since the Moon moves so quickly, we can see that Moon going into the eighth house and getting into touch with the diurnal Mercury and Sun. We also see diurnal Mars is coming to a conjunction with natal Saturn, and these being two degrees apart, we can assume the emotional deprivation making itself increasingly known and felt by the young prince after his mother's death. You might check and see that a diurnal for her ex-husband Prince Charles also shows viable diurnal touches. But even though her death was so violent, a diurnal for her chart is not very satisfactory.

Mother Teresa

Modern saint Mother Teresa, died September 5, 1997, as the media was holding its wake over the death of Princess Diana. Her birth data is given us as 2:25 p.m. MET, August 27, 1910, Skopje, Yugoslavia. She was a Virgo Sun, Moon in Gemini, with Sagittarius rising. She died just after her eighty-seventh birthday with transiting Saturn on her natal

IC and the diurnal Sun on her natal Mars. There are but two diurnal touches, diurnal Chiron and Moon are on the diurnal Midheaven. Notice that diurnal Chiron is trine natal Chiron in zero degrees of Scorpio and Pisces. But diurnal Moon was also going over diurnal Venus and in opposition to diurnal Saturn, and diurnal Jupiter is opposed to diurnal Vertex. The thing this diurnal chart most stresses is that diurnals are transits to the natal chart.

Compliments of:-
Joseph Silveira deMello
1755 Franklin Str #204
San Francisco CA 94109
Tel (415) 775-8939
email jsmgemscorp@juno.com

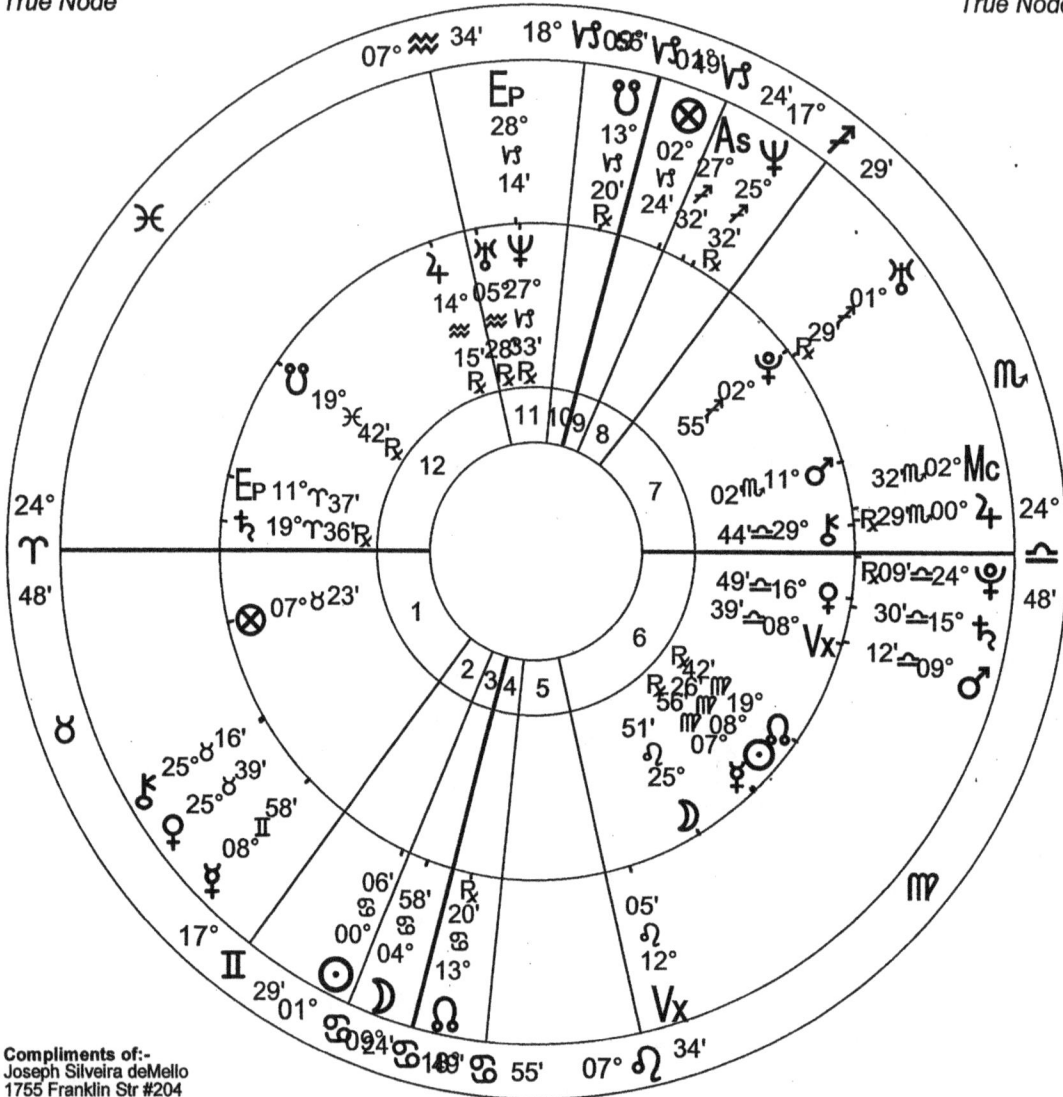

Inner Wheel
220. Pr William diurnal
Natal Chart
Aug 31 1997
9:03 PM BST -1:00
London, England
51N31 000W06
Geocentric
Tropical
Campanus
True Node

Outer Wheel
Pr William Mountbatten
Natal Chart
Jun 21 1982
9:03 PM BST -1:00
London, England
51N31 000W06
Geocentric
Tropical
Campanus
True Node

Inner Wheel
221. Pr Henry diurnal
Natal Chart
Aug 31 1997
4:20 PM BST -1:00
London, England
51N31 000W06
Geocentric
Tropical
Campanus
True Node

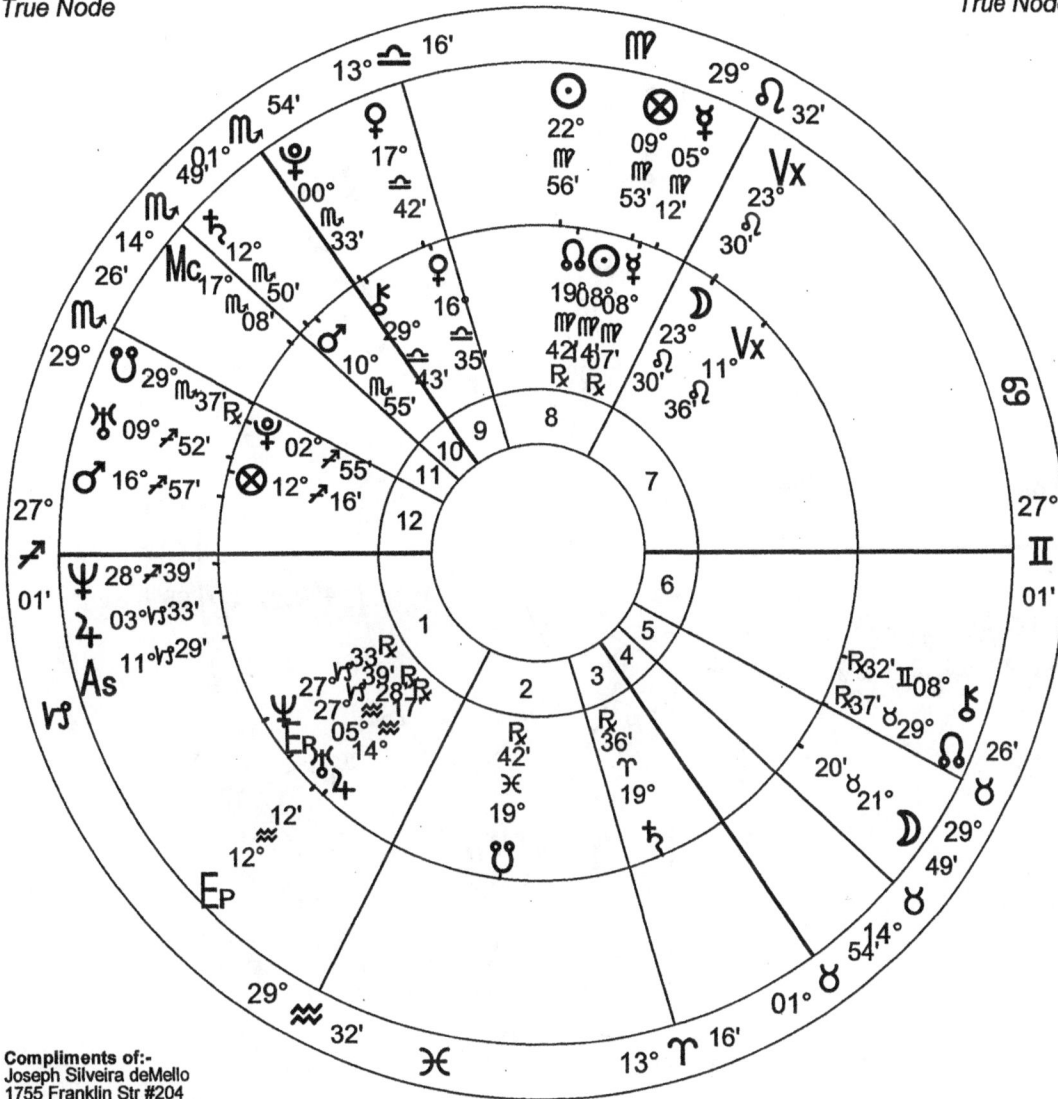

Outer Wheel
Pr Henry Mountbatten
Natal Chart
Sep 15 1984
4:20 PM BST -1:00
London, England
51N31 000W06
Geocentric
Tropical
Campanus
True Node

Compliments of:-
Joseph Silveira deMello
1755 Franklin Str #204
San Francisco CA 94109
Tel (415) 775-8939
email jsmgemscorp@juno.com

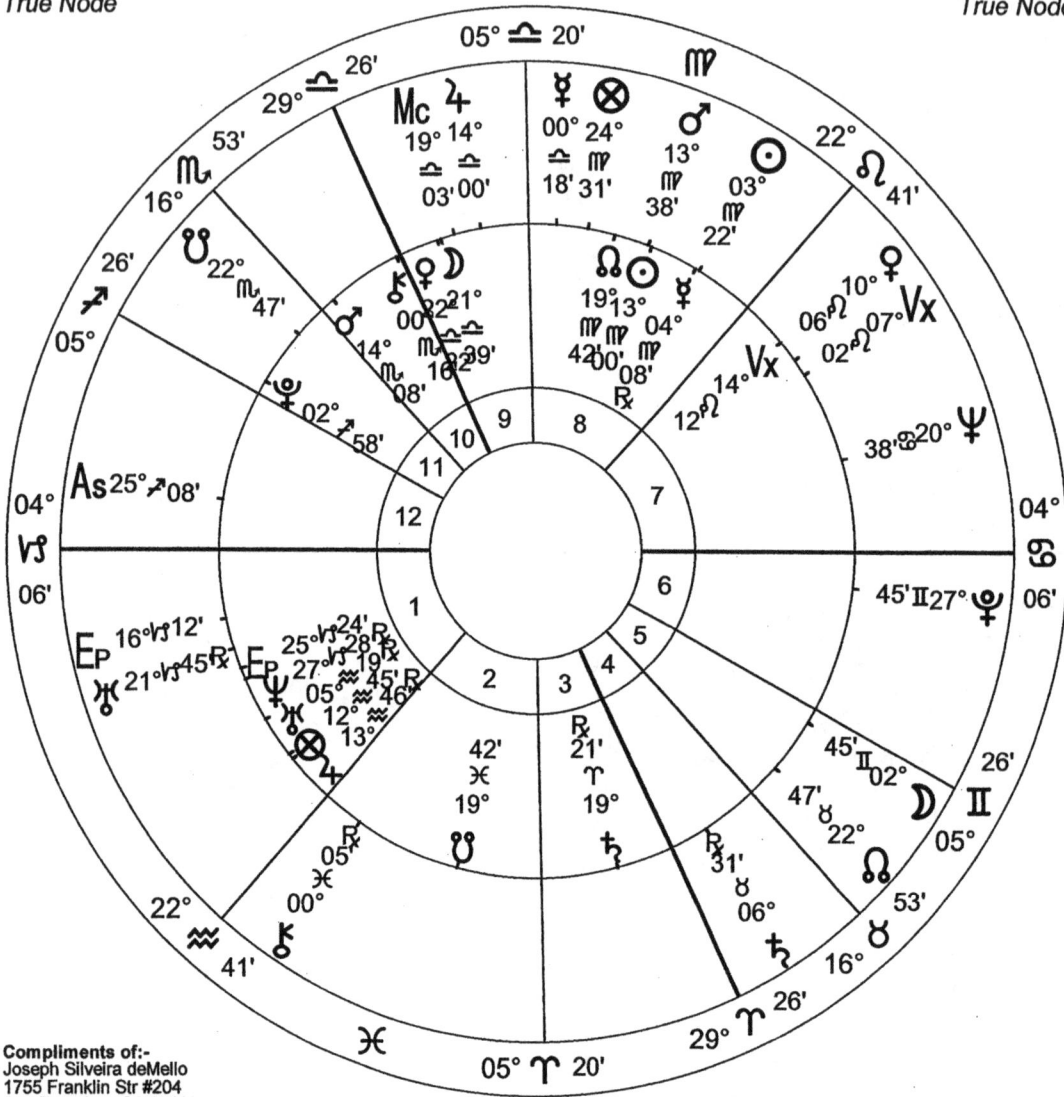

Inner Wheel
222. Moth. Teresa diurnal
Natal Chart
Sep 5 1997
2:25 PM MET -1:00
Skopje, Yugo
41N59 021E26
Geocentric
Tropical
Campanus
True Node

Outer Wheel
Mother Teresa
Natal Chart
Aug 27 1910
2:25 PM MET -1:00
Skopje, Yugo
41N59 021E26
Geocentric
Tropical
Campanus
True Node

Compliments of:-
Joseph Silveira deMello
1755 Franklin Str #204
San Francisco CA 94109
Tel (415) 775-8939
email jsmgemscorp@juno.com

The Wedding

An astrologer who contributed to various parts of this book sent me the data for a diurnal of her wedding day but later had second thoughts and asked me not to use this chart with any identification to her. I could hardly believe my eyes when I first looked at this chart. Every planet that can go retrograde, except Venus, was retrograde in the chart. No astrologer I know would have counseled marriage under such conditions. Marriage is both rite and contract, and I have known astrologers to be spooked by a mere Mercury retrograde for a wedding chart. And here we have a chart loaded with retrogrades for a marriage which has lasted better than fifty years. Granted it happened well before this lady began to study astrology or had astrological advice in the matter. The further surprise was that as a diurnal this chart had no angular contacts although there were conjunctions between diurnal and natal planets.

This wedding chart was the culmination of a wartime romance during WW II. The bride and groom had met, and he had immediately made up his mind that she was the girl he was going to marry. He kept right on proposing marriage on every date they had until she finally said she would. As usual in those days, things were arranged in hurried and tight schedules and involved daunting circumstances. He got transferred to a base in the Midwest, and she decided she would marry from her parent's home. There was no time to arrange for the presence of his family. It was dubious he could even get a two day leave from his base well south of Chicago. The guests would be her family and childhood friends none of whom he had ever met.

The lack of diurnal angular touches may have been due to the bride considering herself married from the moment she accepted his proposal. The times were hectic and feverish with men suddenly shipping out to war without much advance notice. There was seldom more than a one-night honeymoon and many couples did not meet again until the war finally ended. Also, in those days, plane travel was a novelty, and roads, even 30 years ago, let alone back to wartime days were far from the super highways they are today. High-crown roads (often well pot-holed and hazardous) went from one small town to another, and fifty miles an hour was unheard of speed. If anyone had known astrology they would certainly have been on tenterhooks. The day before the wedding, the Moon had gone over a Mars and Uranus conjunction opposite Venus. Granted the square in the chart is mutable and the nodal axis makes trine and sextile patterns to this opposition, there is also a grand trine involving the South Node, the Mars-Urnaus conjunction and Neptune.

Rectification with Diurnals

When I first lectured on diurnals at Seven Hills, I used the chart of the sister of a friend of mine for examples of rectification with the use of the diurnal technique. She was a very tall, straight backed, senior citizen, a lady who had taught French in a large eastern university and lived across the street from the lovely campus in a stately Victorian house. She was the widow of a doctor, but had her own career and interests. She had told me when we met, and as tactfully as she could, that she did not see the validity of astrology, but she gave me 11:08 p.m. as her time of birth. The chart I did for her had Capricorn rising, and I had expected Aquarius rising. Aquarians may often be astrologers, but when they are not, they will be the first to tell you they do not believe in astrology. At any rate, I had felt from the first that the original chart I did for her was not correct. Eventually she got around to telling me that my prognostications for her were always correct but always three weeks early. Aha! I thought. Now if I had a couple of dates of past serious events, I could perhaps rectify her chart with the use of the diurnal technique. She did not quite see her way to furnishing me past events in her life.

Unhappily, she fell and broke a hip on June 1, 1986, about noontime, so I did the diurnal for the previous day. And the following year, In February 1987, this time on snow and ice, she fell and broke the other hip. Where she had been operated on for the first break, the second break was left to mend naturally. Unfortunately I have mislaid the chart for the second accident.

The great thing about diurnals is that however many charts you do for the wrong birth time the planet significant to the events will always be wrong at the same distance to the angles. So I had not been surprised when I noted this was so with these diurnals, and I began the work of rectifiying the birth time. Using a computer makes this quite easy to do. Both diurnals had an error of eleven degrees. One diurnal degree equals four minutes of time correction one way or the other, and since I was predicting ahead of time, it meant I should increase her original time of birth by $11 \times 4 = 44$ minutes to be added to change her birth time to 11:52 p.m. Now I had a good birth chart for her.

In trying to recover information to reproduce the second accident diurnally for this work, I spoke to the lady but she was not able to remember it even when I mentioned it had been in February and in the snow. So I asked for another event and learned the date her husband died, November 15, 1974. Understand that it would have been better had I been able to use two similar events. It is also preferred that one have more than two events on which to base a rectification, but I was originally on such a high of success I felt as bees in clover, especially with a non-believer on my hands.

Having done the first fall with the corrected time, I now had the diurnal IC as the midpoint of diurnal San and Chiron and her natal Mars-Jupiter conjunction neatly in orb and around the diurnal IC. This chart was done for the day before the event to cover the Noon time of the event itself since she was born so late in the day. The diurnal Moon would have advanced from zero Aries and significantly aspected trine diurnal Saturn and square diurnal Neptune and natal Uranus. Diurnal Mercury is on natal Pluto. When a bone breaks in an accident, one expects Mars and Saturn to be involved. The sudden unexpectedness would involve Uranus, and the injury to the hip should give us a Jupiter or Sagittarian involvement. She told me that she was simply not paying attention to where she was stepping.

223. Marriage chart
Natal Chart
Jan 7 1944
9:23 AM CST +6:00
Chicago IL, USA
41N30 087W38
Geocentric
Tropical
Campanus
True Node

Compliments of:-
Joseph Silveira deMello
1755 Franklin Str #204
San Francisco CA 94109
Tel (415) 775-8939
email jsmgemscorp@juno.com

Inner Wheel
231. Catherine's 1st fall
Natal Chart
May 31 1986
11:52 PM CST +6:00
South Haven MI
42N25 086W15
Geocentric
Tropical
Campanus
True Node

Outer Wheel
Catherine rectified
Natal Chart
May 15 1906
11:52 PM CST +6:00
South Haven MI
42N25 086W15
Geocentric
Tropical
Campanus
True Node

Mc
27°
♏
04'

As 03°♒47'

27°
♒
25'

05♍16° Vx
03♍04° Vx 27°
♍

09°♍

♏
♎

27° ♉ 42' 12' ♊

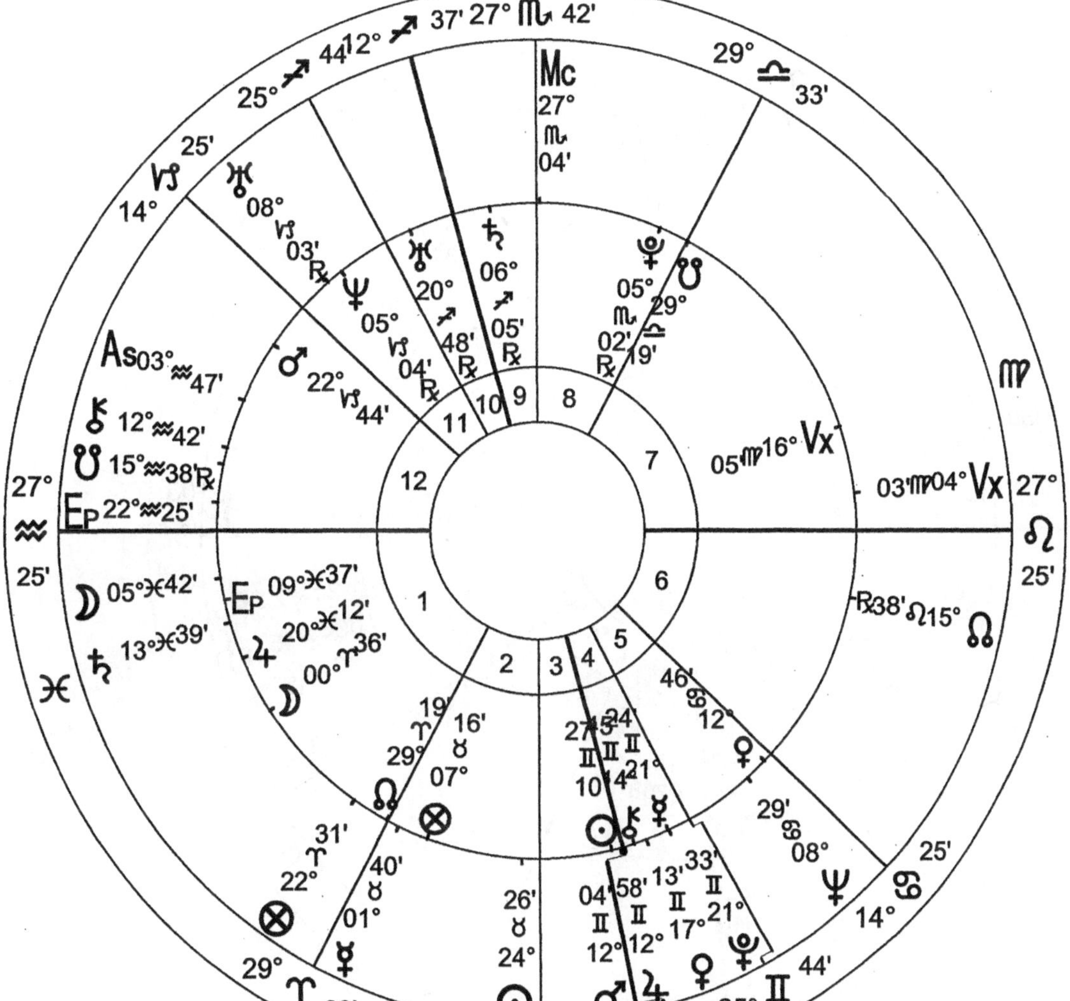

Compliments of:-
Joseph Silveira deMello
1755 Franklin Str #204
San Francisco CA 94109
Tel (415) 775-8939
email jsmgemscorp@juno.com

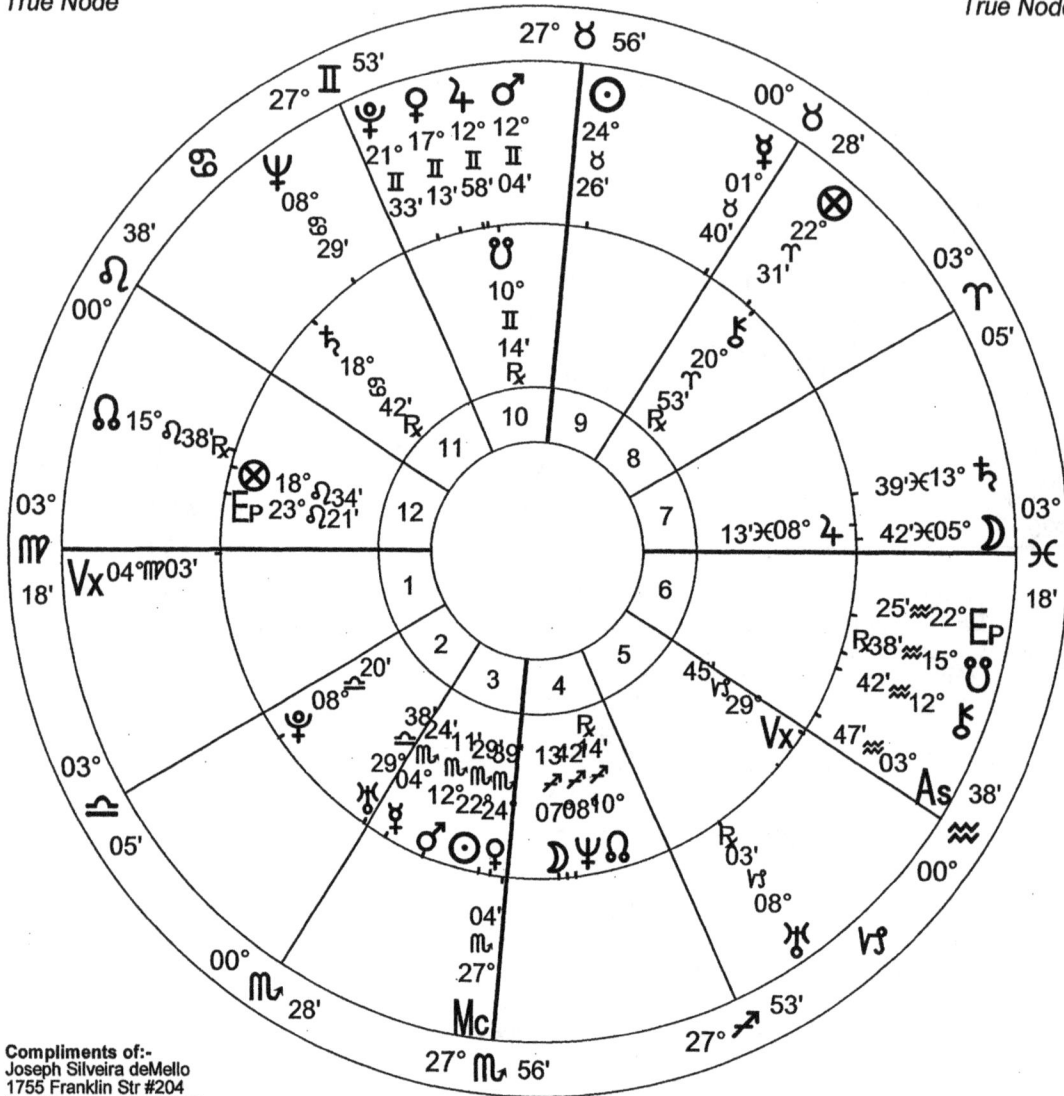

Compliments of:-
Joseph Silveira deMello
1755 Franklin Str #204
San Francisco CA 94109
Tel (415) 775-8939
email jsmgemscorp@juno.com

In the diurnal of her husband's death (chart done for the day before the event), her natal Midheaven is on the diurnal IC, the natal Vertex is in orb of the diurnal Ascendant. While there is nothing on the seventh house cusp, her natal Moon falls in the seventh with diurnal Jupiter and natal Saturn. On the other hand, I have found that diurnals in angular houses are more significant than natals in diurnal houses, so in this case we find diurnal Moon with diurnal Neptune close to the North Node to be of interest in the diurnal fourth house. The diurnal Moon and Fortune will move at equal speed to touch other points of this chart. You can even see that it was not an event which physically happened to her, there being no placements in the diurnal first house. After I check conjunctions between both rings, I then check other lunar aspects.

When doing rectifications with diurnals, it is always best to begin with a recorded birth time or one based on family lore. If time is unknown, you will have altogether too much correction to make. You also have to have some idea of which planets are going to be significant of the event. Her personal status was much changed at the death of her husband at the culmination of a serious illness and there was no element of surprise connected with the event. We must always be prepared to find that other planets than those we expect will bring their own shade of significance to an event. This is how astrology always tells us more.

We habitually work in diurnals allowing only one degree of orb to the angles. If the diurnal shows a significant planet to an angle but one degree either side, these will be considered to be in orb, and only after you try other events and find them falling the same way consistently, I would not hasten to rectifying for a mere four minutes plus or minus the birth time. I dare say this depends on how you handle the Virgo quotient in your lives. But the usual problem for many people is that they cannot get specific angular positions in their diurnals. We cannot be so rude as to say that perhaps the event was not as significant as originally thought to be. It is also difficult to suggest that an official birth data with which someone has happily worked with in other techniques could possibly be incorrect. One thing is certain. If one diurnal chart shows no angular coordinates, diurnal or natal, neither will any other diurnals done for the same person with the same birth data.

Moreover, all diurnals will be incorrect at exactly the same distance from an angle. This consistency of error is good news. If it happens that one event shows just fine, and all others do not, then you have to revise your ideas of which planets were valid to the particular situations.

There is always the problem that a client might not remember the right date of an event, as in chart #175 where we had the month and day but the choice of two years. Happily in that instance the lady was an astrologer and had excellent recorded data. Doing a diurnal for both years quickly settled which year was correct. If people, astrologers included, all kept desk diaries, work would be so much easier.

The funny story about this rectification exercise is that my academic lady could live with an astrologer who so inexactly forecast three weeks ahead of time, but she was less amused when suddenly I produced a chart which was right on. She has never asked me another question about her chart. How-ever, she had me do charts for her son, his ex-wife, and her two grand-daughters.

Begin, always, by studying your own charts and your own events. The very first thing working with diurnals will teach you is that you may have to revise your thinking of how specific planets work for you. Some will work more mildly for you than they do for someone else, others more strongly. Perhaps your most beneficent planet turns out to be Mars instead of Jupiter, that is possible, you know. Planets you don't expect to be significant may show up, and then your are put to find their importance to the event. After all, why should the demise of a relative show up as favorable to your chart?

Perhaps you inherited, or perhaps you did not inherit, perhaps your life was changed for the better by the event, or not changed at all. Do enough of these charts, become studiously critical and try for objectivity, but satisfy yourself and develop your own philosophy in ways which will work both for yourself and for your clientele.

Rectification of charts somehow meets with disapproval from other astrologers who seemingly would rather continue to use an officially recorded time of birth even though it has been proven to be incorrect. When I rectified my chart by a very long and tedious process, I got a time consistent with the memory of my father and a chart that has always worked for even minor events. But in the last more than thirty years, I must have had at least a dozen astrologers furnish me with correct rectifications on my chart according to some style or theory they favored.

Astrologers each have different ways they work. For clients I do the natal chart, secondary progressions and solar arc directions, and the current solar return. Often for the day of the reading, I do a diurnal chart. I do this because, some years ago, I had uneasy feelings while giving a reading, a gnawing sense of foreboding. I was sure I was missing something. When he left and returned to his car, it had been burglarized. Now I find that clients enjoy seeing their chart come up on the computer monitor. Computers, if you can make your fingers work properly, are a boon to astrologers. Imagine going out and taking your own measurements of the heavens, especially in San Francisco where the heavens are too often obscured by fog. How on earth did Lilly function in London? But the point is that to all this some astrologers add solstice points, fixed stars, asteroids, heliocentric charts and give fabulously correct and interesting readings to their clientele. Never be heard saying that a techniques which works well for others does not work for you, for it only means that there is something you are not doing as well as you might do it. Myself, heavy with Mercury significance, must confess to days when nothing seems to click and everything turns to dross. In those cases, I simply wait for another day when my head is clearer, and watch with amazement as everything falls into place. I am glad I found astrology and all its techniques. The study still amazes me.

Appendix—Saturn Cycles

From the beginning of any study of astrology, we learn to see the nature of Saturn in its role as karma, lesson teacher, obstructor and delayer. In short, we learn all the heavier features of Saturn long before we can see Saturn as a source of stability and conservatism, and as a rewarder when we alter our attitudes to work as Saturn demands. Anything which can punish must also have an ability to do us some good.

The total study of astrology is a study of cycles, and since Saturn is almost always on time, but with one exception, any astrologer can do quite a valuable lifetime report for any client based entirely on Saturn. The study of any planet as it aspects its own natal position can be very revealing. The normal cycle of Saturn is about twenty-eight years, so we are seldom going to have more than three in a lifetime. Twenty-eight years is also the cycle of the progressed Moon around the chart. As one astrologer put it long ago, the Moon chases Saturn.

We are going to concentrate on the cycle of Saturn as it makes hard aspects to itself—first, a lower square to itself, then the opposition, around to an upper square, and finally ending the cycle with a Saturn return to its natal position. The Saturn return is always considered an ending, but bear in mind that any ending is also the start of something new. In the cycle of Saturn to the natal Sun, we get Saturn working on the ego and a closer individual layout. We will do it and term it the same as above—lower square, opposition, upper square, conjunction to the Sun. But here we have a different situation. Saturn opposite the Sun is considered an ending, while, when transiting the Sun, it is considered a high point in the life. The opposition of Saturn to the Sun is the only time Saturn is not exactly on time. A serious culminating event will happen either just prior to opposition or just after exactly on it.

The final insight Saturn gives us in this cyclical study involves Saturn as it touches the four angles, and with that we must think about the entire pattern of Saturn as it goes through each house in turn. Saturn has definitive messages to give us in each house. It makes different demands on us as well as some alteration of method and approach.

Take a chart blank or draw a circle bisecting it with the horizon, Ascendant-Descendant, and, thinking of the whole 360 degree circle, estimate and draw a vertical from where your own Midheaven to IC would be. Unless you were born close to the Equator, your chart quadrants are not likely to produce quadrants exactly ninety degrees wide. Whatever house system is your choice—Placidus, Campanus or Koch—most of us will have a pair of intercepted signs which will give us smaller and larger house areas. Saturn stays two and a half years in each sign, but its length in each house will vary. Saturn will spend about fourteen years in each half of your chart, whether it is the upper or lower half, the right or the left side of the chart, but seven years in each quadrant is rare.

Although I will show what this diagram does to my chart, I want you to think in terms of your own chart. I want you to keep your own charts in mind, enter your positions rather than mine to quickly grasp your own individual placements and patterns. Label your angles with degree and sign. Now think of where your natal Saturn is. Mine is at 16 Scorpio, so I will mark it and proceed around the chart and mark out the lower square at 16 Aquarius, the opposition at 16 Taurus, the upper square at 16 Leo. Now enter your Sun, mine being 11 Scorpio, so I go around to mark the lower square to the Sun at 11 Aquarius, opposition at 11 Taurus, upper square at 11 Leo. Having done this, we are now prepared to examine the individual pattern. Notice the first thing Saturn will do is hit my Descendant at 9 Sagittarius. Then, in my case, I go around to the next mark at lower square the Sun at 11 Aquarius, conjunct the Midheaven at 15 Aquarius, and a lower square to Saturn at 16 Aquarius. What a busy time that is for me. Quite close to each other. I have major hits over the top and also over the bottom of my chart. Next is finding the opposition to the natal Sun at 11 Taurus, the opposition to natal Saturn at 16 Taurus, and later the coming to the Ascendant.

Take a moment to shake your own head in wonderment that while Saturn is doing one thing, as in all astrology, something else is gong on at the same time. Because hard aspects provide action and events, and soft aspects often slide by unnoticed, this study concentrates on the former.

As astrologers, we have some idea of how to evaluate Saturn. We have noted its sign and location. Is it dignified by being in its own sign or being in its own mundane house. We must have a clear grasp of its easy or difficult aspects or lack of connection to the rest of the chart. What does Saturn rule in the chart? We note that the affairs of that house are worked out through where Saturn is placed and the things of that house.

Until I studied astrology I had no idea what was my karma. In our evaluation of any planet we see that my Saturn is in a cadent house, and cadent houses are study areas where we prepare ourselves for the eventual transit of Saturn into the next angular house where action begins. I can now see that from the earliest my lessons of life were in learning how to interact with the other people and also for me to learn what those other people expect of me. Quite a load for the newborn infant. At that point of life we probably did not know about all that specifically.

We cannot all have our beginnings in the first house, where we learn to develop our personalities, and neatly go around the chart in house order. But learning about our particular situation will, when we can absorb the idea, tell us of our jumping off place into life. The baby who has a tenth house Saturn comes into life the cynosure of every eye, the darling to all around and not having to lift a finger or do any special thing to get going. Consider all you know of your own Saturn. Saturn is your conservative self, your father, your teacher and the planet which often delays and obstructs.

Consider also whether Saturn at birth be direct or retrograde. One out of every three will have Saturn retrograde. This is not a disability. Those with Saturn retrograde have an extra job. They come into the world with the belief that people do not relate as well as they might to each other or the world around them. Therefore, it is the mission of Saturn retrograde to aid social relatedness. As you work with this idea you will notice that people with Saturn retrograde are very aware of all that goes on around them and avidly interested in many things. But what really makes this retrograde important is that in your early days Saturn will finally transit direct and make a very early Saturn return situation. This very early Saturn return sets the clock so that the next Saturn return will be pushed on a bit later, giving each person his or her own timing.

One more special consideration involves those born with Saturn in the twelfth house. It is well documented in astrological lore that those born with a twelfth house Saturn will have a difficult start in life. Of them it is customarily said that parents and doctors will wonder if the infant is going to adapt and survive infancy all the time it takes until Saturn gets out of the twelfth and crosses the Ascendant into the first house. By the same token, if we wisely correlate the rest of life to the difficulties of a twelfth house natal Saturn, we will not begin any new project while Saturn transits our twelfth house. Beginnings at that juncture are going to have to be restarted after Saturn goes over the Ascendant. Those of you with astrological experience will have discovered client problems for those who start new jobs or new businesses during a twelfth house Saturn transit.

Assuming you have thoroughly evaluated your own Saturn, there are a few more cautions. If you were born by day, Saturn rules Capricorn, and those of you born by night will add that Saturn rules Aquarius.

In working with the mundane areas potentially ruled by Saturn, it is the tenth and eleventh houses. If a planet is in the house it rules mundanely, it is as well off as if it were dignified or exalted. If Saturn is in the house behind that which it rules, there will be a situation of twelfth house fears toward the things of the house it rules mundanely, which would say a ninth house Saturn location toward tenth house matters. If Saturn is in the house after that which it rules mundanely, Saturn is an excellent help toward the future of the things of the house it rules. Always remember the mundane rulers are strong and not off in a distant secondary background.

Saturn Upper Square Saturn

This happens when we are seven years old. It will repeat again around ages thirty-five to thirty-six and sixty-two to sixty-three. The first time it happens, puberty is behind us and we have a year or two of school. If we find ourselves in a situation we do not like, we have to find a way out or a new way of looking at our everyday life. Usually it marks a point of dissatisfaction, a feeling we may be on the wrong track, a need to make new beginnings. Later on in life, how you feel at this aspect is the result of what changes you made after your Saturn return. If you made good or correct choices, you will not be much bothered at this time. You are on the way to Saturn opposite Saturn, which is a point of maximum attainment. This lower square is a wayside sign asking you to pause and see if there is any need whatsoever for adjustments or have to rethink your basic goals. Do not look to others at this point for answers because the answers are all within yourself. Set aside personal whims and fancies and stick with what is most practical and always in line with your natal Saturn. Make your turn toward the most conservative actions, tone down temperament and ego and get on with basics.

Saturn Opposite Saturn

The oppositions come when you are fourteen to fifteen, forty-two to forty-three and seventy-two to seventy-three. Each of these times is quite different in expression.

The first time you are the proverbial sophomore or wise fool. You seemingly reach an apex of achievement, have the world by the tail, about to become an adult. A lot is going on during this dangerous age. There is a lot of peer pressure. The maintenance of an image is vital. A bit cocky, you push all buttons to see what you can get away with. You are ready to be an adult but with no idea that adulthood means taking responsibility for your actions. Most teenagers deny that peer pressure exists, but then we see them in thrall to it at the mall. Psychologists, in their infinite wisdom, tell us it is far better that those going through this period meet the challenges of their peers, join in their didos, dare to do a bit of shoplifting or toke a bit of weed. The worse that can happen is one gets caught and makes a visit to juvenile detention, and first offenders usually get away with a slap on the wrist. This is said to be the best way to learn social responsibility, find out those things with which we cannot get away. The other course is to retreat from peer pressure, retreat into special interests, hobbies, perhaps books. Psychologists regard this as a scardy-cat cop-out. They say we should take the initiative rather than hide from social intercourse. I disagree with them, but that merely places me in the fuddy-duddy category.

The second time it happens, it also happens that Uranus is close to opposite its natal self. We are in the well-known mid-life crisis, and the high point we expected has perhaps passed us by. It is sometimes more difficult to tell at this juncture whether it is Saturn or Uranus tugging at our tail. We may be stuck in some duty to management, job or family and, instead of being cocky youth, we are now thoroughly bored by not having become big leaders or big stars. We would like to kick over the traces, get thoroughly unharnessed, go into something that in the past we dismissed as a wild dream. Bad enough to deal with Saturn, but now we have Uranus demanding instant electrical action. Our real aim now should be to aim toward security in the future rather than getting involved in further aggressive action. Notice how this dovetails with proper advice for teenagers.

Now our concerns should be material, and Uranus is pushing us to get out of Dullsville. Saturn insists we aim toward the most favorable retirement position we can achieve, get some IRAs, look toward the pension plan. And the pull of Uranus for more excitement may be greater and leads us to believe we might be able to do both at the same time. Some go ahead and take the chance, while others do not and spend the rest of their lives with regret they did not make the leap. And, of course, psychologists again side with those who try to shoot for both at once.

The third time this opposition comes along, some of us are retired but still quite active. Now the tendency is to do things to suit ourselves. Pretty soon, if we successfully run the gamut of ill health, we will be in the so-called golden years which are supposed to be years of soaking up and enjoying small pleasures. To have big plans now is really unrealistic. The succeeding years are beginning to pass more quickly than the forever long summers of youth. Even if we are active, there is hardly time enough to do all we want to do. Some of us get our energies curtailed a good bit, so we do what we can do, and although we may seethe at it, we are at a time of life where, if we cannot do something, then it probably wasn't very important and the heck with it. We easily realize that we do not need any more public recognition and, being comfortable and managing to get about with some degree of ease, are far more important to us. This is the period where grandfathers become such great mentors to the youngest generation. In any case, each time we get to this point, we are forced to make personal choices to suit personal needs.

Saturn Upper Square Saturn

This happens at ages twenty-one to twenty-two, fifty-eight to fifty-nine and, if we manage it, eighty-seven to eighty-eight. The first time this happens we are college students headed toward a specific career or doing our level best to stay in the academic womb. The second time it occurs is in the last years prior to retirement, which seems like it is never going to come. In any case, if we concentrated on the personal rather than the material during the opposition period, we should find ourselves where things are going to be smoothly moving ahead to our satisfaction. If we did not move along secure lines when we got to the opposition, now we have then chance to do it right and according to Saturn. When Saturn gets to this upper square it is time to eliminate all dead wood from our lives and it is best to do this right now during this upper square because, if we do not divest ourselves piece by piece now, when we get our Saturn return seven years down the road, we will be forced to clean up our situation in exacting Saturn terms. The truly senior at this point for the third time is making personal choices, simplifying life, hopefully not having to make the kind of decisions that lead to having to toss our cherished possessions to move into assisted living.

Saturn Returns

Saturn returns to its natal place at approximately age twenty-eight. This is so universally

dreaded that a Saturn return without dire events is looked upon as a miracle, although

we all know someone who escaped dire events. Such an escape is due to having a well-aspected natal Saturn. What is happening is that we are at the end of a cycle, the onset of the next cycle, so this has to be an important astrological landmark as if knocking on our heads to make sure we are paying attention. The first reason this is devastating is that we are not well equipped to specifically forecast what will happen and how to stave it off, for Saturn is a force all its own. The astrologer has to do the best possible to decipher this return. I have found this return to occur exactly to the degree and minute.

No astrologer should ever bypass comment on a Saturn return. The client must be carefully warned but not frightened or programmed. I put it that an astrologer can ask careful questions of any client for clues as to how past actions of Saturn has expressed in the client's history. Foreknowledge cannot be depended upon to minimize a Saturn return. Whatever will happen at a Saturn return will be due to actions taken or not taken when and since Saturn was upper square to itself.

For those having a second Saturn return at approximately age fifty-six, astrologers can check out what happened in the client's previous return. Each cycle is somewhat repetitive. Events at subsequent touches may not be the same, but the mood of the person and his general circumstances will have a visible similarity. Thus the astrologer can go into this knowing certain things. What was going on in the world twenty-eight years ago? Where was the client then? We can be sure the client has some memory of being zapped by Saturn in the past when he temporarily took the wrong turning or tried things not in line with the Saturn of his natal chart. We can be very blind to Saturn benefits, but Saturn lessons are remembered. If we sail into the Saturn return thinking life will continue smoothly, Saturn appears to say he is still watching.

There is one great bonus about any Saturn return, whether serious or not. Right after it happens, a person feels really free to do anything he wants to do. It is like the relief from a serious headache. The hammer has stopped beating on our heads. This sense of freedom can be so great that we sail ahead with no need to consider possibilities of failure. Since these times only happen after a Saturn return, these times are precious rare times in our lives. I like to watch actions taken after a Saturn return, and I can report that in no case have I ever seen evidence that such actions ever came to further difficulties. Of course if any corrective measures become necessary, we can make these on the next lower Saturn square. It is important, therefore, that the person who has had a Saturn return not stay in any aura of self-pity. Action is demanded. He must do something and thereby take advantage of this rare bonus period. Even though we may make corrections at the next phase, there will not be with the correction period the great freedom that comes right

after the Saturn return. The point of fact is that life must change. There are other times when astrology signals changes. One of them is when Pluto transits the chart angles, and that is another infrequent happening.

Saturn Lower Square Sun

Remember as we embark on this that Saturn to Sun is operationally different. Sun is the ego, Saturn the stabilizer. Perhaps, if Saturn conjunct Sun is a high point, there was a pre-natal high we know not about unless it was ridiculously far back before the birth date. When Saturn gets to a lower square to the Sun it is time to make a new start, and doing so as if you are going into new and uncharted seas. Proceed slowly because you are reorganizing and making new personal adjustments. By all means, at this outset, tone down any desire to achieve quickly. Trying to hurry things along will only make you tense and keyed up. Remember that Saturn insists you be slow and deliberately steady. Saturn is timely and cannot be pushed. Pace yourself toward long-term gains which will culminate seven years onward when Saturn comes opposite Sun. If you go into something which cannot stand the length of this time test, abandon it in favor of something more serious and realistic. To keep on with it, to get tense and anxious, is going to be counter-productive and may get you an ulcer. Patience is the Saturn keyword. Take on only what is going to be long range.

Saturn Opposite Sun

When Saturn comes opposite to the Sun, the halfway point between the two kinds of squares, it is difficult as it is never exactly on time. Action happens days earlier or days later, and it will manifest differently if you are an introvert or an extrovert. In any case, this time of opposition is the time when the whole world seems to be against anything and everything you are trying to do. The most heavily afflicted will be the extroverts, who will respond poorly and negatively when the ego is assailed. Usually this involves a material setback or an onslaught of ill health. We will find our vitality at a low ebb, and we will find it suddenly difficult to impress others with our personalities, our will, our ideas or our feelings. Among further negative results there may be needless arguments, quarrels or separations. We can throw up our hands in disgust and retreat or separate from others, as we tend to be unwilling to see that the events of this time are faults of ourselves and our responses. If the spirit suffers, so does the body. Extroverts may get stuck with this bad response for quite a long while after the aspect is past. We will see them around us as people ever at war with the world, against everyone and everything, brooding and resentful, never seeing the problem was one of unrealistic expectations.

Introverts early realize they are on the wrong track, that they cannot push themselves on others or control them. Introverts get the message of this aspect. They have less trouble ceasing with ego activity. They are being told that the only person they can really control is themselves. This is specifically the time for growth of character, for karmic development and for mature personal development. They realize

they have to take whatever path will make it easiest to live with themselves, get on with being the best person they can be. Having gotten to the bottom of the problem, they can come out of this aspect with new reassurance.

Saturn Lower Square Sun

Here you get the results of the work done in the most recent seven-year period, the results of your changes when Saturn was opposed to the Sun. If you made realistic changes and rolled well with the punches, you will find yourself now at a high point of importance and material gain. If you avoided the need for change and struggled along less realistic lines, what will happen now will be a complete collapse of your hopes. Having made the choice of reorganizing yourself and your way of expressing yourself, you will now be at a point where you can further consolidate your gains. This means that now you can stop pushing yourself, ease off a bit, relax and enjoy life. You have come to a peak of accomplishment, and after any peak there is nowhere to go but down. Now you ease off material expansion. If you have achieved power, let it go and see what else you can try. Now be less public, get more personal, find another sphere of activity and ambition.

However, if at this juncture, you are dashed down into the pit for insisting on hopes of a less realistic nature, this is the time to realize that the wrong choice was made, a choice not exactly in line with that for which you are exactly suited. Now will be a good time to revise your aims and methods, be less material, go with the more idealistic. Be less grasping, depersonalize your wishes, stop your demands on others and the world, but increase your demands on yourselves in order to get away from this setback. A large problem at this lower square to the Sun is that its message can be overlooked by those who persist in the idea that they are always right and the rest of the world is wrong.

Making the proper choices at every touch of Saturn is going to be even more important since Saturn next will conjunct the Sun. When this happens, Saturn brings you the rewards you deserve or exacts a toll on your ego.

When the astrologer Grant Lewi first wrote on Saturn cycles, he foisted onto astrology a difficult and misleading concept. He looked upon the transit of Saturn from the Ascendant to the bottom of the chart, to the IC, as everyone's most difficult Saturn period. He did not take the Ascendant location as a new beginning. He saw the IC as a real beginning. I submit that real beginnings happen to a very real extent at Ascendant, IC and Midheaven, and sometimes at the seventh house. I say "sometimes" because the seventh house refers to those closest around us rather than to ourselves.

Philosophy has to follow the pattern of astrology. Action happens in angular houses, is maintained through succedant houses, and cadent houses are areas of study for the changes we are going to make in the next angular house. Every cadent house is an area of planning. In the third house we plan for future security and a home, in the sixth we plan how we will meet and relate to those close around us. The ninth house, originally the house of long distance travel and vacations, is where we take perspective on where we are to see where we want to go. It is not necessary to remove ourselves thousands of miles away. But if we have to gain a new perspective by standing on our heads, then that is what we have to do in that area. However, when we get to the twelfth, first we make assessments of what went right or wrong in the previous cycle. We do not do this with any need to place blame on others nor on ourselves. The plain assessment is the whole thing, and an honest assessment is going to lead us to plan a personality image revision.

It is true that Saturn through the first three houses of our chart is not exactly glorious. In fact, it tends first to be highly dissatisfying. We look around and everyone else is getting total reimbursement of the goodies going around, and those with Saturn going through the first quadrant are having many ups and downs. They may get eighty percent and then only fifty percent, but not a full bag of goodies. First of all they have made alterations to their personality image. In the second house they are seeing if they like the result but also grubbing for material resources, which appear somewhat short. And then in the third house they are figuring new ways to communicate and assessing how exactly things or the status quo is for them as swell as planning a more secure future in the next area. When I first did this workshop, a leading astrologer submitted that she had planned, designed and built new homes each time her Saturn went through her first quadrant and moved into them when Saturn got past the IC of her chart. This is an example well worth repeating for your consideration. So many people make serious residential changes when Saturn is going through their fourth house. I moved into my present residence in October 1976 when Saturn was just into my fourth house, and I have stayed there. Hardly any apartment dweller stays that long in one place except to profit from rent controls.

The fourth house transit of Saturn is indeed like a fresh breeze. Everything does seem to open up to you at that juncture. Your money is good, you social life crowds your calendar, and I can say this when I have a fourth house that includes an upper square to the Sun, the entrance into the fourth house, and an immediate upper square to natal Saturn. We can make a residential change any time in our lives, but the change we make in the fourth house is always the change of greatest importance.

Into whatever house Saturn moves, Saturn is going to teach us its lessons. We are now in a position to add to our basic cycle study. Now we can watch as Saturn touches all other natal placements on its way around the chart. Saturn will have particular impact when it touches the planet it aspected when you were born. Otherwise the touch will be of

light importance. The Saturn lesson will involve the things of the house involved. We must always bear in mind the way our natal Saturn expresses. Saturn through the fifth house may block our creativity or speculative ventures. In the sixth house, trouble with work or coworkers. In the sixth we decide what we need or no longer need in the way of performing works or services. But we are also planning things to be done when Saturn gets into our seventh house. In our seventh house, we have people problems. But bear in mind that if we marry with Saturn transiting our seventh house, such a marriage can be forever. The eighth house has to do with gains from other people, which can either be difficult to make or, again, lasting. In the ninth house, well, we should get away from advising people to travel distantly or at all. Our job as astrologers is to get them to schedule themselves properly or in timely fashion, Saturn timely fashion. The ninth as a planning area for changes to be made in the tenth house, is therefore a career planning area. If you are the least dissatisfied with your career, it surfaces here. This is even a time to acquire some formal education to enhance your career position. In the ninth house, putting yourself into a quiet space, try to distance yourself from everyday activities to give a real long range look at the career situation. If you have done the right work in the ninth, you are immediately rewarded on the Midheaven. Saturn demands attention to details even when it is not in Virgo. In the eleventh house, the area of gains from career, the area in which you meet new friends and new interests, join in a community, savor the gains from the tenth house, can be a very relaxing period. This is your last free breath before you have to deal with Saturn in the twelfth house. And, again in my case, going toward Saturn opposite Sun and opposite itself.

There are bits of astrological knowledge that require more investigation and research before actually being carved in stone. I have found that when transits go through the intercepted areas of my chart, the problems I have are interior or private to me. Thus when Saturn has gone through Taurus and Scorpio, I have not had large public problems. At first I thought this might be due to having a fairly well-aspected Saturn, but if that were true, why am I bothered more when the transit is not in the intercepted signs. I would like to learn if astrologers who are sensitive to such things have found that this is true for themselves or their clients. When Saturn transited my twelfth house, it was felt far more when it was in the degrees of Aries and Gemini. When Pluto went through my sixth house, it troubled me more while in the degrees of Libra and Sagittarius.

www.ingramcontent.com/pod-product-compliance
Lightning Source LLC
Chambersburg PA
CBHW081232090426
42738CB00016B/3275